INVENTING NATIONS

Recent Titles in
Contributions in Philosophy

INVENTING NATIONS

Justifications of Authority in the Modern World

TERRY H. PICKETT

Contributions in Philosophy, Number 56

GREENWOOD PRESS
Westport, Connecticut · London

Library of Congress Cataloging-in-Publication Data

Pickett, Terry H.
  Inventing nations : justifications of authority in the modern
world / Terry H. Pickett.
      p. cm — (Contributions in philosophy, ISSN 0084–926X ; no.
56)
  Includes bibliographical references and index.
  ISBN 0–313–29891–2 (alk. paper)
  1. National state. 2. Nationalism. 3. Authority. 4. Legitimacy
of governments. I. Title. II. Series.
JC311.P47   1996
320.1—dc20   95–42920

British Library Cataloguing in Publication Data is available.

Library of Congress Catalog Card Number: 95–42920
ISBN: 0–313–29891–2
ISSN: 0084–926X

First published in 1996

Greenwood Press, 88 Post Road West, Westport, CT 06881
An imprint of Greenwood Publishing Group, Inc.

Printed in the United States of America

The paper used in this book complies with the
Permanent Paper Standard issued by the National
Information Standards Organization (Z39.48–1984).

10 9 8 7 6 5 4 3 2 1

CONTENTS

INVENTING NATIONS

1

CACOPHONIES OF MEANING: PARADOX AND AUTHORITY

The modern age began in high hopes that humankind had moved to center stage. The great theistic explanations of Christianity were replaced with an anthropology that depicts human nature as the source of order. The reigning authority was to be humankind's inner voice, conscience, passion and desire. The new elites were no longer to be people of birth but rather people of heart and mind—a renewed nobility: those of intellect and sensibility. They were to be like those who worked to formulate modernity. Goethe attempted to be the living example. He would show the way through his own genius, spiritual ambition, and restless striving.

The new age began with optimism and hope. The dead mechanisms of ancient rule were to be swept away in a new order of individual freedom and self-expression. Yet, within a generation, the advocates of the new anthropology were turning to the mediative force of the state. Many were proving themselves more than willing to shift full authority over human affairs from the human heart and mind to governmental mechanisms long established. They hoped only for a few modifications and changes in government's organization. The bureaucratic-military complex they had despised became the instrument of modern authority. The despised instrument of princely oppression became the cherished source of freedom and self-expression, and all people required was a new story that justified it.

This book is about that new story, which is indeed comprised of stories or, perhaps, three chief variations on the one basic story. Herder told the basic story as an encompassing anthropology that explained how humans came to be among the animal kingdom and, yet, what distinguished them from the other animals. It is a story about the intrinsic goodness of the human being who is set into motion by nature's having planted in him or her an impulse for improvement. The new story proved so persuasive that it began to eclipse the older stories. It was not long, however, until it became apparent (at least to some) that authority cannot effectively speak as a single individual, no matter how powerful the inner voice, generous the heart, strong the spirit, brilliant the mind. To influence the behavior of others, an individual requires a larger mechanism of force.

NEW STORIES: DREAMS OF DOMINION AND COOPERATION

The coterie of individuals we will call the founders of our modern age despised the state but loved the nation. In the British colonies of North America, they forged a new kind of dynamic government consisting of rival authority centers that was supposed to be anything but static, that was not to act, in other words, like a state. In France they swept away the old monarchist state and threw themselves into a flux that soon became a terror. Germans watched the events and became wary. Perhaps human nature did need the restraints that only the old bureaucratic-military mechanisms of the state could provide.

There was a rub. No modern person could accept an authority presumably representing a prince. Princes were simply too ludicrous. It would have been like obeying a buffoon, a braggart, or a martinet. The new cognitive elites were men of achievement. They numbered among them men of a caliber seldom matched in history, names that resound even today with the magic and power of genius. Princes were pigmies by comparison. To be an acceptable authority for the new age, the state had to represent some other person, class, or idea. Moreover, the new ideal had to draw on modernity's anthropology for inspiration.

Herder and his fellow moderns had celebrated the idea of nation as the counterethic to the dead authority of princes. Each individual human being was driven on a quest for higher community in which human relations are noninjurious. It was that state of cooperation, encouragement, and tolerant respect that Herder termed Humanität, or humanitarianism, in which the nation was born. If the state were endued with the nation, invested with the national will, then it could exercise convincing authority on behalf of all that was newly sacred to modern men and women. It was thus that the second generation came on the justification for authority we have since called nationalism.

In modernity's anthropology, nation is a serious business because it represents the potential ideal state toward which all human behavior is striving. If the state becomes the vehicle for that world historical progress, it is justified. Whatever force or power it exerts by way of facilitating the project of humanitarian fulfillment can be sanctioned. The new story about the nature and destiny of humans developed a political dimension in nationalism, and its advocates, who were known as liberals, became in some cases devotees of the idea of the nation-state. They began to work to transform the princely states into instruments of the nation.

Although it was apparent to some, who remained doggedly devoted to maintaining the integrity of individual self-direction and autonomy, that the state was in all its parts still the same bureaucratic police state it had been under the princes, others continued to see the state only through the prism of their hopes for its transformation. As the nineteenth century progressed, there were numbers of people who identified the state with the nation and lost sight of the fundamental anthropology of individual self-direction. It was no longer liberty that mattered but the celebration of national culture, language, and destiny. The purpose of the state was to assure not merely the prosperity of the nation but its internal and external dominion over others.

The original modern story developed subplots that involved surprising metamorphoses. The feeling heart and strong spirit of the individual was projected onto a collective national culture that subsequently became imperious about its place in the world, insistent on its superiority, and arrogant about its right to dominion or authority over human affairs. Individual autonomy was converted into the political coin of sovereignty (a princely concept), which involved a complex of assumptions about coherent language, history, race, and then entitlements that grew into demands for homeland, resources, access to sea lanes, standard of living and so forth.

Not everyone followed in rapt faithfulness the progress of these subplots. Many fell by the wayside, unwilling to participate. Others began to spin other stories. While few abandoned the idea of nation or a belief in the ideal of humanitarianism that makes up modernity's orthodoxy, stubborn liberals refused to be drawn into the arrogance of imperialism. They did not give up the original ethic of individual self-expression or surrender their belief in the authority of the innervoice. The main plot continued to be a tale of liberty, a story in which each individual struggled against the external obstacles inhibiting the development of humanity, hearkening always to the true innervoice. The main plot continued to be a suspenseful story of emancipation, the triumph of freedom over great odds.

Confronted with the lethal consequences of nationalism, on the one hand, and the impotence of good-intentioned liberals, on the other, there were those who began to develop a third variation of the modern story. If people's intentions were essentially good and governed, furthermore, by the good impulses with which nature had endowed them, then was it not true that what was needed was a social system more congruent with the essential goodness of human nature? If men and women were naturally cooperative and unconflictive beings, then was it not reasonable to devise communities in which these attributes could find their proper expression? Communities that must be fundamentally at variance with the bureaucratic-military police state that had been reinvigorated by a nationalist justification.

The third subplot was a story of human's sociability, which had been, according to these new authors, subverted by a system of government hostile to human's true nature. These new authors employed basic narrative devices used by the modern founders who had first declared the unsuitability and the unnaturalness of the prevailing political (and social) system and called for its abolishment. The nation-state had since proved as contrary to human nature as the dynastic state, perpetuating inhuman practices built on avarice, such as private property, markets driven by profit, and coerced labor. If these practices were replaced by cooperation, distribution according to need, and free and friendly labor, the goodness of human nature could find scope to develop into true humanitarianism. Such is the story that came to be called socialism.

Authority in the modern age is established on some variation of the anthropological tale of human dominion over itself and the world. At the heart of the story is a belief that conflict is not good, that it is best eradicated because it represents an obstacle to self-expression and dominion. Woven like a constant thread through the whole fabric of modernity is the need to eliminate every opposition to the full and free expression of human desire. Since the challenges to self-expression are depicted as external and in no way impugning the integrity of the innervoice, the enterprise of modernity is colored by a strong inclination to totalitarian structures within which mutually benevolent behavior can supposedly be enforced. Force is, therefore, employed—regardless of its justification—to effect monolithic behavior patterns, or conformity.

The characteristics of modern institutions are complete transformations, as they claim to be, of traditional government. It is not so much merely that the person of the prince has been removed or his character reduced to that of one without authority. It is that the purpose of government is the obverse of its premodern regime. Force is no longer employed to assure the benign survival of the world of human relations but to effect what is often called total change—in practice, the abolition of existing networks of human relations. In the modern age, authority, to be accepted as legitimate, must be pledged to abolish the present for the sake of the future; it must employ force to destroy existing networks of human relations for the professed purpose of instituting new networks ostensibly superior to those already real and established. Authority in the modern world is quite simply dedicated to its own replacement by a new and future regime.

The development, in the meantime, of new technologies of destruction and coercion has immensely enhanced the ability of the state to carry out its charge. When certain nation-states are great powers and have at their disposable immense arsenals, complex industrial infrastructures and large populations, there is no counterauthority sufficient to restrain their drive to dominion that is, after all, encouraged by all the tenets of modernity's orthodoxy except the admonishment to humanitarianism. The universalist vision of that original Herderian humanitarianism has long been obscured by the vigor of the particularist ethic so integral a part of both nationalism and many varieties of liberalism. Herder portrayed the innervoice and nature's impulse as predestining us for a universal civilization in which the very best prospers and exists in symbiosis. Voices since have depicted the innervoice as ever more stridently demanding the satisfaction of its idiosyncratic appetites.

WHEN DID MODERNITY TRIUMPH?

A great deal of attention has been addressed to the question about the origins of modernity's anthropology. In the following chapters, it will become apparent that there was not a single moment in which modernity emerged to seize the Western imagination and transform public authority throughout the Western world.

focus on the lives and works of Herder and Goethe as representatives of the founders of a new view of human destiny, but one must imagine them in a larger company of notables whose lives overlap and touch during a period spanning roughly four or five hundred years. Of the three individuals I have chosen to represent the chief ideologies spawned by modernity, only F. L. Jahn produced a seminal text. Varnhagen and Brisbane are more representative of individuals who subscribe to and attempt to live out the prescriptions of the modern faith.

The first generation rethought authority and the question of human order as an enterprise designed both to maximize license (i.e., liberty, freedom) while at the same time guaranteeing an acceptable level of social cohesion (they assumed human nature preferred it). They believed that the good passional drives assured an efficacious movement upwards toward a general state of humanitarianism. Only in the second generation did the advocates of modernity's anthropology perceive the state as the instrument by which both social cohesion and progress could be achieved. Their willingness to support state machinations came only after they formulated a justification for the exercise of its authority that suited their agenda of increased self-direction, autonomy, and liberty.

Autonomy is to be achieved at any price. Even if all its established relations must be destroyed, the new faith demands that it be done. The individual is to be released from the bonds, loyalties, commitments, and interests of the world of old Europe, liberated from the constraints of religion, rank, and family. All the associations once maintained by tradition and the interconnections of natural affection, familiarity, and deference are to fall before the might of arbitrary force. The modern moral imperative mandates that each individual seek to maximize the scope of self-fulfillment at every price. The expressed objective of the first generation of modernity's founders was to establish the individual in liberty qua autonomy. Such was and remains the main theme of the modern story of human destiny.

The only way to accomplish the radical change the new anthropology demands of the faithful is to eradicate human relations as they exist, thus eliminating the true source of conflict. The authoritative use of all force in the modern age has as its purpose the abolition of an ancient definition of human nature. The story with all its three only apparently divergent subplots turns out to be about a denial of certain immemorial patterns of human relations. To avoid a fall into nihilism, it finds reason and inspiration in the idea of aboriginal virtue. In a primeval state of nature, according to the idea, human beings were true to their intrinsic virtue, obeying the authority of the pristine innervoice. The history of our age is, in other words, the story not only of an attempted eradication of everything counterfeit that shackles and constrains us, but also of the restoration of aboriginal virtue.

The liberal seeks with the nationalist and socialist to remove the accumulated counterfeit of the ages in order to liberate aboriginal human nature. The layers of external corruption are percevied as lying heavy on the honest heart, smothering the spiritual clarity of which human beings are capable. Human nature is to be reconstituted only after the work of eradication is accomplished and everything external to its inner goodness removed. Nationalists first, then numbers of socialists, and, finally, too many liberals joined in the struggle to amputate the traditional defining relations from the individual in order to render him or her an unencumbered and compliant subject of the modern state.

The continuing work of dominion involves the state in the work of eradicating rival authority. The great threat to the authority of the modern orthodoxy comes not from liberalism, nationalism, or socialism, however, but rather from the ancient, theologically-based authority of a world operating through divine will. In the West Christianity has been the dominant theism for two millennia, and it constitutes the only authority to threaten the hegemony of the state. The uneasy compact between Christianity and the state came to an end in our century. Though the circumstances were more complex than popular story admits, the first successful move in co-opting the church was made by Henry VIII of England. In one manner or another the state has worked ever since to neutralize the rival authority centers of Christianity.

On American soil the government has been engaged for more than half a century in a campaign to reduce religion to a private matter. Religion is being redefined in the courts as a species of human concern and experience with no public relevance, with no authority over the actions and behavior of human beings except in the few instances still left to the domestic sphere. Although neither the founders of the United States nor its government during the first one hundred and sixty-four years shared the recent hostility to religion repeatedly demonstrated in the American courts, the effectiveness with which religion has been banished from the American public forum by court mandate during the past three decades is remarkable.[1]

The American story is encapsulated in the controversy surrounding recent court interpretations of the First Amendment. Originally intended to accomplish three purposes, the meaning of the prescriptive text began with Cantwell v. Connecticut (1940) to be radically altered. The language of the amendment speaks for itself: "Congress shall make no law respecting an establishment of religion, or prohibiting the free exercise thereof." The national government is prohibited from establishing a national church such as existed at the time in most European states, while freedom of conscience in religious matters is safeguarded and, furthermore, the individual states are left with discretion to deal with questions of religion as they see fit.

In a series of decisions from 1940 until the present, the meaning of the amendment has been subverted and replaced by a literature built on recent judicial opinion. The subversion of the original text and its replacement by a new text that prescribes behavior radically different has not gone without criticism. Even within the federal judiciary the disjunctures in meaning have been elucidated in an opinion written by Judge Brevard Hand in *Jaffree v. Board of School Commissioners* (1983). In the new text the free exercise of religion has been substantially diminished. Today we have arrived at a point in which any reference to a creator (much less any more specific concept of God) is forbidden in schools and other public places.[2]

There is only one way to understand how sincere, intelligent, and right-minded people can believe that they contribute to liberty by mandating that matters of religious concern are publicly unutterable; one must consider the devolution of philosophy in the modern age. A judge who believes that religion has nothing to do with public policy or with civil behavior is like a preacher who cannot understand the importance to Christian ethics of political behavior. The judge bans religion in school and government; the preacher forbids his congregation political action. Each fails to understand that what is now called Judeo-Christian religion is about nothing so much as it is about the nature and quality of justice.[3] All our standards of mercy and judgment are devolved out of one great religion. Without it we would still be locked in animistic superstition or cycles of clan vengeance. The standards we profess to cherish are owing entirely to our Judeo-Christian legacy and its fundamental view of the sacredness of our personhood. Appeals to questions of natural rights that occur in the current debate are irrelevant to any question of justice or law since the notion of natural rights is itself a spinoff of secularized Christian culture and the attempt to substitute nature for God as a kind of causative agent.

Our problems are problems owing to the disintegration of philosophy and to our own consequent inability or unwillingness to comprehend the whole picture. The dismantling of philosophy was well under way in the West by the founding of the American Republic. People on either side of the Atlantic tended to believe in the efficacy of Christian values but no longer believed in the authority of divine revelation. Rather than question the source of standards, the modern habit of mind preferred to interpret values as being merely "reasonable" prescriptions for humanitarian behavior; one derived them from the business of living just as one catches a fish from a moving stream. The very term standard became anathema and values took its place in moral discourse, values being presumably contrived by human beings in response to the demands and conditions of life in this world. Religion was tolerated in the public forum for a long time because it was viewed as a useful mechanism of control for the new cognitive elites, providing the general population with incentives to civil compliance.

There is a word for philosophical devolution, and that is obfuscation. Obfuscation is only one of the tools of arbitrary authority, but it depends upon the dismantling of philosophy (i.e., the desire to achieve a more comprehensive and integrated view of human existence). A number of authors have shown us in ominous portrayals of the future just how governments subvert language and meaning. Here we have seen it at work in our own court cases concerning the First Amendment. Obfuscation aims to distort meaning and through that destruction to disrupt human behavior, leaving the state as the only mediator of order and thereby enabling it to accede to absolute authority over human affairs.

Since most of us resist information that alarms us, the story must be told before it can be believed. One of the most important subplots of the modern story has been to justify the ascession of the state to monopoly authority by connecting it to, among other things, the idea of nation. The result of this odd marriage is the nation-state, which our schools present as an element of nature, much like mountain chains, rivers, and oceans, a motley permanent fixture of nature. On school maps the world is carved into color-coordinated nation-states as fixed in the impressible young imagination as any geologic feature on the globe.

Although the original Herderian anthropology stressed the universality of humanitarian impulses which move us all, subsequent subplots changed our apprehension and gave us a new understanding in which each individual listens only to his or her innervoice, and each culture obeys only its unique destiny. The corollary of such a particularized anthropology summons a view of a world cacophony in which each entity is chirping its own eccentric tune. The only method of transforming a picture of such anarchy into order is by suppressing any confidence one might have in the applicability of generalized (or universal) ethical precepts. The modification of the modern story suggests that any one of the individualized chirps represents its own peculiar expression and is, therefore, justified in terms of the authority of the innervoice. The other chirpers have only to forbear criticizing and to accept, in other words, the integrity of each chirper's tune on faith that cacophony's discord is actually a symphonic harmony on the theme of humanity's glorious diversity.

The call to accept discord as a legitimate expression of diversity serves the aggrandizement of the state, which remains the only mediator of meaning. No other rival entity exists with the authority to interpret the significance of the cacophony. The celebration of discord as a function of state institutions undermines the last security of individuals, who are urged to believe that they can cherish and believe anything they choose, as long as they behave publicly as if it did not matter. A totalitarian wedge is thus driven between what one thinks and feels and how one behaves.

ETHOS AS CULTURAL ECOLOGY

As a scholarship student in Germany, I learned that Amerika is more an idea than a real place to Germans, generating ideas of how I should, as an American creature, behave. Who I was, depended on how Germans chose to read the world.[4] The time I spent as a student in Central Europe convinced me that Europeans are determined to impose their anthropocentric vision on the world. No other civilization has managed so successfully to convince itself of both the correctness of its own view and the need to translate it everywhere into the sole reality. Nowhere can Europeans believe there is another civilization quite as real, authentic, sincere, and legitimate as their own. In their fictions of extra-European worlds of more authentic virtue, the primitivist utopias turn out to be just another projection of their own view.

Every ethos contains a mandate to action that circumscribes its permissible scope. In the ethos of old Europe, behavior was mandated, for instance, that required obedience of the individual. The crisis came when Europeans chose no longer to obey an authority that failed to persuade them. God had vanished from the cosmos, and the princes were left to absurd gestures. The new state regime maintains its authority not by demanding obedience but by persuading us that we lack the authority required to make moral judgments. We are left in a quandry: Either we rebel (which we are free and even encouraged to do), or we acknowledge the supremacy of the state and its ancillary institutions to perform as arbiters of our relations. The resulting impotence I treat in the following chapters, assigning it a name: modern plebeianism.

The modern plebeian who emerges in Chapter 5 through works like Goethe's *Sorrows of Young Werther* as the new, negative actor is a self-pitying, plaintive individual disposed to blame everything and everybody but himself. His posturing narcissism is mixed with petulant demands for autonomy. Goethe's character initiated in the early 1770s a new, plebeian tradition of self-indulgent pessimism that continues as an important tradition of modern literature and cinema. Life is never enough for the modern plebeian. He or she will always want more and even make a virtue of dissatisfaction. Werther's sorry career is a burlesque on the Herderian ideal and, if we stretch a point, might have been a kind of Goethean warning to us. Since it was generally understood not as a caution but rather as a brave, new agenda, we now have every occasion to proceed with our examination of its history.

NOTES

1. Robert L. Cord, Separation of Church and State: Historical Fact and Current Fiction. New York: Lambeth Press, 1982.

2. John S. Baker, Jr., "The Religion Clauses Reconsidered: the Jaffree Case," 32–49 in *The Assault on Religion*. New York: University Press of America, 1986.

3. Two recent arguments for banishing all religious expression from the public forum can be found in Jesse H. Choper, *Securing Religious Liberty. Principles for Judicial Interpretation of the Religion Clauses.* Chicago: University of Chicago Press, 1995, and Marvin E. Frankel, *Faith and Freedom. Religious Liberty in America.* New York: Hill and Wang, 1994.

4. America is as often a metaphor as a place for Europeans: T. Pickett, "The Bruderkrieg and the Crisis of Constitutional Government: The Treatment of the American Civil War by Georg von Cotta's German War Correspondents, 1861–65," *Schatzkammer der deutschen Sprache, Dichtungund Geschichte* XX (1994), No. 1, 13–25. The abiding ambivalence in the treatment of the United States becomes even more apparent when the image of America in the German press during the pass forty years is the subject, as in Heinz D. Osterle, *Amerika! New Images in German Literature.* Bern: Peter Lang, 1989. The question was the subject of a colloquium, "Amerika at the Crossroads: Changing German Perceptions of the U.S.," which I organized at the University of Alabama in March 1991.

2

ETHNOGENESIS: THE EMERGENCE OF A NEW POLITICAL AUTHORITY

Every age chooses or inherits a political order that both reflects and determines its fundamental view of human destiny. The order can provide a relatively benign context for the realization of human needs and desires or it can make existence a living hell. History provides examples from each end of the spectrum and every point between. We moderns have been taught that there was a growing consensus by the middle of the eighteenth century that the existing political order of Europe had failed to provide adequate scope for the expression and fulfillment of a new view of humankind. In the new anthropology associated with thinkers like Locke, Rousseau, Herder , Goethe, and Kant, the meaning of human existence lies in the achievement of individual self-direction or autonomy. History came to be viewed as the process through which whole nations proceeded toward emancipation. The nation-state is the individual writ large, an entity seeking sovereignty (autonomy) and emancipation from constraint that will enable it to achieve an adequate expression of its will and desire.

The emptiness of terms like *freedom, autonomy*, and *emancipation* can be easily demonstrated, pointing to their unfitness to serve as pivotal ethical categories. B. F. Skinner—an avowed determinist—has written that freedom is the absence of causation. People are thus unfree when their behavior is determined or predictable. But people acting predictably often feel free. Architects obey certain rules of geometry, carpenters obey physics, farmers obey the laws of climate, soil, water; yet they all can feel free while exercising their vocations within certain predictable limits. If autonomy means to be utterly free of any causative factor, it is a state that is impossible in nature since every living human being must continue to attend to the business of nourishment, digestion, defecation, etc.

If moral autonomy or the much praised state of individual self-direction is behavior within the context of human relations that is ungoverned by behaviorial prescription, such behavior must also be utterly unpredictable and thus a form of acting freely.[1] Here is where language becomes a vital component in the new,

anthropocentric morality. The new person does not live within the rules of physics, geometry, or the weather. The new person behaves out of some inner necessity that he or she conceptualizes along the way. Herder describes this inner
necessity as a *Trieb* (impulse/urge). The impulse is the motor, and the conditions
one encounters are acted on and shaped by the concept-building power that mani-
fests itself in *language*. Through language individuals create their own reality as
they go, urged by impulse, engaged in manipulating conditions into meaningful
patterns expressed in language.

Modernity's anthropology begins as new kind of optimistic determism. Herder
portrayed humankind as being destined by the finer impulses or urges to Humanität,
a concept we quickly identify as humanism or humanitarianism, which is to say a
benevolent, noninjurious, encouraging, charitable behavior. Others of the same
century formulated the same optimism in different ways. Language came to be
regarded as the conceptual building block through which humans construct meaning—that is, culture. Culture becomes that meaningful pattern through which we
live; it is, furthermore, both the artifacts and the shared experience (i.e., history
and language) out of which the idea of nation arises.

In the Herderian scheme of optimistic determinism, ethnicity is determined
by membership in a national, language-based community characterized by shared
language and culture. Ethnicity is macrocosmically a predetermining factor of
meaning for the individual who is—at least in the European understanding—born
into a nation. We shall see how organic metaphors are used to express the assumed
goodness of ethnic aboriginality and purity, especially in the nationalist ethnogenies
generated in the next generation and the next century after Rousseau, Herder,
Goethe, and others to explain and formulate national destiny and purpose. The
determinism is expressed in two different fashions: macrocosmically (because
the individual enters an existing ethnic/national identity at birth) and
microcosmically (because the motive force of the individual through time and
space is determined by an impulse or urge which has a humanitarian relationship
as its ultimate optimistic goal).

The fundamental ethical problem lies in the unexplored source of the natural
urges and impulses that animate humankind. Do they originate in nature? Many
have thought so. Indeed, the failure of this optimistic determinism to account for
the escalation of lethal and destructive behavior during the past two centuries has
baffled modernity's faithful. Things should be getting better, but they seem to be
getting worse. Determined partisans of modernity have answered the problem
with a couple of explanations:

1. Things are not really getting worse. That is merely an appearance. In fact, things
    have always been very bad, but people tend to romanticize the past and think it was
    better. This answer is exemplified in my son's belief that I am not really telling the
    truth when I relate how downtown Atlanta was perfectly safe forty years ago, that
    people could wander its streets at will without fear of being murdered or mugged, that
    people in most of Atlanta did not even lock their doors. "Dad," he remarks indul-
    gently, "these are all just childhood memories for you." Since he cannot envisage a

time when threats of murder, mayhem, and robbery did not lurk in every urban landscape, he cannot believe my story. It is in this fashion that each generation accomodates
an escalated level of violence and discord.

2.   There is more crime and social disorder, but it is the price of freedom and, therefore,
     not intrinsically bad. At other moments, my son will say, for instance, "Sure, neigh-
     borhoods were safer, but the police could stop a strange pedestrian casually strolling
     through and take him into custody for no reason at all." This is a version of the
     modern myth of the nasty past in which freedoms were abridged and general misery
     prevailed; it is exemplified in "democratic" myths about the unrelieved ugliness of an
     old European order in which arrogant aristocrats lorded it over abject peasants, who
     longed to be liberated from their destitution and slavery.

3.   A variation of point 2 admits that social disorder has become a problem, that earlier
     days might have been more ordered and even happier. Increased effort (and expendi-
     ture) on public education and the general welfare will, the partisan urges, finally change
     the unfortunate present into a happy future. We have only to continue in the faith and
     believe. No matter how bad it seems, modernity's recipe is correct and history will
     prevail.

There are a number of other answers, but these will suffice as examples.
Now we turn to the process through which the state (shaped during the period of
Absolutism) was subsequently co-opted as the instrument of national self-expression. In so doing, we must turn back a moment to the concept of ethnogeny,
which has proved to be an important sanction for the exercise of political authority in the West, providing an explanation and justification for the use of force to
achieve ends it has shaped and defined. The French Revolution can be viewed in
this connection as an expression of emerging French national self-identity, for it
was, after all, an assertion of France's peculiar mission of bringing civilizing
principles to the rest of Europe.

Our focus will not be French but German ethnogenesis, which has a particular urgency for reasons that must first be considered. Paul Massing points directly to the central core of our reason in his study of antisemitism in Germany:
"There remains a quality in German racial nationalism which seems to elude a
purely politico-economic explanation. How is one really to understand a philosophy or religion that, in the nineteenth century, makes "blood" its Holy Grail?"[2]

An exploration of German nationalism offers an opportunity not only to evaluate the most articulated tradition of ethnogenesis and one of its earliest examples,
but to examine its actual course into the horrors of National Socialism. It provides a worst case scenario to test the shortcomings of modernity's most earnest
attempt at creating and justifying a new political authority. German ethnogenesis
also provides an opportunity for us to consider the enormous contrast between the
original anthropology that was formulated by the great minds of "high" culture in
the eighteenth century and the emergence within a century of its terribly disturbing popular reality. It is a descent from the heights of Goethe's declaration that
"the human being is noble and good" to acts of systematic genocide and general
conflagration. The apparent contradiction in the moral quality of the inception of

ethnogenesis and the full-blown horror of racist nationalism should become more explicable to us as we proceed.

HISTORICAL CONDITIONS AND A FEELING OF SPECIAL DESTINY

German ethnogenesis was set off in reaction to the aggressive assertion of French authority and developed an ethnogeny of linguistic and cultural self-promotion, a sense of its own *Sonderweg* or "special path." Fichte departed from Herder's anthropological coexistence when he delivered his *Reden an die deutsche Nation* (Discourses on the German Nation) in 1808, for he depicted the German nation as being pitted against other nations in a struggle for survival. J. S. Chase writes that

The classical myth of German culture was translated into the belief that Germans were the only contemporary people in Europe who still possessed the legitimate ethnicity that had been the underpinning of Greek civilization. Their internal political divisions notwithstanding, Germans for Fichte formed the only true nation because they were the only people who had not been corrupted by foreign principles of universalism.[3]

Germany's special destiny became such an established idea that English and American historians have begun to use it in their studies. The notion has been rejected by some recent German historians, however.[4] German ethnogenesis is actually part of a larger movement that signaled a radical departure from the existing European political order taking place in the nineteenth century. What we have come to regard as medieval European civilization had achieved a functional mix between the Germanic ethos and Christianity's complex theism by the twelfth century. Warrior virtues and the Christian ideal of noninjurious behavior had introduced a higher level of civilization crystallized and encoded as chivalry. Two centuries later, however, a new ethos centering on cynical self-interest had begun to deprive the earlier vision of its compelling ethical vision.

Works such as Machiavell's *The Prince* (1516) mark the rise of a new perspective that rejects a government grounded in prescriptive behavior in favor of a ruthless system of aggrandization on the part of a person or persons. The prince came to be both the source of authority and the force that animates the *state*. Authority and social and political force were to serve the prince's or rulers' interests. The institutions of the modern state were put together for no other purpose. There was, at the same time, a recognition that tranquility within a realm was necessary to maintain a tolerable level of order. Subjects could, in other words, be pushed only so far before they might jeopardize state ascendency through some form of rebellion.

If morality was seen as having to do with one's considerate relations to others, it necessarily involved the exercise of self-restraint and the acknowledgment of the rights of others. Nevertheless, new emerging elites thought they recognized in the princely states of their day little inclination to prudence but much dedication to selfish tyranny. Their states seemed to them dedicated to arbitrary amorality and a willingness to apply force to stop the growth of any moral consciousness or rival authority. Most of the leading German-speaking thinkers were no different from their English or Danish-speaking equivalents: They welcomed the French Revolution in its first stage on its own terms, as a liberation movement for all humanity. Only after the excesses of the Terror became news did they draw back their support. In turning away from the Revolution, they found their way back into habits that supported a continuation of the state as the medium of authority; there was consequently no complete break with the state or its methods of exercising control through force. Konrad Repgen has shown that arguments employed over four centuries to justify war have continued into the modern era to be the same as in old Europe.[5]

It was during the period of dynastic rivalry following the postchivalric decline that the state came into being. The state became the instrument of royal authority and implied in its name a kind of immutable permanence or *stasis* that was designed to depersonalize the authority of the prince. *Auctoritas* was the vote of opinion passed by the Roman senate; it was personal and, therefore, accountable; the authority of the modern state spoke in the third person plural and used the passive voice to absolve itself of responsibility for the acts of its agents.[6] Whereas the authority of the medieval noble depended on his approaching Christian-chivalric ideals of comportment, including showing mercy, giving quarter, and protecting the weak, especially women and children, as well as his being bound by a complex matrix of obligations to nobility, aristocracy, and church, authority vested in the postchivalric state became free of external moral restraint.

Power was personalized for a while in the person of the prince, as we know from the famous dictum of Louis XIV, "L'etat, c'est moi." That personalized force presaged the anthropology that took general shape three centuries later because the ruling prince was unaccountable to anything but his own impulses, urges, desires, or needs: in short, his interests. God no longer fit seriously into the equations of power. One acted as one saw fit and as conditions and political logic dictated. A system of absolutely subjective authority was constructed that became the political analogue of an existential metaphysics still yet to emerge and that can be subsumed in the declaration "Each man his own ruler."

The emphasis of such early absolutist and princely authority was on static mass of stupendous (and in retrospect, perhaps, oppressive) size and weight. The ruling elite seemed determined to embody such an ideal in their own persons, for they ate themselves into great masses of flesh and were compelled by sheer bulk to move with a ponderous gravity they soon idealized. The fascist and socialist art, sculpture, and architecture of our century recapture something of the static mass of that earlier era, although it preferred its own version of muscular rigidity.

The fearsome majesty the absolutist princes sought to effect in their state (the word resonates with immovable mass) lies in the convergence of all earthly power in a single authority. The moderation requisite to mercy is hardly suggested, either by the Baroque or the Nazi forms. The sheer size of the buildings strongly suggests the insignificance of individual consciousness. Obedience was no longer the wonderful privilege of the worshipful creature but became the coerced behavior of the subject(ed). The relentless nature of such public power generated a countercurrent of moral dissatisfaction, an underground current of grumbling at first that surfaced with great force in the genius of modernity.

The state is characterized by an impersonal will to exercise violence. It is, furthermore, out of that willingness that the modern police power emerged during the course of the nineteenth century as a key instrument of domestic governmental control. It is one of the ironies of history that in our modern age the institution of the state was preempted to serve as the instrument of an international order in which the majesty of the crown bowed to the primeval and originating power of an ethnoculture. The state was incorporated to the use of the nation, and its character was transformed. While the crown had sought to represent an unchanging authority anchored in a static political order of inherited roles that were touted as being congruent with nature or God, the nation is based on a dynamic and growing ethnolinguistic culture with a vested interest in change.

In the new political landscape, change is sacred and achieved through the continuing destruction of clearly defined personal roles. The systematic destruction of identity is regarded as a positive process, a progress. No individual is permitted to rest in any given identity. Autonomy turns against the person, who moves from role to role while being buffeted by the mechanisms of state force that, except for occasional humanitarian appeals (to a welfare state, democracy, the establishment of general affluence, etc), lack any convincing justification. Even those who serve the state insist that they are in profound opposition to its purposes of control and rule. Every new politician loudly proclaims his or her devotion to change and the reduction of government.

Education is the chief conceptual tool of control in the modern state. The insatiable quest for new identities is celebrated in state-sponsored education as reflecting the natural chaos of the world and the primacy of the individual ego. Any competing authority is excluded from consideration, and history is altered to suit these purposes. The conceptual heritage of modernity places a number of configurations at the state's disposal, including a hostility to the authority of religion, the deification of passion and desire, and a habit of mind that rejects tradition. Coaxing its citizens to live within these configurations is the primary business of state-sponsored education and serves the purpose of eliminating rivals and reducing persons to blank slates indifferent to all authority but vulnerable to state force. The work of neutralizing all opposition is accomplished, at the same time, while seeming to promote human liberty. When the person has become an individual cipher striving for autonomy over a destiny that has been co-opted by the state, ethnogenesis shifts the focus of human activity from the existent order, the present, to a potential and future reordering.

AGNOSTICISM AND THE STATE

The only stable entity in the dynamic and changing constellations of existence is the state. It is the state that has substituted impersonality for hierarchy; it is the state that serves the purpose of destroying any substantial and satisfactory identity before it can become established. That which is established—the *establishment*—is considered an evil in the new scheme and equated with everything that is wrong with the present, thus justifying the need to change as well as the urge to look only to the future. In ethnogenesis only one order is recognized: a future, pending order. Yet an order that is not in existence cannot be known. Ethnogenesis is, in other words, hostile to knowledge at worst, agnostic at best.

If in ethnogenesis knowledge is anathema, then the unknown is favored. In its commitment to the future, ethnogenesis denies the assurance (i.e., the goodness) of things known and understood. The person known in the confluence of social and natural reality is exchanged for the individual identified by nothing more than references to moral abstractions. These references are taken from a state presumably desired but not yet achieved, things considered "natural," though they are hardly observed in the nature of society, such as equality, individual self-direction, and so forth. Such an individual does not exist. The identity that contributes to personhood, which has everything to do with the unequal, discriminate place in which we find ourselves in life, is subverted in the name of a future no one knows and entitlements to a state that is nonexistent.

The modern individual is alone, unattached, and undefined, existing in an autonomous desolation. On closer inspection the desolation proves real, but the autonomy is, however, a chimera. The emancipation that promised to unencumber human nature actually strips it of meaning. The modern state has also devised strategies through which it has detached millions from their homes and moved them hither and thither about the landscape for new purposes no less abstract than the "rights" that originally detached them from their identity as persons. The individual has become a cipher waiting to be assigned some attribute and some place that will reendow its existence with significance. Of all the institutional arbitrators that once existed, it is the modern state, which is utterly pledged to an agenda of intrusion and control, that has assumed the task of dispensing such meaning.

As the nationalist telos shifts from a focus on the existent to the potentially future, the person to the individual, so also does the structural ideal accomodate it by discarding established (and already meaningful) hierarchy for (presumably potentially meaningful) anarchy. Ethnogenesis produces a new scenario in which the present wages war against itself on behalf of the future. The instrument of this warfare is the state, which alone has authority to enforce and to legitimate acts, which alone has consistent, unified, established identity and a condoned role in the flux of international life. The state is much more real than individuals and certainly an institution with vastly more impact on our lives than any of its former rivals, such as the church, the nobility, or the commercial and economic interests (even the much discussed and much maligned international commercial interests).

Although each nation defines its own particular and presumably unique mission, every national mission seeks not the protection of an existing but the initiation of a new order of the world. With the French that mission was the extension of the blessings of the Enlightenment to all Europeans. Germans sought to establish and spread their own culture: "am Deutschen Wesen soll die Welt genesen" (an approximate rendition into English: "German being will heal the world") is the virtually untranslatable popularized motto of the superiority of the German way of life which I once found in a photograph of a prisoner-of-war camp in Alabama. The prisoners were veterans of Rommel's desert campaigns and had exerted themselves in arranging flower plantings so that the cosmos alone, or a passing airplane, would be witness to a floral expression of their faith in their national ethnogeny, even in a moment of desperate defeat and incarceration an ocean away from home.

Faith in the felicity of ethnolinguistic cultural nation runs deep. At the beginning of the new order there was a widespread expectation that the causes of conflict would be obviated or, at least, drastically reduced once the dynastic order had been replaced. With the princes gone, it was believed, a new era of peace would arrive. The representative cultural class, the bourgeoisie, would have latitude to apply its humanistic common sense to the task of government. The state would become the servant of minds—not persons—subject to the laws of mundane commerce. The once arrogant aristocratic lust for power and glory would be vanquished, and the absolutism of the church would be neutralized. Discord would vanish; international trade could flourish, spreading a general affluence that would create a new age of good feelings.

Stephen McKnight has shown that these heady expectations of a new age were not, moreover, confined to the immanent sphere of politics and commerce but included a belief, especially among the interpretive elites of the Renaissance, that humankind might regain a lost partnership of cocreativity with God, as human beings reassumed their rightful (and former) role as terrestrial gods with control over nature. These expectations underlie much of the expository literature written during the first century of ethnogenesis, the late eighteenth and early nineteenth centuries, when the rise of the national state established a new Western political order built around the sanction of ethnolinguistic culture.[7]

The bourgeoisie was soon drawn into the maelstrom of change and redefinition and did not replace the nobility as the ruling political elite at the apex of the social pyramid. The socialist analysis is wrong. Ethnogenesis did not introduce a new stage in the class war but rather created the circumstances for the absolute triumph of the state over all contenders. There can be little doubt that the process of ethnogenesis continues to dominate the scene at the end of the twentieth century. Totalitarianism is one product and the spread of nationalism across the globe is another. The world order has become an international order, with new nation-states entering the fraternity every year and many more still in various stages of incubation. Each nation strives for a purification of its national body, culture, language, and ethnogeny and bears in itself the essence of totalitarianism, in which diversity is vilified.

ETHNOGENESIS AND THE END OF THE POSTWAR ORDER

The continuing viability of the idea of nation as a sanction for political authority in the heart of Europe was once again apparent in 1989, when East Germans shifted their clarion call to liberty from the chant, "wir sind das Volk" (we are *the* people), to "wir sind *ein* Volk" (we are *one* people). In spite of the ambivalence of the West German intelligentsia toward nationalism, events were triggered which led to German unification and a profound new shift in political relationships in Europe. Nationalism in general and German nationalism in particular continue to be important forces not only in the European Revolution of 1989–1990 but in subsequent developments.

Prior to the nineteenth century the West was a society governed by a universalist Christian vision. The notion of Europe as a concept was preceded by the notion of Christendom. The demise of the old universalist European order, with its several competing authorities, territorial and moral, did not occur, however, before a similar territorial state was planted in the new world. The United States is founded on a territorial order of diffused or multiple authorities and stood alone for a long time in the new order of Atlantic civilization in opposition to the idea of nation. The Civil War (1861–1865) radically altered its character, however, destroying the presumptions of authority rival to the central state. The Civil Rights Movement of the 1960s eliminated any vestigial pretension to regional or local authority. But that was not the end of the central state's aggrandizement. Since the 1950s, a series of federal court decisions have practically removed the authority of religion, as well, from public life, leaving the state in unrivaled authority and in a position historically analogous to that of the absolutist princes.

The difference between the present triumph of the federal government and the majesty of the absolutist princes of eighteenth-century Europe lies in the continental reach of central authority in North America. Communications and logistical technology have made it possible beyond the dreams of any prince to command and control a population and territory of vast proportions. Neither is the span obstructed by the populist nationalism so prevalent in Europe, for the political order of the United States was built around a universalist humanitarianism consistent with prevailing Western views, devolved out of Christianity and articulated, moreover, in a social contract or constitution. The Constitution established certain basic human rights that took precedence over ethnolinguistic factors. It is, therefore, within easy juristic reach of Federal authority to quash the assertion of ethnolinguistic rights or interests as soon as they clash with the interests of the federal state.

In spite of all federal efforts to homogenize the populations within its enormous realm, a regional autonomy lingers, in some places (like the South) still at times fiercely cultivated. Even technology has not afforded the means to obliterate completely the deep human ties to neighborhood, place, and its traditions everywhere on the North American continent, in spite of repeated ruthless efforts on the part of federal authority. In one respect, the universal monarchy which

Europeans were always ready to oppose was accomplished on the far side of the Atlantic under the guise of republican freedom and general civil rights.

SOCIALISM: THE PRETENDER TO UNIVERSALISM

Socialism, the other heir presumptive of ancient universalism, is, in important respects, a charlatan because it has repeatedly failed to transcend the exclusivist habits of authority endemic to nationalism. Striving toward an essentially materialist ideal of social justice, it has repeatedly attempted, at the same time, to transcend ethnocultural, linguistic, national, and even historical limits in the establishment of an order concerned only with fair distribution of the world's material goods. Since the world is posited as the only scene of relevant human activity, possession of the space and resources available is a key issue inexorably tied to any question of justice. Socialism is obsessed with greed, however, though it generally assigns that vice to a class of human beings rather than to general human nature. By externalizing its chief vice, it is able to vilify an outsider group as a pariah "class" that must be eliminated.

Socialism sets up a configuration of good and bad that is morally incoherent. The possession or control of the space and resources of the world is depicted as a good, but only when it is achieved by the superior in-group (those willing to share). If the wrong class of people, those presumably not willing to share, achieved control, then possession is bad. In the socialist scheme, history becomes a struggle for power between the generous and the greedy over the world's resources. Success is possession and control. The moral incoherence lies in the fact that the generous and good are self-declared and self-annointed; to hide their own greed, they are forced to initiate a regime of hypocritical totalitarian control which censures any statements that contradict their version of history.

Socialism oddly shares several of its fundamental assumptions with nationalism, being pledged to a progressivist design for history in which the good (success) is achieved through effort and sacrifice at some future date. Humankind is, furthermore, divided into the good in-group and the bad others. The moral mission is to eliminate the bad others or, at least, their effective influence over events, thereby changing the corrupt present into a felicitous future. The bad others are, moreover, depicted as vicious and cunning adversaries who can only be defeated through tremendous sacrifice. The reward for such sacrifice is a glorious future of general concord and happiness, a final stage in which human existence will find its fulfillment.

In spite of the apparent successes of socialism in our own century, it became clear that the idea of nation has proved the most durable in determining East German and later other identity in 1989. The failure of the idea of socialist internationalism does not end with Germany, however, for the first move to collapse the Soviet house of cards began with the reassertion of Polish nationhood. The successful establishment of the Solidarity movement shifted the instrument of Polish nationality from the Catholic Church to an exclusively political organization. Since that moment the Czechs, Slovaks and others have reasserted their own sense of national entitlement. A number of peoples are setting up their own independent governments within nation-states dedicated to and representing their unique ethnogenies.

The collapse of the *Pax Sovietica* has exposed even the most determinedly internationalist Westerner to the importance of a resurgent nationalism throughout Central and Eastern Europe. The disharmonies that had formerly been suppressed and internalized by the captive populations of Eastern Europe are now seeking external expression in interethnic conflict. If interethnic conflict has exploded into civil war in a number of spots, including Georgia, in the more sophisticated civil societies of Hungary, Bohemia (The Czech Republic), and Slovakia it has thus far been contained and rechanneled. Slovenia, long attached to German civilization and power, also seems to have escaped being drawn into the volcano of Balkan civil war. In retrospect, at any rate, the hegemony established under Russian-sponsored socialism appears as ephemeral as the French hegemony under Napoleon;. But whereas the French left at least a heritage of representative government, the Russians left behind a demoralized and devastated urban wasteland situated in the midst of an utterly polluted natural environment.

Such historical examples lend weight to the view that modern attempts to universalize political society have proven destructive; they also seem, moreover, to serve as mere pretext for the exercise of nationalist hegemonies. One might expect that the rhetorical millennarianism these two examples paraded as their excuse for the exercise of unbridaled force would have placed such enterprises in disrepute—this is, unfortunately, far from true. Serbs have been known to justify genocide by insisting that they are protecting the heart of Europe from the heathen.

Here again one can only observe how the durability of the North American territorial state has not come without some accomodation to the demands of the national idea. In the north, the Canadian federation has been threatened by a nascent Quebecoise nationalism, and political society in the United States is presently rent by increasingly intransigent demands made by rival ethnic constituencies asserting their right to a portion of the federal pie. The American view of the international scene is actually distorted by our identification of nation and state. Since we fail to recognize a difference, we are likely to confuse or misread assertions of nationhood as legitimate claims to statehood or sovereign government. We may, by the same token, be gullible to claims made by tyrannical plutocracies that they represent a nation.

The geopolitical fact that there are numerous distinct peoples,—clans, tribes, families, communities, and neighborhoods - which lack the resources to be independent states has escaped a number of people since Woodrow Wilson helped to originate the principle of self-determination as paramount to guiding international behavior. With the principle of self-determination was born a new entitlement that runs counter to another concerned with the sanctity of established borders. Operation Desert Storm was justified by the latter principle, while Slovenia and Croatia were recognized according to the former. Much mischief remains, no doubt, to be done in the service of one or the other of these fateful notions. Certainly the acceleration of conflict between rival ethnicities striving toward their own statehood is evident since they received such powerful encouragement from the United States. What must be recognized at the end of our own century is the fact that the globe is populated with states which lack the resources to provide even the most basic services to its citizenry.

Ethnogenesis nudges people to aspire to statehood when the resources are not necessarily available, or when other obstacles make such statehood imprudent, dangerous, or threatening to rival peoples. Often national aspirations are humored by one or another of the great powers who see its own interest in their promotion. These are some, but there are many more reasons why ethnogenesis has not proven a stable foundation on which to establish an international order. What we shall see in the chapters that follow is how little interest anyone in the modern age has shown in international stability. Much of the discussion that dominates the public forum urges us to celebrate instability. Even among literary scholars now the prevailing critical mood urges a decentering of authority, and a posture of absolute skepticism. These are, of course, ivory tower scholars who have little real power, but their rhetoric simply reflects the realities set up when two contradictory principles were established as the basis for a global political instability rather than order.

1945–1989: THE INCUBATION OF AN AMERICAN FANTASY

The Western political heritage has been one of progressive destabilization throughout the globe. Western Europeans were enouraged by a benevolent American hegemony after 1945 to believe that the age of nationalism was finished. The Russians propagated the same message in the East, and any expression of nationalist sentiments was censored. Since ethnic divisions were not real to Western Europeans, who were convincing themselves that the age of ethnolinguistic nationalism was over, they could not matter in the division of the postcolonial third world. With characteristic arrogance, the colonial powers withdrew from their colonies without giving adequate attention to the reality of tribe, regional distinctions, resources, or traditions of the indigenous peoples they abandoned. They permitted themselves to be harried out by aspiring new plutocracies on site that were often made up of European-educated locals, who themselves felt contempt for the customs and other tribal realities of the native inhabitants and who had come to their positions of influence as clients of the colonial powers.

Under the umbrella of American protection, Western Europeans were able to set about constructing a European Union and striving for commercial hegemony abroad and unprecedented affluence at home. Western Europeans wanted to believe that World War II had concluded the ravaging of international order initiated during the Romantic period and the Napoleonic wars. Prompted by the Americans, the Germans, French, Belgians, and Dutch were absorbed in constructing an exclusive trading club. Once they had shed the burdens of colonialism, they came to enjoy an unprecedented period of prosperity that continued until the monumental shift in late 1989.

In August of that year, I was among a group of Fulbright scholars in Bonn-Bad Godesberg who heard the U.S. Cultural Minister say at dinner that we had chosen our scholarship year well since we were likely to see the collapse of the postwar status quo before Christmas. My West German friends laughed at the notion and attributed it in their knee-jerk fashion to American naïveté. The Wall was there to stay, they insisted, ironically demonstrating their agreement with the Stalinist leader of East Germany, Erich Honecker, who had said that the Wall would separate Germany for at least another century. How out of touch either of these parties was can be measured in the remarkable events that followed shortly.

The West German attitude reminded me of what I had heard Poles insist when I spent two research semesters in Cracow in 1981 and 1985. Many times I had been told that Western Europeans were simply not interested in liberating their East European brethren from the Soviet yoke. There were comments about the Germanic peoples of the West versus the Slavic peoples of the East, but more important to their arguments was the idea that Western Europeans had a profound stake in the status quo and would not care to change it. Many Poles were convinced that Western Europe provided tacit and actual support for the Soviet-controlled order in Eastern Europe. After all, the postwar order had brought West Germans, Italians, and French an unprecedented period of peace, prosperity, and freedom, the Poles would add knowingly.

The certainty of my German friends was shattered in November of 1989 when the Russian-sponsored governments of Eastern Europe began to collapse in rapid succession. Ethnolinguistic nationalism went on to reignite conflicts throughout the region and beyond. The savage level of violence raging in former Yugoslavia, in which a quiltwork of ethnic groups had enjoyed four decades of peaceful coexistence under the disciplined tyranny of Tito, is the worst scenario come true. Today Croats and Serbs have caught hundreds of thousands of innocents in their nationalist crossfire. Further afield, there is enough war and bloodshed to dishearten the most optimistic observer of the political scene.

NOTES

1. Renewed concern with these questions is evident in John Staddon, "On Responsibility and Punishment," *The Atlantic Monthly*, February 1995, 88–94.

2. Paul Massing, *Rehearsal for Destruction: A Study of Political Antisemitism in Imperial Germany*. New York: Harper, 1942, 82. Also quoted in Jefferson Stuart Chase, *Representing Germany: The Literature of the J. G. Cotta Publishing House and the Genesis, Dissemination and Legitimization of German Nationalism 1815–1889*. Dissertation: University of Virginia, 1994, 8.

3. Chase dissertation, footnote 2, p. 18.

4. Kurt Sontheimer, "Der historische Sonderweg—Mythos oder Realität," *Von Deutschlands Republik. Politische Essays.* Stuttgart: Deutsche Verlags-Anstalt, 1991, 55–63.

5. Konrad Repgen, "Kriegslegitimation in Alteuropa," *Von der Reformation zur Gegenwart*, 66–83. Analyzing the various texts of declarations or justifications of war, Repgen finds that the reasons given can be divided into twelve categories, including the following: warding off universal monarchy, opposing rebellion, protecting hereditary rights, commercial interests, preventive actions against threats, defense actions, and defense of feudal privileges, treaty commitments, revenge of past injustice, defense against Turkish incursion.

6. Samuel Haber, *The Quest for Authority and Honor in the American Professions, 1750–1900*. Chicago, University of Chicago Press, 1991, 12–13.

7. Stephen A. McKnight, *Sacralizing the Secular. The Renaissance Origins of Modernity*. Baton Route: LSU Press, 1989, 110–111. In pointing to problems in the history of modern historiography, McKnight writes that "this study [Paolo Rossi, *The Dark Abyss of Time: The History of the Earth and the History of Nations from Hooke to Vico*, trans. Lydia G. Cochrane, Chicago, 1984] examines the reactions of seventeenth and eighteenth-century historians and philosophers to geological and anthropological evidence of a time span considerably longer than the biblical tradition permitted. The data opened fresh approaches to historiography and the comparative analysis of ancient civilizations. Rossi shows that these materials also stimulated interest in Ancient Wisdom's myths and symbols of a Pre-Adamite time. According to the tradition, this Pre-Adamite time is followed by a period of alienation through the influence of the Judaeo-Christian tradition. This dark age is, in turn, superseded by a new age of enlightenment in which man regains his true humanity as a terrestrial god. This historical construction, obviously, reinforces Petrarch's conception of the medieval epoch as a "dark age" and the Renaissance and Enlightenment celebration of a new age in which man (re)gains the knowledge and power to reign as a terrestrial god." He then calls for a fundamental reconsideration of eighteenth- and nineteenth-century historiography.

3

THE WORLD THAT MODERNITY SPURNED

Perhaps there were two nations-states that actually did emerge organically, slowly, in the natural maelstrom of events, as the Romanticists said that nations should. Yet even these two nations—Britain (or England) and France—were anything but racially or even linguistically pure. England had had waves of invaders over the centuries, mixing Celtic, Roman, and German stock. A number of dialects and languages were spoken as well. In our own age, the difference between the Germanic French, descendents of the Franks, and the Gallic French is still evident. There are also a number of other distinct ethnic and language groups within the realm of France, places such as Brittany, Alsace, Gascony, and the country of the Basques. The modern consciousness of belonging to the French nation is indeed a belief hardly more ancient than the notion that being German should have to do with politics.

Generally, it hardly matters where one looks: The idea of ethnolinguistic identity coalesced around the idea of the nation-state and became a decisive factor in the political allegiance of many European peoples in the nineteenth century. Before that, political loyalty or obligation had little or nothing to do with nation. The kings of England have not, for instance, been English since Harold fell before the Normans. The present ruling house of Windsor is actually an ancient ducal house originally seated in the area of Lake Constance.

Europeans did not even think of themselves first as Europeans until well into modern times. The majority were Christians at the most profound level of identity; next they were members of a particular estate: nobles, peasants, or townsfolk. Authority in the premodern European world was the ordered spirit of Christendom making itself visible in history and particularly in the persons of those whose charge it was to govern. One confronted the world into which one was born not as something to be changed and unhappy with, but as something to revere and be thankful for. As the crown governed on earth, so was it governed by and limited to the parameters of the Christian ethos and its moral vision.

The fact that the theocentric moral vision governed behavior did not mean then, any more than it can today, that there was not deviance. The existence of wicked or destructive behavior does not nullify the ideal of goodness and mercy in the Christian vision, any more than the existence of benevolence, cooperative sharing, and acceptance nullifies modernity's ideal of dissatisfaction and angry rebellion. Old Europe was built on a story that has two connected parts. The first story is about Socrates, the second about Jesus.

SOCRATES AND THE GOOD LIFE

In the story of Socrates the mind returns to the primary focus of the ancient tradition of wisdom literature upon a practical concern for the welfare of the person within a community. The story of Socrates (as told by Plato) professes a morality of self-control, service, and obedience at the expense of one's own life; it is a story not of expedient management but of sacrifice that is the natural outgrowth of a reverence for order. Order can be many things, but most important for our purposes is its connotation of endowing relationships with discriminate meaning. Order does not merely facilitate understanding, it imbues that understanding with significance, and that is precisely what distinguishes it from disorder.

The story is told that, while Socrates is awaiting execution, his friend Crito comes to him in the hope that he can convince him to escape before it is too late. The way is prepared. Socrates' friends have paid the necessary bribes and have made expedient arrangement for his escape. To Crito's surprise, however, he finds his old friend quietly sleeping instead of awake and worried. When Socrates wakes up, they debate whether he should try to get away or allow himself to be killed. Crito urges Socrates to avoid death for the sake of his friends and children. Socrates replies, "If, acting under the advice of men who have no understanding, we destroy that which is improvable by health and deteriorated by disease, when then that has been destroyed...would life be worth having?... Could we live, having an evil and corrupted body?"

Crito declares, "Certainly not."

"And will life be worth having," Socrates goes on, "if that higher part of man be depraved, which is improved by justice and deteriorated by injustice? Do we suppose that principle, whatever it may be in man, which has to do with justice and injustice, to be inferior to the body?"

Again Crito can only say, "Certainly not."

Then Socrates focuses on the nature of honor as he explains that "we must not regard what the many say of us: but what he, the one man who has understanding of what is just and unjust, will say, and what the truth will say." When Crito agrees to the sole validity of the opinion of the good, virtuous, and honorable, Socrates takes that decisive, moral step to ask, "And may I also say that not life, but a good life, is to be chiefly valued?"

After Crito agrees, it is easy for Socrates to explain his indifference both to the opinion of the many and his lack of fear that they can also kill him. Since he had voluntarily chosen to live in submission to Athenian law (and to enjoy its privileges and protection), he must also obey it even when it is not comfortable for him to do so because honor, reason, and consistency demand it. Without honor, according to Socrates, life is not worth living. Honor is a commitment to order, and it is testified to by a select few who are virtuous. It means that one must submit to its dictates even if it proves personally disagreeable. What honor has no need of is the stamp of approval of the many.

The equation is elegantly simple: The virtuous few uphold honor by maintaining order, which enables the many to prosper and to find fulfillment. Honor is a notion the modern sensibility associates with elitism; if it has its advocates, they are generally special cases and may be branded as conservatives, as was Goethe during his lifetime. The notion that virtue is a rare commodity strikes the modern mind as undemocratic. The problems having to do with the character of order are circumvented today because we generally deny either the existence or desirability of order. In fact, democracy does not require that we deny virtue. The idea of democracy affirms order and posits virtue in the bosom of every citizen: Every man and woman a Socrates. The obligations of a citizen pledged to civil virtue are not left ambiguous in Plato. Socrates drives to the central issue when he asks, "May we do evil, Crito?"

"Surely not, Socrates."

"And what of doing evil in return for evil, which is the morality of the many — is that just or not?"

"Not just," Crito says with decision, not questioning Socrates' lack of faith in large numbers of people.

"Then we ought not to retaliate or render evil for evil to anyone, whatever evil we may have suffered from him" Socrates adds, and Crito agrees. There is no mistaking that Socrates (i.e., Plato) also believes that such a principle will be comprehended and appreciated by very few people and misunderstood by many; furthermore, he knows that there are many who deny the existence of evil, so he adds a warning to his friend and his reader:

"But I would have you consider, Crito, whether you really mean what you are saying. For this opinion has never been held, and never will be held by any considerable number of people; and those who are agreed and those who are not agreed upon this point have no common ground, and can only despise one another when they see how widely they differ. Tell me, then, whether you agree with and assent to this, that neither injury nor retaliation nor warding off evil by evil is ever right. Shall that be the premise of our argument?" Here Socrates states the principle of honorable conduct, and, whatever else is contained of significance in the dialogues of Plato, the ethic of honor is made uncompromisingly clear and restated in a number of other contexts. To seal his faith, Socrates chooses to die by it.

THE VIRTUOUS FEW LIVE BY HONOR

In the traditional story, the sanction for honorable behavior is established when somebody stakes his or her life on its being right in the same way the nationalist is prepared to die for the nation. Again, a willingness to die for a certain idea or kind of behavior speaks for its ultimate importance. Furthermore, though Socrates makes his own decisions and sticks by them, he does vaguely appeal to the "gods" as a final warrant for his self-abnegating behavior. There is the implication that the order for which he chooses to die is anchored in a divine plan. In drinking hemlock Socrates is doubly affirming for Crito and his friends that the continuation of order is more important than his own survival.

The legacy of Western civilization is built on this principle of honor, which involves both individual discretion (Socrates chooses) and self-abnegation (Socrates willingly dies) in the service of meaningful order. The ethical vision of the West can be understood in this Socratic moment. It is the same moment in which a significant extension of the moral vision taught in the ancient wisdom literature takes place. Honor permeates Western history after Socrates and only falls into disrepute in our own times.

Civilization in the West is understood to be the active consequence of honor. When honor's component parts—discretion and willingness to serve—become dysfunctional, civilization is disrupted. Aristotle argues at the outset of his *Politics* that every community is "established with a view to some good," so that its support and maintenance becomes a duty for any individual who cares for life— even when he or she must die in that service. Honor assumes that the larger ethos is just and that behavior congruent with its prescripts will be moral (i.e., considerate and constructive). If a people or generation indulges in behavior that divides family and inflicts general pain and suffering on people, then they are dishonorable and civilized behavior is absent.

Since Socrates, it has been impossible in the West to separate ethical vision from the moral quality of human existence; the two pulsated together and nourished one another. The character of the ethos was informed by a vision of God as holy love. God equaled the ideal toward which all right-thinking human beings strived. When a person behaved a certain way, there was a consciousness of congruence or incongruence (i.e., which is to say moral or immoral conduct) that had nothing to do with the expedient. Society governed by an ideal of God, who epitomizes a belief that the aim of community is good because the most profound thing in life is love or noninjurious, encouraging behavior, became an anachronism in the nineteenth century. The mundane faith that it is our vocation to work for good has been discarded. As ersatz we have the modern notion of a self-consciously secular society that deliberately removes any consideration of the sanctity of the ideal and devotes itself to efficiency in maximizing material production—and all for the sake of satiating humans' most vulgar desires. The new faith is in the healing power of a proliferation of goods and services. Satiation equals fulfillment.

EXPEDIENCE CHALLENGES HONOR

In the modern disorder one is presumed to act according to the dictates of natural expedience: The human species circulates across the breadth of history with no more mind than a teeming colony of ants. The motivating force in behavior imposes an expedience quite different from the practical expedience taught in the ancient wisdom tradition since it centers not on the mutual survival of individual and community but rather on the dynamic self-aggrandizement of the individual in a ruthless "natural" quest for satiation. In the modern order, every individual is both potential tyrant and mindless ant, hopelessly torn between a ludicrous hubris and abject acts that accommodate the totalitarian demands of others infected by the same titanic delusions. It is the perennial naturalism of the modern view that vastly separates us from our ancestors.

At the same time, the modern era is not the first moment in history in which honor offends a certain sensibility. Ever since Socrates' time, there has been a powerful opposition to the main tradition of honor. The main offense lies with Socrates' assertion that there exists a "man who has understanding of what is just and unjust" and that, furthermore, the wise will listen to "what the truth will say." There was always a minority view that Socrates' death offends by confirming the uselessness of idealism. Socrates chose death and, therefore, did not survive; his act of accepting the verdict of his peers is, in the minority view, a mere meaningless gesture because Socrates gained nothing and lost everything.

With the change from theology to anthropology in the eighteenth century, Socrates' example appears folly. If the autonomy of the individual is the telos of existence, then giving up that autonomy and existence is an act of madness. Honor is futile. In the modern age there is no certitude that "one man who has understanding of what is unjust and just" can overcome the torment and absurdity of death, thereby clarifying the muddle of disordered experience. Socrates had already contended with such a point of view in the Protagoras, a dialogue named for a man who had come to Athens to teach the young men how to succeed.

In the Protagoras, Socrates argues that success is neither a discipline nor a state with any specific content and cannot, therefore, be taught. The teacher of success, the sophist, promotes a view that cannot account for personal relations, that finds it must convert the person into an individual who is *ipso facto* dishonorable (i.e., who cannot respond appropriately to human need). Protagoras' success represents an unaffirmable and, therefore, defective ethical vision because it cannot accommodate a moral life. When Protagoras says that he is teaching success, what he really means is that he is teaching expedient survival through self-aggrandizing acts perpetrated at the expense of others. Such a habit of mind will, says Socrates, amputate the imagination from the greater part of the person's humanity: his or her connection to others. Success leads to the nonexperience of mere survival.

In his answers to Socrates, Protagoras could easily be a spokesman for modernity. First, he negates knowledge, and then he insists that survival is the only thing that can truly be known. Virtue is thus a meaningless term; honor is empty. One can only know whether one has triumphed over the emptiness of experience by subordinating or removing all obstacles to one's survival, thereby establishing meaning in one's own hegemony over being. What Protagoras fails to remark on is that, no matter how often and through what means one survives, all success is made hollow by death. Socrates recognizes that sophism denies the grounds of rational discussion and excludes arguments; thus does he finally simply fall silent.

Socrates' silence has been interpreted as his conceding the argument. In his incisive interpretation, *The Tragedy of Reason: Towards a Platonic Conception of Logos* (1990), David Roochnik argues that Socrates perceived the pointlessness of argument with a person who denies the existence of order (and, thus, the possibility of knowledge and truth). The dichotomy between Protagoras and Socrates was, at any rate, established in the constitutional moment of Western civilization. On one side are gathered the forces of disorder and dishonor, while on the other are congregated persons of honor like Socrates. Finally, one can and must make a moral choice between the two.

If Socrates is right and society (or civilization) depends on honor and collapses in dishonor, the central question seeks the identity of the few who know the difference. Protagoras sees only a terrible disorder in which relationships are reduced either to subordination or to domination. He leaves no scope for moral action or its public corollary, civil order. For Protagoras, discourse is the art of hostile manuever. His modern counterparts have made subterfuge the mode and urged deception to masquerade as politic persuasion. They have turned their bickering immorality into a public ethic called competition, ultimately undermining civil order by encouraging injurious behavior as the only recourse for the expedient opportunist. Socrates shows us the alternative to Protagoras' desolate egoism when he interprets his ill-advised indictment by the Athenian council as a mere aberration that true community will correct when a balance of justice and honor is restored. There is indeed no doubt that Socrates' execution is the emblematic sacrifice that returns civil counsel to its right mind, not merely in Athens but ever since through the efficacy of his example.

THE COMPONENTS OF HONOR: TRUST AND FAITH

What Socrates demonstrates is that trust is essential to honor. And trust is faith. It is on the ineffable goodness of existence that Socrates wagers his life and Aristotle thereafter constructs a whole treatise on politics. In submitting to the decision of the tribunal, Socrates affirms not only his ethical vision but his moral faith in its indomitable reality. What Socrates ultimately teaches in both his life and his death is that true judgment is given to us so that each person can locate himself or herself to the self; when that is done, moreover, death no longer matters. Judgment is not served as punishment but becomes a disposition of love. Socrates' humility reflects the character of the prescient mind, which apprehends how truth waits beyond the limits of experience and knowledge but is manifest, at the same time, in active benevolence, in mutual support, and in compassion.

Yet Socrates never claims that he is that "one man who has understanding of what is just and unjust," a witness to the truth of what virtue really means when it acts in honor to uphold both the integrity of one's personhood and the civil order. The man who made that claim is in the second story that flows into the mainstream of Western civilization. It was four hundred years after Socrates died that civilization had once again arrived at one of its many low ebbs. Rome was a true ancestor of the modern state, affording a lethal mixture of emancipation and control through a governmental mechanism largely devoted to cruelty and force. The *Pax Romana* drew on a swiftly diminishing pool of moral inspiration. The great ethical energy provided by the vision of ancient Greece had been virtually expended in those days at the end of what we now think of as antiquity. There was dire need of a new infusion to be supplied from a corner of the Roman world that nobody expected and from a most unlikely person: an obscure Nazarene carpenter named Jesus.

ONE GOOD MAN: JESUS OF NAZARETH

Sympathetic contemporaries believed Jesus began his public career as a prophet or interpreter of Hebrew Scripture. His public statements called attention to the original meaning of the Law, to the nature of God and his creation. Today we might call his a voice of reason during a period of intense and often misleading controversy. It was an urgent time when the Hebrew community was under massive assault from a politically dominant pagan order. Jesus called on his contemporaries not to forget the Law but to remember its spirit and his nation's unique call to obedience. Jesus reminded the various theocratic parties that God for the Jews was the originating and personified source of all things, a God of mercy, understanding, and justice and thus completely different from anything Rome represented. The thrust of his admonitions was to recall that the Law was given not to enslave, bind, and confine human beings but to define for them the parameters of their humanity, thus providing them a clear sense of their immortal destiny.

While the warring and rival factions at the top of Jewish society were locked in a quandry of collaboration, betrayal, and expedient resistance to Rome, Jesus provided devastating refutations of their various positions, pretensions, and pedanticisms. When confronted with the Roman governor, Pilate, a man who was the devoted servant of expedience, success, and power and who from all appearance held the power of life and death over him, Jesus responded with more confidence than Socrates had done. He responded as the man "who has understanding of what is just and unjust." The following interview between the Roman governor, Pilate, and Jesus is taken from the Book of John, chapters 18–19 and can be found in any translation of Christian Scripture:

"Are you the king of the Jews," Pilate asked.

Jesus' responses are firm and confident: "Is that your own idea," Jesus replies, "or did others talk to you about me?"

"Am I a Jew?" Pilate responded impatiently, "It was your people and your chief priests who handed you over to me. What is it you have done?"

Jesus said, "My kingdom is not of this world. If it were, my servants would fight to prevent my arrest by the Jews. But now my kingdom is from another place."

"You are a king then!" said Pilate.

Jesus answered, "You are right in saying I am a king. In fact, for this reason I was born, and for this I came into the world, to testify to the truth. Everyone on the side of truth listens to me."

"What is truth?" Pilate said. It is almost possible to see him shrug, unaware of the terrible irony of his words. With this he went out again to the party outside the gate and said, "I find no basis for a charge against him." In a shrewd measure to absolve himself and yet to gratify the community, Pilate permitted them to choose between Jesus and another prisoner. Their choice fell so that Jesus could be executed. Pilate then turned him over to the soldiers to torture and thereafter returned him to his accusers, saying, "Here is the man!"

As soon as the chief priests and their officials saw him, they shouted, "Crucify! Crucify!"

But Pilate answered, "You take him and crucify him. As for me, I find no basis for a charge against him."

Afterward Pilate was even more afraid, and he went back inside the palace. "Where do you come from?" he asked Jesus , but Jesus gave him no answer. "Do you refuse to speak to me?" Pilate said. "Don't you realize I have power either to free you or to crucify you?"

Jesus answered, "You would have no power over me if it were not given to you from above. Therefore the one who has handed me over to you is guilty of a greater sin."

From then on Pilate tried to set Jesus free, but the Jews kept shouting, "If you let this man go, you are no friend of Caesar. Anyone who claims to be king opposes Caesar."

When Pilate heard this, he brought Jesus out and sat down on the judge's seat at a place known as the Stone Pavement. It was the day of Preparation of Passover Week, about the sixth hour.

"Here is your king," Pilate said to the Jews.

But they shouted, "Take him away! Crucify him!"

"Shall I crucify your king?" Pilate asked.

"We have no king but Caesar," the chief priests answered.

Finally Pilate handed Jesus over to them to be crucified. The text continues with its profound associations as Jesus is driven to the cross. The cruelty of the execution process is described and then Jesus' cry of agony, "My God, why have you forsaken me?" In these last words, Jesus actually cites the first line of the Twenty-Second Psalm, whose resounding phrases of hope bring comfort:

> From you comes the theme
> of my praise in the great assembly;
> Before those who fear you

> will I fulfill my vows.
> The poor will eat and be satisfied;
> They who seek the Lord
> will praise him. . . .
> For dominion belongs to the Lord
> And he rules over the nations.

If the power of Rome and the anxious ambitions of the Jewish elite are put into devastating perspective, Jesus' resurrection which follows shifts the focus from the mundane to the cosmic. The petty machinations of his enemies, the moral incompetence and careerism of Pilate, and the majesty of the Roman power Pilate represents all are suddenly diminished beyond irony, beyond cynicism, beyond significance. His true character as logos stands revealed. Socrates' restless conscience need seek no more.[1]

THE DIVINE UNDERPINNINGS OF HONOR

It is his quiet, almost reluctant manner, his gentle compassion, and the clarity with which he peels away the layers of insignificance that persuade the reader about Jesus. Here was a man moving among ordinary people, driven only by his merciful concern for the afflictions and blindness of those around him. Here was a man who demonstrated that he "has understanding of what is just and unjust." Unlike Socrates, the gadfly of Athens, he was not under compulsion to engage in constant discussion and argument. Indeed, when he was confronted with questions, his replies cut through to the fundamental issue and left his interlocutors baffled and breathless. Even before his own execution, he had shown more than once, but especially in the case of his friend Lazarus, that death has no power over goodness.

In Socrates' part of the traditional story, virtue (i.e., the way of the honorable person) was discerned by the wise few in Socrates world (i.e., the *aristoi*); in Jesus' story virtue is *revealed* in a quieter dialogue underpinned by the loving benevolence of an actively merciful and caring God. It is a benevolence unmitigated by the generally uncomprehending ambivalence and pettiness of human beings who cannot know what they do. While people worship power, wealth, and influence, God himself turns out to be the suffering servant the world ignored.

The varied depth of the two stories is also apparent in the difference in status and education between Socrates' inner circle and Jesus' followers. The Greeks were educated and recruited from among the elite. Their hope lay in the active pursuit of the knowledge of virtue. Jesus chose his disciples without regard to status, from among simple men. Their hope lay in obedience to God, in whom virtue was incarnate (i.e., in which both knowledge and truth were united in one person).

Jesus is the answer to Socrates' query. The person with the knowledge of good and evil is God. The source is, as Socrates had hinted, divine. Obedience to God is also virtue, and that is what constitutes honor. Noninjurious, merciful, charitable behavior is sealed by divine sanction. Human beings can trust that such action is good regardless. To deny it, one must no longer merely deny Socrates but God. The Western vision of human destiny was established first in the Greek search for virtue and confirmed in the divine revelations for which the Jews served as intermediaries. The consequence was a new ethos that encompassed the Western community and was known as Christianity.

CHRISTIANITY AND CIVILIZATION

Substantiated by the Christian ethical vision, moral relations made a quantum leap toward civilization after the barbarian encroachments and the collapse of the ancient world. Injurious behavior was stripped of its pretensions and exposed in all its pernicious reality. Henceforth, when human beings acted to injure one another, the subtle (and less subtle) deceptions traditionally employed to justify injurious behavior were more readily exposed as lies; the purpose of the law is, after all, to expose the difference between good and evil, justice and injustice, mercy and cruelty. Most important, however, is the fact that the credibility of the law is tied inextricably to the trustworthiness of its source.

One by one, the pagan societies of Europe acknowledged the Christian message. Traditional Western literature is full of stories of encounters between pagans and Christians during the period that has been misnamed the dark ages. It was a time of conversion, and Christians did not always win at first. There was plenty of room for dramatic suspense in the sometimes violent encounters between evangelizing Christians and pagans. The reaction to the Christians' work was frequently as savage then as it can be today. Much of the Christianizing effort was launched from the edge of Europe, where learning and civilization had kept a tenuous hold while the achievements of antiquity were consumed in general barbarism at the European center. Irish monks set out again to the continent. Men of erudition and mighty intellectual gifts, like Alcuin, who went to serve Charlemagne. Others founded little cells that eventually became great centers from which Christian civilization spread: Cluny, St. Gallen, Reichenau, Fulda, then Paris and others.

The stories of conversion always involve conflict and confrontation. There is, for instance, the exemplary story of the Icelandic chiefdom, Kjartan, who, while stranded for a winter in Norway and subject to King Harald's benevolent influence, was converted. Kjartan misunderstood Harald's overtures at first as attempts at domination. Thinking himself locked in a power struggle, Kjartan wrestled the King in the water of a fjord and tried his wit against him in other ways. Finally, when Harald discovered that his proud guest was plotting arson and murder, Kjartan saw the true character of mercy. Expecting to be killed, the Icelander was confused when King Harald forgave him. There was something more to the King's new religion than Kjartan had expected. In the end, with Harald's pardon assured, Kjartan and his men converted. Kjartan decided that a morality of mercy and forgiveness was to be preferred over the vicious cycle of pride and vengeance.

OLD EUROPE AND THE IDEAL OF CHIVALRY

In a world of pervasive conflict, the warrior was transformed by a new concept of Christian chivalry that matured no later than the eleventh century and became the governing ideal of the political elites in what was then Christendom. The honor of the Christian knight depended on his acknowledging the priority of mercy, which included helping weak and innocent victims and granting quarter to vanquished foes. The Roman idea of the majesty (and cruelty) of state justice was mitigated by the Christian vision. New behavior was the result. The slaughter of noncombatants and innocents became anathema for all with any claim to being civilized; furthermore, it promoted the humane treatment of prisoners and discouraged general acts of savagery. The ultimate and persistent message of Christ's life, death, and resurrection turned the world upside down. No longer was the power of the high and mighty sacred; rather was the lowly servant holy: Service, not domination, was the ideal. The bully lost his claim to any true eminence.

These principles entered the moral vocabulary of the West not because of any sudden but inexplicable change of sentiment, such as must today be imputed to those of humanitarian inclination, but rather through faith in the nature of the divine as depicted by and through Jesus Christ. The example of the justice and truth long sought in the Greeks' tireless quest for a dependable knowledge of virtue was present in a single man. The entire political elite of Christendom was bound for centuries by a vision of chivalric honor that had begun as a Greek ideal of the true *aristoi* (i.e., those chosen to act in the best interest of the community).[2]

THE AFFIRMABILITY OF AN ETHICAL IDEAL

Finally, the affirmability of an ethical vision and its moral ideal can only be judged by the behavior of those persons who most closely approximate it. If we find ourselves in an age in which there are more violent and savage knights than there are those who live up to the Christian ideal of chivalry, it says nothing about the integrity of chivalry itself. Exercising mercy to noncombatants, giving quarter to vanquished foes, and showing civility to prisoners is a good in itself, apart from whether any knight actually does any or all of these things in combat; to act accordingly takes great courage and self-discipline and involves enormous risks. An individual is not likely to make any effort to live up to such an idea unless he or she firmly believes that it is true, right, fair, or just—in short, good. At the same time, believing in the ideal, one will know to what extent one has done wrong when one errs into unacceptable behavior.

Without an ideal of behavior a person simply cannot know whether actions are right or wrong, good or bad. Ideals cannot, at the same time, be simply concocted, for they must be believed; but to be believed, they must be more than the product of our attempts to deal with the disorder of our lives. We must have faith in the source from which they come and in those who have acted most congruently with them. Socrates never pretends to be more than doing the best he can to discern what is right and good. He is not the source. He can persuade us, but we cannot completely believe in him because he does not insist on his authority.

Jesus insists on his unerring ability to discern the will of God as the source of both the right and the good. He seals his claim by overcoming death. There are numerous stories that recount how he acted in different situations. From his statements and his behavior we can impute—and that is the crux of the moral message—the mind of God or, at least, that part of the mind of God that we as mortals need to know. What we learn is this: worldly power does not have absolute power over life; its end is death, and death is denied dominion.

The modern deconstruction of the ethical vision is aimed at subverting what we have learned through Jesus; it can achieve its aim, so it supposes, only by launching an offensive against the institutional structures of Christian theism and its fundamental vision that the good and the right are anchored in the nature of the source of all things. Atheism is, therefore, at the heart of the modern age. The belief in the Christian God (i.e., his goodness, mercy, and justice) had to be undermined; otherwise a Protagoras would have no scope in which to promote the expedient relativism which he hopes to substitute for moral behavior. If Protagoras and Pilate were to be resurrected and given a new chance of domination, Christ would have to be killed in earnest.

NOTES

1. Excerpts from the *Holy Bible. New International Version.* Grand Rapids, Mich.: Zondervan Bible Publishers, 1984: The Book of John, Chapter 18, pp. 1682–1684.

2. Chester G. Starr's study, *The Aristocratic Temper of Greek Civilization* (Oxford, 1992), considers the nature of such aristocracy in delightfully elegant prose.

4

J.W. GOETHE AND THE RISE OF THE NEW, PLEBEIAN IDEAL

In both the Greek and the Judeo-Christian tradition, it is honor that requires the individual to despise the morality of advantage precisely because it consists of rendering calculated injury wherever it proves expedient. Expedience is viewed as a destroyer of relationships; it is, therefore, rejected as being hostile to community. It serves an ethic of individualism devoted to the promotion of desire and governed by the appetites of the heart. Authority exercised on behalf of expedience and antagonistic to honor is viewed in either tradition as being *ipso facto* dishonorable, usurped, and illegitimate. Modernity's characteristic justifications for rebellion are derived from the obverse argument on behalf of expedience (how can we best achieve our programmatic goals?).

In the postclassical age, Christian honor was integrated into a moral system that mixed religious and political sanctions for authority, provided the emerging political elites of a new European order with divine sanction for their authority, and imposed absolute constraints on all who possessed the means of maximizing injury. Men of the sword and seal, the military and political elite, came from the paladins of the Carolingian hierarchy. The twofold traditional story of honor, at least in its clarified Christian form, retained sufficient force to channel authority in directions productive of order and thus material prosperity. The great material and cultural blossoming of the High Middle Ages was a dazzling moment in the career of civilization and continued the life of Western community.

CHRISTIAN RADICALISM AND CIVIL DISORDER

Whereas it is strongly implied in the Greek legacy that the object of honor and virtue is to serve an affirmably civil order, Christianity's eschatalogical focus has helped to produce traditions at times radically indifferent to any consideration of the immanent, secular, or civil order. The chivalric achievement depended on a realism that ignored or downplayed the millenarian aspects of the faith and concentrated on the ancient aristocratic concern for delineating and delimiting conflict. The faith continued, nevertheless, to incubate various radicalisms that often showed potential for being politically lethal.

In retrospect, it appears that some Christians have exhibited a frequent and continuing urge to abrogate the civil order. They appear as sponsors of disorder. There is at the same time a strong tradition in Christianity for supporting order and the status quo. Thomas Molnar has suggested, moreover, that civil order truly begins with Christ's admonition to "render unto Caesar what is Caesar's and to God what is God's." At that point, Molnar believes that the business of government was detached from the sacral, though Christ's words did not settle the question of who actually is to rule in the world.[1] Constantine tried to rejoin the sacral with the secular power when he made Christianity the official Roman religion.

From our perspective, the antihegemonial tendencies in Christianity came more and more into play as the pendulum began to swing in the fourteenth century toward mysticism and the revival of dualistic heresies. The strong elements of dualism in postmedieval Christianity were subversive to order since they involved a rejection of the world; furthermore, the two dicta of Christian realism were often ignored. Reformatory leaders often forgot that of primary consideration is a belief in the permanent nature of the human self and, second, that God will continue to respect human freedom and to act in human history as in the past. The new dualism separated existence into two parts; on the one hand, there is the "bad" world, in which humankind was given over to evil forces, and, on the other, a "good" hereafter or spiritual realm.

The dualistic scheme was then transposed into the conventional modern view of secular progress: All things good come in the future; all things evil belong conversely to the past or present. Ever since, all ideologies have shared the basic assumption that change is mandated by a valueless (or corrupt) present (or past) reality. Whether rightist or leftist, modern ideology is founded on the view that conflict is unnatural. Since the world is full of conflict, it must either be overcome or rejected. Rejecting the world as evil became a standard attitude among numbers of reformatory Christians before it became the habit of socialists, liberals, and miscellaneous other ideologues.

Since a portion of Christianity was abandoning any faith in the goodness, meaning, and intelligibility of the world, it is not surprising that the intellectual elites of Europe set to work to devise their own secular affirmation of life. By the early eighteenth century, they had rejected Christianity and erected in its place the great edifice of science, a system predicated on the belief that human life can be made complete by human effort. When science was built on the empirical method, stupendous strides in technology were achieved. Such achievement came naturally as some of the finest minds devoted themselves to its service. Yet from the beginning there were skeptics who did not believe that science and its ancillary technology were the answer. Some of these minds sought meaning in their work, career, marriage, or community with other people. Others became simply cynical and pessimistic about life's purpose.

Natural catastrophes like the Black Plague and human catastrophes like the Thirty Years' War seemed to confirm the growing consensus that life is a desert of unrelieved suffering and anguish, a desolation to be held in utter contempt and to be exchanged for something better when an opportunity arises. When the best of people turn away from worldly affairs, one can be sure that the business of running society will fall into the hands of the cynical and opportunistic. Corruption accelerates in periods of decline when those of moral integrity turn their backs on the public sector. Things only become worse, and the concomitant belief that authority is corrupt disposes circumstance to fulfill the prophesy. As early as the thirteenth century, the chivalric poet Walther von der Vogelweide wrote that

> Dishonesty sits in the saddle
> Violence rules the streets,
> Justice and peace are sorely wounded. . .[2]

Only an occasional voice was raised to answer Walther von der Vogelweide with optimism, as did Johannes Heermann, some four centuries later:

> Great, oh Great God
> Is the plague that has struck us,
> We have guzzled injustice like water,
> But there is still the consolation
> That you are full of goodness. . .

In spite of the disarray of Christianity and the consequent ascendency of the state in Western society, European humankind was still very far from having either means or, perhaps, will to commit the heinous acts we have witnessed in our own twentieth century. The path had been opened, however, and time would bring in a harvest of savagery.

THE BATTLE BETWEEN THE SACRAL AND THE SECULAR

The old tensions within Christianity divided its adherents, and its internal battles contributed to the reaction against it that gathered steam by the eighteenth century. The legalism of some, the dualism of others, and, finally, the self-righteousness that masked an increasingly inflexible defense of what seemed to many a self-serving plutocracy throughout Europe turned many of the best minds to look for meaning this side of paradise and outside the confines of orthodox and institutional Christianity. The mathematical and scientific genius Leibniz produced in his *Studies in Theodicy* (1710) arguments which preclude other than empirical evidence being admitted to the scrutiny of "correct" reason. Matters of faith, according to Leibniz, are not real.

The battle between the sacral and the secular may have, on the other hand, begun in the struggle between king and pope during the Middle Ages. The successful thrust of the crown was achieved when Roman law was resurrected and given precedence over ecclesiastical law, the argument being that Roman law was of greater antiquity and, therefore, more venerable. Jurists trained in Roman (pagan) law could argue for the king's temporal power over and against that of the church, an argument tatamount to claiming that the state is not subject to moral constraint. The only thing that retarded the crown or state in its rush to supremacy was its common cause with the church to maintain order. When the church fell into disorder, the state no longer had reason not to co-opt it and seize a sovereignty it had already demanded as its just due.

The assault on the fundaments of the Christian faith that became commonplace by the eighteenth century were partly an attack on its theism and partly a reaction against the excesses of its disarray, hypocrisy, and dualism. Although this catalog by no means exhausts the causes of the collapse of the old order, it shows how Christians participated in its demise. Out of the resulting chaos a new hero was emerging who would inhabit a new story and provide the ideal for a new order. It was no longer Socrates or Jesus submitting to aberrational injustice in order to prove the unconquerable triumph of goodness and justice. The new story began with the telling of how Luther steadfastly defied the combined secular and sacral authority of Europe.

It is not the complexities of Luther's theological arguments or what he believed that interested a new generation; it is his defiance of the established institutions and the existing order of things. The romance of Luther is the spectacle of the autonomous individual asserting his or her own unique authority in opposition to the combined powers of the world. If it is a distortion of Luther's real story, it initiated a new tradition of the rebel, the maverick, the defiant and angry individual standing up to and against a corrupt and hostile established world. The hero's anger is aroused by the apparent corruption of the world which is in contrast to his or her own innocent integrity. The hero's defiance is a righteous assertion of his or her determination to oppose the corruption of the status quo at any cost.

THE PLEBEIAN AS HERO OF THE MODERN AGE

The new heroes seem to be against an ethic of expedience. They seem willing to sacrifice themselves to a better future. They refuse to lower themselves by compromising with a world they condemn. In the new story, the world responds to the new heroes' anger and defiance by attempting to destroy them. There is a caution, however, for the story is ambivalent about the outcome and lacks the profound faith of either Socrates or Jesus. Sometimes the hero wins (though it is usually a tentative victory), and sometimes he or she loses. The unrelenting nihilism of the new story is only temporarily relieved by the Pyhrric victories of the new hero. The ambivalence merely reflects a total lack of assurance that there is a benevolent (and, therefore, meaningful) conclusion to human life.

The crisis was intensified by the emergence of pantheistic thought first during the period of rationalism. The conjunction of Pan (world) and theism (god) provides a number of insights into the nature of reality, such as the absoluteness of God, God's immanence in the world, and the unity of being. It is, in many respects, an intelligent worldview. The problem lies in the stress pantheism places, on the one hand, on the unknowlability of God (i.e., ultimate reality), leaving the human imagination groping for an explanation of the deepest meaning of human life. On the other hand, pantheism encourages a "way of negation" hardly suitable for a healthy civil order. Worst, pantheism finds it impossible to distinguish between good and evil, justice and injustice, right and wrong, since it sees an identity in everything. The world is god and everything in it is just a facet of god.[3]

The revival of interest in Spinozan pantheism that occurred during the 1770s in Europe reflected the intense search for a new warrant with which to justify authority after the rejection of Christian theism. A famous and much-publicized dispute between the Enlightenment critic, G. E. Lessing, and philosophical defender of Christianity, F. W. Jacobi, gives us a clear indication of the passions at play at the time. Lessing commented in a conversation that he sympathized with Goethe's perspective in his poem "Prometheus," which was circulating in holograph among friends. Jacobi took the comment to mean that Lessing had joined the anti-Christian forces rallying around Goethe's Promethean hero. Ninety years later the topic was still controversial enough in England to obstruct G. H. Lewes and George Eliot (alias Mary Ann Evans) from getting their translation of Spinoza published.[4]

MONISTIC PANTHEISM IN THE FOUNDATION OF MODERNITY

The rise of modern versions of monistic pantheism are the essential precondition to the development of ethnogenesis. The divinization of the nation, the rejection or externalization of evil, and the anchoring of authority in the human passions are crucial conditions for the creation of an environment hospitable to a revival of Roman-style state authority. Pantheism also underlies the faith in science and is expressed in a belief in everything from technology to the environmental movement. During the nineteenth century, the scientific community developed in Darwinism an explanation of cosmic dimension, a metaphysics, as it were, that has since become its public and hotly defended philosophical dogma. In popularizing works like Richard Dawkins's *The Blind Watchmaker* (1986), the parameters of modern pantheism are promoted religiously and an eternal world is depicted in which humankind is merely another tiny, insignificant component.[5] In popular psycho-scientific lore, humankind and life generally began to be depicted as a kind of cosmic accident.

A Cartesian demand for absolute certainty became the governing principle of rationalism which led to a rigidity of mind previously impossible in the traditional order. The truth requirement of absolute certainty translates into a belief that, in order to know anything, one must know everything. There is also an existential corollary belief that, in order to be anything, one must be everything. Under the burden of such a demand, knowledge and substantial identity prove impossible to establish, much less to maintain. When an ego or self can be anything, it loses all discriminate sense of who it really is in relation to the conditions and circumstances of its mortal life.

In the old order the shortcomings of hubris were commonly known and part of folk wisdom. In the new, modern order such knowledge has been lost in the deification of human ego; the worst of it is that it came only to be rediscovered in devastating moments of profound existential self-loss. Modern literature is full of accounts of such dark moments of the soul when the infinitely ambitious self discovers that, in abandoning its discriminate limits for infinite self-expansion, it has lost everything it might have otherwise really been, and is left with nothing but nebulous pipe dreams at best and the disillusionment so dear to the heart of many moderns. The Horatio Alger stories notwithstanding, the quest for a self-generated immortality leads in the modern myth to self-extinction.

Not every writer has been able to follow through to the nihilistic end without flinching, but modern critics generally judge writers and their texts by how subtly they sketch out and hint at the final demise of hope. Throughout the literature of the last two centuries, one can trace a global myth of the death of hope that can be subdivided, in my view, into two subsidiary myths. I call the first the myth of humankind's hopeless grandeur because it teaches that truly good men and women are those most determined to defy mortal limits *even when they know it leads inexorably to the destruction of their own world.* In the myth we are urged to admire the courage, audacity, and integrity of such behavior; it is touted as a form of self-abnegation. The second I call the myth of humankind's pathetic dilemma because it teaches that striving is the only admirable behavior though its inevitable end is extinction. Both myths are pessimistic and interpret human destiny as a journey that is ultimately pointless.

The optimism that modernity has been able to summon has nothing to do with a revival of hope; rather is it a feigning of hope and optimism through a celebration of the indifferent and presumably eternal forces of nature. Such hope is of dubious value to human beings since its optimism is centered on the continuing and exclusive reality of the nonhuman world, and it includes among its company everybody from worshippers of mother earth to physicists who relish the utter impersonality of the universe and humankind's absolute insignificance within it. It is hardly surprising that, in light of such pessimism, the individual has lost a sense of personhood. Loss of identity has been one of the major literary themes of our age. Other themes signifying disorientation continue to preoccupy writers. Concepts of confused dislocation play a central role in our public forum, and we try very hard to turn them into virtues.

THE MORAL BANKRUPTCY OF MODERNITY'S FAILED HUMANISM

If behavior must first be warranted before authority can be established, the fundamental question of all civilization is "why do you do this?" To which one must answer, "because. . . ." If one lacks an answer to the instrumental question, there is no warrant for the behavior. One can only say, "I don't know why I do this." Unjustified behavior can only be sustained by celebrating ignorance and fate: "I don't know why I do this, and it does not matter, anyway (because nothing matters in the end and because everything happens as it will)." The relishing and, perhaps, masochistic physicist studies the cosmos because he or she derives a self-denigrating pleasure in "observing" (viz., postulating) humankind's insignificance. Self-denigration is not a building block of civilization and ultimately erodes human order by undermining any justification for authority.

If an act or behavior is unjustified and unexplained, it lacks meaning. Without behavior that is somehow warranted, there can be no credible authority. Without authority, there can be no meaningful framework within which one can act or behave. The philosopher Charles Taylor has remarked that "the assumption behind modern self-exploration is that we don't already know who we are." Taylor believes, furthermore, that the awkward and generally fruitless inward quest so characteristic of our age began with Augustine, who thought God could better be met in the question of meaning than anywhere else. The modern quest is an immanentized version of Augustine's "intimior intimo meo et superior summo meo." If one does not expect to meet God there, then, at least, one might hope to find the self, or a cogito of some kind.[6]

I suggest that it is not so much that we have no warrant for acting. It is rather that our warrant is inadequate or unaffirmable. More often than not, we can (and do) answer the moral question forcefully enough: "I do this because I want to do it." Our warrant is our desire. We both justify ourselves by desire and appeal to appetite: "I need this (to satisfy my desire)." Using desire as the warrant for behavior is consistent with pantheistic fatalism. As components of nature/god, we are impelled by natural forces and presumably have little discretion over or choice in what we need, want, and do. A number of modern writers, scientists, and thinkers have sought to give some substance to that desire. Sigmund Freud translated it into the pleasure principle (*Lustprinzip*). We will see how the American socialist Albert Brisbane works out—with the help of his mentor, Charles Fourier—an elaborate theory of the passions. Schopenhauer believed that we are driven by a desire to avoid pain. Herder/Goethe & Co. thought we are impelled to humanitarianism by the very nature of our "higher" impulses.

The most obvious countercivilizational compulsion in the pantheistic worldview to which I have alluded consists of its depiction of Nature/world as a battlefield on which beings are compelled by their appetite to survive. There is no prescriptive mechanism with such a view to contain lethal self-aggrandizement. Those whose passions are strongest will prevail whatever the cost. In the calculus of human order, passion-driven self-assertion means domination. *Advantage* is the primary instrumental value in life, according to the ethics of desire. Oliver Wendel Holmes, Jr. wrote in his uncommonly influential work, *The Common Law* (1881), that we might cherish the "divine folly" of honor and civility while, at the same time, he believed that the *ultima ratio*, not only of *regum*, but of private persons, is force, and that at the bottom of all private relations, however tempered by sympathy and all the social feelings, is a "justifiable self-preference."[7]

Holmes's comments actually conclude a development that began at least as early as the Scottish Enlightenment and can be followed through Benthamite thinkers like John Austin and pursued beyond to William James and John Dewey. The recitation of these names already suggests the profound influence the ethic of expedience has had on the Anglophone world. The world depicted is like a stage on which individuals and groups vie for advantage, seeking to subjugate or eliminate rivals. In such circumstances the ability to deal calculated injury is a valued behavior. It is not difficult to imagine how such views spawn titanic and imperial fantasies encouraged by movements such as New England transcendentalism and especially by its chief spokesman, Ralph Waldo Emerson (1803–1882), who helped to translate German idealism into an acceptable American jargon of self-reliance.

Emerson's myth is only one of a variety built on the idea of the heroic (and defiant) autonomy of the individual. We can locate variations of the myth on both the political left and the right. The engine of the myth is an egoism committed to the primacy of desire and appetite. Conflict is viewed as being abhorrent because conflict really means that appetite is obstructed by the desires and needs of others outside the primal ego. Righteous indignation and rage is directed at the demands and claims of persons outside the desiring individual or his or her immediate circle of sympathizers. The thrust of warranted behavior is to subvert, destroy, or subjugate those external claims and needs. Totalitarianism is the objective: a *Gleichschaltung* that brings all desire into congruence with that one, primal ego desire.

CONFLICT BECOMES THE NEW EVIL

In sum, ideology, whether from the right, the left, or even presumably politically neutral positions on the spectrum, is based on the proposition that the existence of conflict in present societal structures is essentially bad. Robert B. Carlisle writes in his study of Saint-Simonian doctrine:

Whatever conditions existed at a given time could, indeed must, undergo change. Change could always be made for the better. "Better" applied to everybody. The Saint-Simonians did not invent a doctrine of progress any more than they invented a creed of nationalism, but they particularized the idea of progress, and they projected a route for it.[8]

The great irony in ideology, whether it comes from the right or left, is that, even while professing that its system can obviate the causes of social conflict, it also teaches coercion or the application of force in creating and maintaining a conflictless society. Such ideology is not limited to politics but can be expressed in every area of life. Even aesthetics, as the work of the American Morse Peckham shows, is not immune.

Peckham sets forth a theory based on the new anthropology of desire. Human beings are depicted as stimuli receptors bombarded by disconnected stimuli. Peckham erects a system like liberalism or Darwinism in which the individual must seek to impose his or her will on the chaos in order to create form and meaning. Art, Peckham writes, "enables us in protected situations in which nothing is at stake...to rehearse the endurance of cognitive tension," which, in its turn, will give us strength to manage the natural confusion of the world.[9]

Peckham attempts the same feat that others in modern pantheism attempt: While denying the possibility of any extra-egocentric or objective ideal of existence, he makes a virtue of self-assertion and willful self-direction. The individual is engaged in a heroic though essentially futile effort of creating meaning *ex nihilo*. By insisting that art teaches us to exert our will successfully, Peckham joins Protagoras and other sophists modern and ancient, denying the ancient morality of noninjurious behavior and putting in its place an antimorality of advantage and expedience. The purpose of art is to escalate the overt expression of frustration, rage, and violence. Civility is in such a worldview, as Thorstein Veblen so cogently claimed, a mere subterfuge by which the dominant maintain their power.[10]

THE NEW STORY OF HUMANKIND

The new story of humankind, the new anthropology of desire and the autonomy of the heart also involves a shift from a logical habit of mind to a historical or perspectival view in which the world is apprehended, no matter what the ideology, as a pastiche of processes and events. Once we invest all value in a future, we deny ourselves meaning in the present. We cannot *know* the actual character of what is to come, we can only ardently desire it. Character is then defined in terms of the forces that shape its development; its integrity is gauged by the vehemence with which the individual promotes the cause of the future. In our relationships with one another, it is the dynamic that is valued and given precedence, not the steady commitment we exhibit to daring relations with others, not what we do but what we intend.

The historical or perspectival mode that results has generated an enormous literature devoted to biographical minutia, with its accompanying psychological explorations of intention. Th unprecedented development and popularity of the biographical genres during the nineteenth century and the durability of traditions concerned with personal development, including genres from the memoir to the gossip column, reflect the focus of the new story. Writers strive to create an ideological configuration devoted to the future that can lend experience coherence. It is not who you are or even who you know that matters any longer; it is who you might become, whom you might meet, and what you might acquire that provide the tantalizing attraction for millions.

Eugene Elliot Reed has shown how the primitivist impulse spawned a literature of displacement long before the eighteenth century. From Thomas More's

Utopia (1516) through an entire Robinsonade tradition, fictional protagonists have been placed in exotic settings in which they discover truer values than they ever knew back home, or with their family, or in their own time.[11] Defoe's story of the shipwrecked mariner initiated a tidal wave of similar stories in every Western language. In the *Island Felsenburg* (which appeared in four volumes from 1731 to 1743), J. G. Schnabel tells the story of a young man forced from his homeland by the devastations of the Thirty Years' War. He sails about looking for a new home and, too, is shipwrecked. Only he is not alone on the island but finds it inhabited and proceeds to establish a utopian state.

Holmes' "justifiable" self-preference had coexisted, at least since the beginning of the eighteenth century, with a strong utopian tendency to work for the common welfare, striving, perhaps, for utopia. In either case, it was human energy and talent that were to direct humankind's destiny. J. G. Herder (1744–1803) gave his unqualified assent to humankind's new autonomy when he wrote that "If we consider mankind. . ., we recognize that there is nothing higher than the humanity in human beings for, even if we imagine angels or gods, we imagine them as ideal, higher human beings." Once it has become settled as common sense that humankind is self-directive and autonomous, that self-reliance is, as Emerson put it, the decisive factor in existence and that humans will seek their own advantage (Benthamite wisdom via Holmes, otherwise known as Utilitarianism or Pragmatism), then there remains a certain expectation that some great individual will appear who can truly direct events, guiding them into the future. Goethe proposed the figure of Prometheus. Napoleon actually appeared as a historical actor and brought with him the terror and devastation of modern warfare. Force and violence were the tools of his trade, and he strode Europe like a horrible god. Since Napoleon, the roll of despotic geniuses has lengthened, and their deeds of infamy have multiplied.

As the eighteenth century proceeded into its final quarter, there were fewer and fewer dissenting voices heard. Historical and anthropological relativism became, in one version or another, the (anti)metaphysics of the new age. One had a choice among a wide variety of value systems and could choose anything from naive materialism to a very sophisticated humanitarianism. The former is too simple to bear much explanation. The latter is a complex belief system that bears closer examination, especially since it ultimately provides the underpinning for ethnogenesis; it can, furthermore, best be summarized by reviewing the thought of J. G. Herder, the mentor and friend of J. W. Goethe (1747–1832).

Like so many of his great contemporaries, Herder believed that truth is revealed in the general laws of nature. Humankind is, moreover, predestined to respond to these laws because it is a part of nature. The sexual urge is the strongest component of the fuel that propels the individual toward congruence with natural law, bringing human beings through the pain and suffering of desire and appetite to consummation in true community. The final state, governed by natural law, is, according to Herder, Humanität (i.e., humanitarianism), which is governed by love and goodness.[12]

Although there are many problems with Herder's humanitarianism, it does attempt to provide a comprehensive explanation for human destiny complex enough to challenge intelligence. Like so many of his contemporaries, Herder also mixes theological language with his new anthropology. Speech is, for instance, a "light from God." Reason permits humans to develop speech. Speech enables us to share our experience and live in community. Community begins, however, with family, which is composed of the natural, reproductive bonds and is driven by sex. Family and speech are the building blocks with which nation is constructed.

Nation is not the final end of history for Herder, but it is the consequence of a natural, evolutionary history taking place because of what he calls *Triebe* (the best translation I find is "urges"). Natural urges impel us to nation and national organization brings us to a level of conscious recognition that goodness and love are preferrable to meanness and hate. Reason may enable us to decide, but it is not clear what reason is to Herder or what he believes is reason's source. Herder also never explains exactly why "higher" urges should impel us to humanitarian behavior and not to something else, while "lower" or animal urges drive us to obey bodily functions.

Like Lessing and other figures of the Enlightenment and Roccoco, Herder was convinced that one could avoid the terrifying aspects of life by being true to one's better, human nature. We may even risk venturing into biographical interpretation by remarking how Herder was born into a relatively benign time and place. The atrocities and suffering of the Thirty Years' War were long past; the horrors and excesses of the French Revolution were still ahead, though, by the mid-1780s when Herder's major work began to appear, not very far away. Experience taught the elites of the period that one could avoid extremes and stay within the boundaries of prudence. It was both prudence and reason—which it is hard to tell apart—that would prove the key, according to Herder, in building the equitable, caring national society he felt was the inevitable destiny of humankind.

Some of the children of more violent and cynical times soon looked askance at the optimism of Herder's humanitarianism, though its influence never completely died and continues to nourish our times and influence those who believe that the modern liberal, democratic national state can solve our human problems. The difficulty with Herderian thought is that it simply cannot account for the noxious forces gathered on behalf of rapine and destruction. Neither can Herder's benevolent picture of humankind's auto-redemption explain the nasty pleasure people derive from doing injury to themselves and their fellow people.

As the enormous upheaval of the French Revolution spread, those of Herder's mind first welcomed it as the tide that would wash away the corrupt structures of the present order. As the atrocities mounted in France, however, they became more cautious, some of them rather simply commenting on the stability of their own community. A denizen of that optimistic territory of modernity's imagination, Christoph Martin Wieland (1733–1813), wrote, for instance, in January of 1793 that "the internal peace that we...have enjoyed in all of the German fatherland proves much for the good side of our constitution and for the respect which both regents and subjects pay the laws" (*Works*, Vol. XXXI, p. 222f). Looking back and cognizant of what Wieland's nation proved capable of committing, it is difficult to accept his complacence with an equanimity proper to historical objectivity. Spokesmen would soon claim even greater virtue and humanitarianism for the German nation in their attempt to rally their countrymen against the French occupation.

J. W. GOETHE: THE EMBODIMENT OF THE NEW IDEAL

One of the greatest stars of the new story had learned from Herder while studying at the University in Strasbourg. Unlike Napoleon, he had no particular interest in political power and appeared at first to be little more than the spoiled only son of an affluent gentleman of leisure in the imperial city of Frankfurt on the Main River. It was not history that pulled the young adult into a larger life but rather his own genius. By 1773, his star had risen in the literary firmament like no other before him. At twenty-four, he was for many the embodiment of the new anthropology that centered on the force and sanction of the human heart. The power of his imaginative language broke the bounds of convention in first one genre and then another. His work was full of the explosive immediacy of the life of the feeling and desiring heart. He was Johann Wolfgang Goethe.

Had Goethe been less gifted, his fame would have fizzled, just as it did with the lesser writers of the Storm and Stress with which he was associated during the 1770s. Members of the group were known for writing histrionic drama and their unconventional personal behavior. In his essay, "Of German Character and Arts," Herder called his younger friend a second Shakespeare, and Goethe aspired to live up to that charge. Those who visited him at his home in Frankfurt discovered that being in the presence of a mind of inexhaustible energy was not relaxing. Goethe drew his visitors into tireless and intensive discussions that could last for several days. He was relentless and never seemed to rest, so that only fairly robust spirits had the stamina for his company. As word spread and each brilliant new work provided new excitement, a myth of the power of his titanic talent came into being.

During the remainder of Goethe's life, from 1770 until the third decade of the next century, he worked at creating a great literature of desire. By 1788, as he explained in a letter to Herder's wife, he had abandoned any belief in anything divine other than the individual human being. The divinization of human nature was thereafter his chief project and drew on the pantheistic anthropology that had begun to be developed in earnest by some members of the previous generation. Meaningful human behavior, Goethe believed, had to be subject to the government of the human heart.

In one respect, Goethe was being true to the Pietism of his youth by secularizing it. He gave life to the metahistorical humanism developed by his precedessors. After a sojourn in Italy from 1787 to 1788, he joined Friedrich Schiller in promoting a new literary and cultural movement devoted to the "new" humanism. Acknowledging their debt to ancient (pagan) civilization, they called the movement German classicism (*Deutsche Klassik*). It combined both a respect for the antique and a belief that German civilization was a continuation of the highest and most cultivated order. The movement could have had no more prestigious leader, for Goethe coupled the products of his rare poetic talents with a will to make his own life story an icon for a new view of humankind.

Few writers before or since have been as intent as Goethe was on turning himself into the symbolical center of a new anthropocentric universe. If humankind was god, then Goethe was anthropos incarnate. It is also possible to approach Goethe's great and abiding fame in less philosophical terms, if we recognize in him the first great modern celebrity, shrewdly adept and wildly successful in promoting himself and his work. He turned himself, after all, into the dominant public persona of an age. The feat is stupendous for any time and place, but it is especially impressive because it was accomplished in a time before the mass media and sophisticated public relations technology were even developed. Goethe managed by styling himself the personification of the new ethic he was promoting. After his death, his celebrity was rejuvenated when a new generation of Germans made him the *Dichterfürst* or prince-poet, a kind of national icon of national culture.

Goethe's new world was not sustained by the disciplined sacrifices of honor, nor was it even nourished by the prudence of reasonable persons; the Goethean world was fed by the longing of the human heart impelled by the promptings of nature's divine laws. In Goethe's new ethos beauty lies in the unwavering pursuit of the object that the heart desires. Especially in *Faust*, doubtless one of the most respected dramatic poems in any language, Goethe developed a morality in which the act of striving to satisfy desire is the most highly valued of all acts. *Faust* was the culmination of Goethe's long career. The work was conceived about the time Thomas Jefferson set out in his life of politics, and it was finished when Andrew Jackson occupied the White House. It has been called the "drama of modern man," and it stands for the universal myth of the human heart.[13]

SHADOWS IN PARADISE

Even with all Goethe's exhuberant energy and optimism and his determination to ignore the more terrifying and unhappy aspects of life, there is a foreshadowing in his own works that all is far from well. There are, for instance, mysterious ambiguities in his Bildungsroman (novel of education) *Wilhelm Meister's Apprenticeship*. When Mignon sings "Nur wer die Sehnsucht kennt," there are hints of serious trouble ahead. Although resistant to translation, the song can be rendered:

Only those who know obsessive longing can understand what I suffer! Alone and separated from all joy, I look to the firmament on the other side. Oh, he who loves and knows me is far away. Bewilderment overcomes me, my innards burn. Only those who know obsessive longing can understand what I suffer![14]

The sinister side of the new Goethean vision is clear: Giving oneself up to the ethos of the human heart leads to alienation, so one finds oneself "alone and separated from all joy." The metaphysical desolation is suggested in the last two lines of the second sentence: "I look at the firmament on the other side." To be fully alone and sovereign in the universe is the price of autonomy. Ever able to bring his point home with a very personal twist, the singer laments: "Oh, he who loves and knows me is far away."

Goethe also made clear the pain and suffering in earlier works just as he expressed the excitement and triumph of individual freedom. He portrayed characters like Young Werther, who ended his tormented quest for love in suicide. An odd kind of optimism, nevertheless, generally dominated Goethe's thought. He managed to avoid the desperate nihilism to which certain Romanticists of the next generation fell prey. His new hero asserts himself, as he does in the poem "Prometheus" (1774), both as an exemplary individual and master of his destiny: "Here I sit and form humanity in my own image, a race like me, to suffer, cry, and experience pleasure and be joyful." His optimism derives, at least in part, from his belief that a rejection of Christianity does not imply a rejection of all moral categories. Goethe saw himself as embracing a neopaganism by returning to classical ethics. The moral warrant for the assertion of individual autonomy is that it will have a particularly beneficial role in the historical process toward humanism. Intervening events have shown such faith to have been misplaced.

NOTES

1. Thomas Molnar "The Liberal Hegemony: The Rise of Civil Society," *The Intercollegiate Review* 29 (1994), No. 2. Molnar believes that a tripartite division into material, military, and spiritual functions "existed in every part of the world, which is a good indication of the structure's validity well beyond the Indo-European tribe and the Middle East" (p. 7). He goes on to speak of a cleavage between king and priest that became "a central reality with the words uttered by Jesus Christ....The ancient Gordian knot was thus cut, and we may argue that 'modern' history began with those words" (p. 8).

2. My translation is taken from Walther's famous poem that begins with the lines "ich saz uf eime steine, und dahte bein mit beine..." The lines translated are

untriuwe ist in der sâze,
gewalt vert ûf der strâze:
fride unde reht sint sêre wunt... (p. 10).

[Paul Stapf, ed., *Sprüche, Lieder, der Leich Urtext —Prosaübertragung*. Wiesbaden: die Tempel-Klassiker.]

3. A concise discussion of pantheism can be found in Norman L. Geisler, *Christian Apologetics*. Grand Rapids: Baker House, 1990, 173–192. The way of negation was popularized by writers like Hermann Hesse, whose primitivism is especially evident in novels such as *Peter Camenzind* (1904). In *Demian* (1919), a novel popular in the 1960s in the United States, the protagonist emerges through suffering to the realization that good and evil are one.

4. G. Vallee et al, eds., *The Spinoza Conversations between Lessing and Jacobi*, New York: University Press, 1988. The revival of interest in pantheism in the 1770s did not abate. Thomas Deegan, "George Eliot, George Henry Lewes and Spinoza's 'Tractatus Theologico-Politicus,'" *George Eliot-George Henry Lewes Studies Nos. 22–23* (1993), September, 1–16.

5. There are also attempts to reconnect cosmological and metaphysical thought by scientists like Gerald L. Schroeder, *Genesis and the Big Bang* (New York: Bantam, 1990), as well as Hugh Ross, *The Fingerprint of God* and *The Creator and the Cosmos*. Works contra Darwinist thought include Phillip E. Johnson's *Darwin on Trial* (Washington: Regnery Gateway, 1991). Arguments from within science for ultimate intelligibility include Wolfgang Gerok, *Ordnung und Chaos* (1990), and Friedrich Cramer, *Chaos und Ordnung: die Komplexe Struktur des Lebendigen* (1989).

6. Axel Honneth et al. eds., "Inwardness and the Culture of Modernity," in *Philosophical Interventions in the Unfinished Project of the Enlightenment* (Cambridge, 1992), 105.

7. Paul F. Boller, Jr., *American Thought in Transition: The Impact of Evolutionary Naturalism, 1865–1900*. Chicago: Rand McNally, 1968, p. 156.

8. *The Proffered Crown. Saint-Simonianism and the Doctrine of Hope* (1987), 235.

9. *Man's Rage for Chaos*. Philadelphia: Chilton Books, 1965.

10. Veblen also remarks that "much of the courtesy of everyday intercourse is of course a direct expression of consideration and kindly good-will." *The Theory of the Leisure Class*. Boston: Houghton Mifflin, 1973, 51.

11. Reed, *The Civilized vs. Civilization. Primitivism in the Literature of German Pre-Romanticism*. Moscow, Idaho: University Press, 1978. Arthur O. Lovejoy et al, eds. *A Documentary History of Primitivism and Related Ideas*, Volume I. Baltimore: Johns Hopkins University Press, 1935.

12. J. G. Herder, *Ideen zur Philosophie der Geschichte der Menschheit*. Leipzig: Johann Friedrich Hartknoch, 1787, p. 306.

13. There are innumerable biographies of Goethe in English, beginning with G. H. Lewes's (1855). Nicholas Boyle's recent *Goethe: The Poet and his Age* (Oxford, 1991) is excellent.

14. R-M Heffner et al, eds., *Goethe's Faust. Part I: Text and Notes*. Boston: D. C. Heath, 1954, 10.The German text:

Nur wer die Sehnsucht kennt,
Weiss, was ich leide!
Allein und abgetrennt
Von aller Freude,
Seh ich ans Firmament
Nach jener Seite.
Ach! der mich liebt und kennt
Ist in der Weite.
Es schwindelt mir, es brennt
Mein Eingeweide.
Nur wer die Sehnsucht kennt,
Weiss, was ich leide!

The disturbing impact of the song depends on the word *Sehnsucht*, which is a combination of "longing" (*das Sehnen*) and addictive behavior (*die Sucht*). The result conveys a sense of obsessive longing. The poem begins with the assertion that the hearts of geniuses (like Goethe) are also tormented by a state of obsession.

5

STRANGE BEDFELLOWS IN A NEW, PLEBEIAN ROMANCE

With the rise of the Goethean hero, a new romance of rebellion was established. From the 1770s until the present, the celebration of hostile and injurious acts has promoted a steady acceleration of violence in every facet of human life. Hostile and injurious acts have found, for the first time since the advent of Christianity, justification in historical and ideological explanations that merely show how they serve some ends, propelling us into a better future. Doing harm has become appropriate behavior, and violence is invested with moral authority. The paradigm that serves virtually every situation depicts the noble maverick struggling to defy a corrupt world.

As much as Goethe was aware of the potential dangers lurking in his new Promethean man, he was shrewdly able to deflect attention from the subversive purpose by way of his poetically powerful depictions of the new vision and its age. After writing "Prometheus," he produced the poem "An Schwager Kronos" (which can be rendered as "Father Time") in which he enlists time in his project to master life. The poem is narrated by a consciousness that is surely the poet's as it hurdles in a frenzied coach ride with Father Time (Schwager Kronos) up and down a mountain. On the way, the narrator seizes the reigns from the coachman, Time, and urges the horses to new heights. In Goethe's works, a Satanic usurpatiousness usually accompanies the seizure of control from destiny, fate, or time and is often described as near frenzy ("my bowels burn"). But Goethe is also a poet of marvelous surprises, and the coachman, Father Time, reassumes control of the vehicle in order to bring it (life?) in a long and sensual descent to an inn, where a friendly innkeeper is waiting to offer his hospitality.[1]

The kindly hospitality of the innkeeper exemplifies Goethe's faith in the inexplicable goodness of the world—or, more likely, the unwavering value of his own behavior as guided by his inspired heart. If he seizes the reigns to reach the rarefied heights of the mountain peak, he also relinquishes them to assure safe passage back down. Goethe's own life reflects, on the one hand, the audacity of his genius and, at the same time, a seemingly contradictory prudence he displayed in establishing and maintaining himself in a singularly long and successful career and elite life style. Still, there is a persistent hubris in Goethe's works and thought, though he was child enough of his class and century not to permit it to violate the conventional social parameters that might have threatened his position. He was also incredibly fortunate to have an indulgent and protective sponsor in Duke Carl August of Weimar.

In "Father Time," for instance, there is a confusion of identities at times between Father Time and the narrator. Indeed, the narrating consciousness shifts from the rider to the driver and back again. Three entities—nature/Goethe (rider-driver)/time—are merged. Goethe's secular trinity is a monistic whole, and one can see why Goethe found pantheism an appealing explanation of existence. If he seldom doubted that the gods smiled on him, it was because he did not always clearly perceive any difference between himself and them.

Such subjectivism has a certain price, and Goethe developed elaborate strategies to evade payment. For one thing, he avoided pain and grief so elaborately that he refused to confront the news of the death of his son, August, in Italy. When his wife was miserably dying under the assaults of a painful disease, he would not go to her side. Social disapprobation did not affect him in his determination to shield himself from anything that might have disrupted his happy balance. Yet how can we lay blame since much of Goethe's talent for refusing to acknowledge the darker side of human relations is reflected in our age? Devastating wars and incomprehensible human suffering are quickly suppressed in the twentieth century. Rather than provoking a radical challenge to the fundamental anthropology of modernity, suppression enables things to continue with more of the same. It is because of this that I hope to make some political connections in this book between events, expectations, and behavior as well as the underlying structures of our self-understanding.

Ancient literature is thematically concerned that the price of self-divinization is annihilation. The archangel Satan sets himself against God and is consigned to hell. In the modern, secularized eschatalogy developed in the thought of writers like Herder and Goethe, the narrating consciousness aspires to full control over destiny. But there is no price. Goethe has his Faust rescued and taken into heaven in the presence of singing angels. The top of the mountain, as Goethe shows in "Father Time" is, at the same time, a surprisingly desolate place; but the welcoming arms of the benevolent innkeeper are waiting down below at more moderate altitudes to receive the weary titan.

There is some congruence between the ancient and the new story. The new literature shows that the peak once achieved is a place where oxygen is thin and caring warmth notably lacking. No matter how much the autonomous and ambitious heart insists on its entitlement, it is not likely to find what it really wants in the willful pursuit of desire. Goethe has his character Faust largely looking for meaning in the exercise of control, manipulation, and exploitation. He has other stories, most notably *The Sorrows of Young Werther*, in which the hero resorts to suicide when confronted with the truth that real life will not yield to his desires. Virtually in defiance of circumstances and conditions, the Goethean hero(ine) never responds to life's limits by adjusting what he or she demands. In a tantrum, Werther rejects life, and Faust is not only saved in spite of himself by a *deus ex machina* but celebrated in some of the most exquisite poetry ever written.

Much of the cultural labor of the modern age has been invested ever since in justifying and promoting the same doctrines of the autonomous and titanic individual, one could add, in spite of the often demonstrated consequences. The tradition of literary thought Goethe initiated has virtually dominated the public forum of the West and is solely devoted to the new anthropology.[2] The question is, How can this be so? Once it becomes apparent that certain behavior is destructive both to the self and to others, how can it continue to preoccupy the imagination of an age? The answer lies in the dynamics of modernity's anthropocentric metaphysics.

Goodness in the context of the old story is vested in noninjurious, encouraging, constructive behavior; in the new story it is good to strive, to have ambition, to seize control of one's destiny, to self-express, to self-direct—in short, to become autonomous and self-aggrandizing. It is not the saint who counts but the self-made individual; not Socrates' concerned wisdom nor Jesus' divine and loving care but the subjectivist's insolent demands. The new scale of goodness is reflected in the symbolic value of money and the self-indulgent life style it makes possible, and this is true not only among individuals but among nations. As long as the moral parameters are thus drawn, ethical objectivity is impossible. Not even the keenest minds can evaluate and understand past failures and atrocities if they are still governed by the values that led to the disasters in the first place.

The chief quality that the new subjectivist hero lacks is a strong sense of the reality of other human beings. Goethe struggled much of his life to equate art with nature, rather than accepting the traditional view of art as a mirror of nature. Assigning art (i.e., contrivance/artifice) coequal status with nature (i.e., other beings as well as oneself), the ego achieves a kind of license to ignore the general welfare. To give artifact, or human production, equal status with the created world, art must be accepted as another natural expression of creation as sacred as life itself. In Goethe's vision productions of human imagination are coequal to natural phenomena—which is to say that artifacts that are born in his experience are as important as relations with other human beings. It is a new moral view that would have been inexplicable in the context of the old story because it exalts ego and its accoutrements over caring acknowledgment of the reality of other human beings.

The next generation would take up Goethe's notion and expand it into a declaration of what Friedrich Schlegel called "Universalpoesie," in which everything is viewed as literature. In one grand leap into the nihilism of modernity, the reality of other human beings and the world itself is transformed into artifice, something neither actual nor truly meaningful outside the imaginative realm of contrivance. No wonder it became virtually impossible for modern human beings, schooled in such habits of mind, to comprehend the meaning of the suffering we have imposed on ourselves in the chamber of horrors we have made of our history.

In spite of the accumulating evidence to the contrary, we almost blithely continue at the end of the millennium to support the structures of modernity's systematic campaign against the human spirit. Goethe's and Schlegel's notion has most recently found articulation in the assertions of a school of critics who have successfully dominated academia and are known as Deconstructionists, or postmodernists. Like midget Berkeleys, these critics carry on in the modern tradition of reductivist dehumanization, maintaining that the world is a text. It is not so much the ounce of truth that interests them in the idea they promulgate, but rather the provocative and disturbing power that partial truth can exercise to erode the grounds upon which we build our empathic insight into the reality of our fellow beings. Theirs is an exercise designed to exterminate compassion.

If the world is art, or a text, or in any way merely some poorer copy of a reality inaccessible to us, or if we are the products of some cosmic accident and lost in an indifferent universe, then we are reduced to being victims of our own unreality — a gaping abyss is opened up between our longing and the impossibility of its fulfillment. Confronted in the new vision with our ultimate insignificance, we no longer can find reason to care. Futility is the posture the new story cultivates, for it encourages the view that we are not only helpless but hopeless. Even in our triumphs we fail to make sense.

THE PARADIGM EXPOUNDED: THE SUBJECTIVIST AS HERO

It was in the novella *The Sorrows of Young Werther* (1774) that Goethe first created the paradigm of the new subjectivist story. The story occurred to Goethe while he was mulling over the suicide of an acquaintance and just after he had fled a hopeless infatuation with a young woman who was already engaged to be married. Written as a series of letters from the protagonist, a young man with a name that sounds very like Goethe's own, the style was sentimental, self-indulgent, and effusive. It depicts the career of Werther, a young adult who obviously belongs to the affluent middle classes, who becomes obsessed with his infatuation for a young woman already engaged to be married. In the work Goethe showed his uncanny ability to touch a resonant chord in his generation, for it was a sensational success and catapulted the twenty-four-year-old author to international fame.

The story begins as the rather muddled and self-centered young man gets himself first into one bad situation and then another. Although he never explains his connection to family or place, Werther hints that he was already trying to escape a problem back home before the story began. He bungles into a town and falls in love with a charming young woman named Lotte. At first, he is not aware that she is already engaged to be married. In an attempt to escape his growing obsession with her, he leaves town and takes employment with an aristocratic diplomat. There he muddles things once again when he stays after working hours and mixes with an exclusively aristocratic company, who recognize him as middle class and ask him to leave. Reeling from one humiliation to the next, he returns to Lotte, who has, in the meantime, married.

The reader never really becomes acquainted with Lotte. She remains little more than a prop in a story focused entirely on Werther. In his letters he does show her in situations in which she appears to encourage his interest in her, but her consternation when he becomes passionate indicates that she, like most normal people, simply has not understood the extent to which Werther's behavior is neurotic. Neither she nor her fiancé and later husband, Albert, can comprehend a person who is willing to go beyond civility in his importunities. Werther gives no indication in his letters that he is aware that his behavior is troubling and wrongheaded. He places responsibility for the debacles he creates on the other people. The aristocratic exclusivity that humiliated him is unjust; Lotte's fiancé is a pedantic bore, and so forth.

In choosing the epistolary narrative, Goethe comes upon the perfect strategy for the subjectivist. Werther tells his own tale; no other viewpoint enters into the narrative, at least until near the end of the story when Werther's mental breakdown is complete. Werther can portray himself in a sympathetic light, disguising his reprehensible conduct, self-absorption, and indifference to the feelings of others. To recognize how obnoxious he really is, one must read between the lines. He shows us himself in charming poses, playing with children, talking with peasants, acting out the sentimental role of a person of sensitivity and feeling.

Capturing and holding reader's sympathy is an important aspect of narrative strategy in the new tradition Goethe develops, especially since the subjectivist protagonist displays objectively irritating and uncivil behavior. Goethe's task is formidable: to make an obnoxious, spoiled, petulant, intruding, and even murderous young man appealing. In addition, the reader must be charmed into finding Werther's pantheistic ruminations on the meaning of life somehow interesting. It is a tall order for any writer, and Goethe manages the task very well by showing how Werther is in touch with nature, how he loves children and enjoys talking to his social inferiors. Although sometimes lethal, Werther can also be spontaneous and childlike. Stressing the "good" side presumably distracts us from noticing that he is more often unfair, self-righteous, arrogant, and inconsiderate. Disabled by his subjectivism, Werther cannot comprehend any view but his own.

Werther insists in each of his letters that he is among the blessed few who are selected by nature to act as its mouthpiece on earth. He is, he boldly declares, an artist without ever having produced a work of art. His sentiment and intentions give him that status. He believes that he is an instrument of nature; as such, he depicts himself as a kind of natural phenomenon. What he does is, therefore, inevitable, even irresistible. His behavior is not subject to the tentative rules of normal human interrelationships which depend on each person recognizing and acknowledging the dimensions of the other. All Goethe's narrative talents are employed to seduce the reader into collusion with the narrator.

If one is able to ignore the seductive strategy of the writer, however, in order to observe the character objectively, it is no pretty tale. Although Werther insists

on his love for Lotte, he has no care for her welfare. Engagement in the eighteenth century was a very serious matter indeed. Lotte's engagement to Albert
makes her legally inaccessible to anybody else. Were she to yield to Werther's
imputations, she would be ruined socially, morally, and legally and subject to
punitive action. These are matters, nevertheless, for which Werther is uncon-
cerned. He can only think about his own "love." In our oblique glimpses of the
other characters—the kind and helpful Count, a patiently civil Albert, the rather
unresourceful and unimaginative Lotte—it is clear that decent people simply do
not know what to make of Werther. They are, as he so contemptuously points out,
conventional people. Comprehending how he can do what he does is simply
beyond them. They cannot envisage willfully destructive behavior such as he
displays. They are people of the old story: decent, moral, concerned with acknowledging and respecting the feelings of their fellow beings, curbing and disci-
plining themselves—in short, conventional.

Lotte and Albert meet Werther on terms of civility. Werther exploits them
shamelessly, despising their civility as he violates it. He is the penultimate hero
in the new, subjectivist story of humankind, secure in his contempt for the structures of civilization, self-absorbed, grounded in his unscrupulous willingness to
exploit and subvert those very structures by destroying the relationships they were
created to sustain. Werther's story makes clear the weakness in civilization Socrates
had recognized in his debate with Protagoras. Faced with ruthless willfulness
and self-aggrandizing ambition, civilization is strangely awkward and inept and
lacks protective mechanisms. Those who cannot recognize the value of empathetic
and benevolent behavior cannot be met on rational, nonviolent terms.

Goethe's work also represents a sophistic advancement for the cause of expedience. Werther disguises his intentions in romantically sentimental language
that appears to disorient Lotte (though Albert is not fooled and meets Werther
with a cool self-possession that infuriates him). While he professes his desire for
her, nowhere does Werther consider an honorable option or explain what he intends if Lotte happens to yield and become a consumed object rather than a desired one. When Werther returns and finds Lotte married, he does not bow out
civilly; rather he gives his obsession full vent. In fact, Lotte's marriage simply
increases the stakes that attracted him to her in the first place. Since she is even
more inaccessible, the potential danger of injury becomes greater for all concerned and attract Werther the more.

Like so many future prisoners of the heart, this hero of the new story shows
himself devoted to maximizing injury. He is pledged to do harm. It is not unre-
quited desire, or even thwarted sexual obsession, that is the theme of Goethe's
most popular work; the story has to do first and foremost with an intent to damage
and destroy. Werther is the apostle of disorder and violence, and he really has
only contempt for the needs and desires of others. That fact did not escape a
number of critics when the work appeared. Goethe was involved in a whirlwind
of criticism after reported incidents of suicide were linked to the influence of the
novel.

FAUST: THE SUBJECTIVIST AS SKEPTIC

Goethe's greatest work develops the theme of the new hero even more fully. In *Faust* he unfolds a larger agenda when he has Faust declare in a famous opening scene the bankruptcy of all knowledge:

> I have thoroughly studied philosophy,
> Jurisprudence and medicine,
> Unfortunately even theology,
> All pursued with intense labor.
> Now here I stand, poor fool,
> No wiser than before!

His Wertherian conceit is intact and vital to the type, for Faust notes, further, that he is "smarter than the other bums, doctors, masters, clerks, and priests," that he is, moreover, "plagued by neither scruple nor doubt, nor afraid of either hell or the devil." What drives him on his course is his utter lack of joy:

> For all that every joy is usurped,
> And I have no illusions that I could teach
> The human race to improve.[3]

What the new hero hopes for is to reimbue life with meaning by finding release from the disenchantment of real and present circumstances. Instead of blaming himself for his inability to enjoy and appreciate life, he blames his condition on the world he lives in. In *Faust* Goethe strikes the new chord Werther had first intoned: to demand of life more than life can give and then to blame life for its failure; next to demand an emancipation from one's condition that can only be accomplished with the help of the devil.

Endemic to the Goethean vision is the belief that life is really only worth the trouble if one can have one's own way, if one's desires and appetites can be fully satisfied. If the world, which is, though inadequate and corrupt, the *only* thing there is (in other words, god), does not respond by granting desire its object, then death is embraced and maximum injury inflicted on everything and everybody within reach, including oneself. The world is converted to an object, and the presumptuous ego attempts to gobble it up as a disposable experience. The deadly ethos is disguised as a new religion of the yearning heart and sensitive spirit. Its influence is still a force in our own time and is expressed in a number of social and political movements and fashions.

PLEBEIANISM AND THE MORAL MANDATE FOR SATIATION

What I have called until now the new subjectivist story, the Wertherian or Goethean vision, the new anthropology, and the new pantheism needs a generic designation. It is the belief that the individual human being can become an autonomously self-directive force, and it entails a rejection of preestablished authority. In practice, it works itself out as a new plebeianism. At its most blatant, a spoiled, self-centered ego petulantly declares its right to satiation, demanding more of conditions, circumstance, and other people than they are willing or able to render. It is for purposes of self-aggrandizement that this ego consciousness styles itself an autonomous individual, for it is fixed on its own appetites and is greedy to satisfy them. The expedient pursuit of these objectives governs plebeian behavior.

Faust is the archetype. He is easily corrupted, ruthless in hurrying from one novelty to the next, hungry for any tantalizing spectacle that includes sex and violence, and devoid of empathic insights into the people he exploits and violates. Faust is the new plebeian man whom Goethe began to develop in the 1770s with *Werther*. The popularity of these works throughout the West shows how resonant was the chord they struck. The literate elites were ready for a new, plebeian hero: the raging ego that insists on the sole legitimacy of its appetites in defiance of the combined established order. The works initiated a new tradition in literature in which writers continue to produce fiction, poetry, and drama.

In the plebeian story, it is the human heart or its passion that is to lead us by the nose, having us follow the dictates of desire rather than reason—reason indeed being used as a mere adjunct to appetite, to justify and rationalize it. The world, the present, the conditions, circumstances, and community in which we find ourselves are viewed as fundamentally bad. The complaints of the new plebeian were conventionalized by the second decade of the nineteenth century into a litany of dissatisfaction that is still invoked today to show that one belongs to the right crowd, those who know the score, those who are literate and sophisticated (and not silly, ignorant, even Christian optimists).

THE LITANY OF DISSATISFACTION

There are a number of ways to communicate the litany in the course of an ordinary conversation, but the litany consists of seven basic assertions:

1. Good is probably nonexistent but certainly irrelevant and can exist (if it does at all) only in the future.

2. Religion (but especially Christian religion) is primitive and belongs to a childish state of humankind's development. Only ignorant people entertain its notions, which are fantastic and unreasonable and have nothing to do with "reality."

3. Earthly life is all there is. Death is final.

4. Life is chaotic at base, and things are pretty rotten and badly need changing.

5. The poor, marginalized, dispossessed, rebellious, and eccentric are morally superior to other (conventionally civil) people.

6. People who serve the conventional institutions of Western society are *ipso facto* corrupt and/or stupid.

7. Philosophy (often called metaphysics) is nonsense because there is really nothing we can know (of any value).

The new plebeianism insists first and foremost on the need to transform human nature. The resulting transformatory ideologies are closed explanatory systems that seek to explain everything relevant in terms of the need for transformation, for complete and radical change, and for the eradication of all present conditions and persons, especially if those people are perceived as not being capable of total transformation. We will turn to these ideologies and justifications of a new kind of anti-authoritarian authority in the next chapters. The new plebeian expresses a profound antipathy toward human relations and the protreptic that promotes them. The plebeian enterprise constitutes an egregious assault on human community that has dominated our age and is encapsulated in the belief that no order (or its authority) is truly valid.

The new plebeian has entered a quarrel between logos (intelligibility) and misology (antiknowledge and pro-expedience) that is at least as old as Socrates. John Schaeffer is one of several recent critics who believe that the quarrel has become more acute with the introduction of literate (written) culture. If writing and not speaking is given privileged status, human activity, to an increasing degree, becomes centered around reading and textual interpretation. Knowledge, which is the act of making something present in speech, no longer functions as the goal of intellectual activity. The relativizing activity of interpretation becomes the central work of every functional person. In the cacophony of resulting voices, it becomes difficult to sustain a truthful account.[4]

The former tellers of the story have become critics who vie with one another to produce the most interesting interpretation. The result is a breakdown of logos (intelligibility) with the rise of divergent interpretations about the (lack of) meaning of the original story. The new story is that the story still needs to be written. There is always the footnote, as Herder asserted, that the real meaning and significance can only be discerned at the end of history, when everything is done and everything is consequently—and for the first time—really known.

The practical consequence of such a shift is that it brings power and privilege to a new class of interpreters, critics, scientists, professors, journalists, teachers, the media, and all others who profess to explain what is meant in the printed text. Werther was admired because he created his own text and insisted on its primacy. Other interpretations were invalid because those delivering them were discreditable. They were corrupt, callous, or empty. Like Werther, the modern plebeian hero(ine) acts out of discontent with life. Furthermore, conflict is, in the terms of the new plebeianism, unnatural because it grows out of a confrontation between the autonomous ego's desire and the unwillingness of the world to satisfy it.

In earlier chapters, I have suggested that the "idols" or ideologies developed to justify some authority and order first require the elimination of conflict and look forward to a future in which harmony will reign. Here is the source of modernity's totalitarian fantasy. Harmony without conflict can only be coerced in a militant transformation of the present order. The only bad behavior in this plebeian story is that which contributes to sustaining the present order of the world. Those who serve existing institutions are especially despised.

THE HYPOCRISY OF MODERN ANTIAUTHORITARIANISM

Since discontent is the instrumental plebeian role, it acts to destroy sanctioned authority. Modern plebeians foreswear authority while courting privilege and power in their careers. A declaration of antiauthoritarian beliefs and actions is indeed the new justification for seeking an office of authority. The hypocrisy is unique in the history of leadership. Plebeians protest that they despise authority and the force it involves as its sanction, and yet it is precisely what they seek.[5] Every human endeavor, including literature, is enlisted in the action to transform the present. "Serious" literature is that which, for instance, rejects the present and points to the future (dis)order.[6]

The new cadre of elite interpreters—people like Herder and Goethe—became the brokers of privlege and power, the empowered directors exercising authority over life. In the earliest stages of the new age, during what we know as the Renaissance, there were the magi who, in their control of esoteric knowledge, held Faustlike the magic key over life.[7] In the next stage the magi become scientists (still conceptually very close to the protoscientists, who sought to transmute mundane material into gold) with the charge of explaining existence. Goethe's poetic genius was the declared third guise of the magus. The (Romantic) artist exercises hegemony through art.

The plebeian vision is actually a fantasy of successful life without risk. The plebeian's passions are sufficient warrant for what he or she does, since the passions are assumed to be the medium through which nature/god/world speaks. The liberties taken by the plebeian with other people's feelings, needs, and lives are sanctioned because they are congruent with passion/appetite/desire/nature. No matter how exasperating plebeian behavior is, it is right because it is a part of the passional force of nature. A new human type is established that conforms to the ancient plebeian penchant for public irresponsibility and that insists on its right to self-expression and gratification without risk or limit.

Underlying the new plebeianism is a pantheism closest to that of Plotinus. The world is created ex-Deo; evolutionism is a characteristic pantheistic (naturalistic) explanation for existence. In his autobiographical writings Goethe refers to his life in organic terms. The motive of much of his scientific research was to discover the primordial existential impulse in the organic life of the natural world. Hegel would bring the tendency of Goethe's thought to fruition in his philosophy. In Hegel history is the very progress of God through time on his way to becoming fully intelligible.

THE PROBLEM WITH MODERN PLEBEIANISM

For all its stirring, cosmic drama, the vision or fantasy of the new plebeian-ism contains insurmountable obstacles to the simple and necessary task of affirming existence. In its pantheistic foundation and consequent belief that creation is ex-Deo, modern plebeianism makes it virtually impossible to differentiate effectively between good and evil. We have already noted that, if all things are part of god's body, there can be no difference between goodness and wickedness; furthermore, if human destiny is really about the individual's struggle toward self-exaltation, any act is justified that promotes the process. The new plebeianism offers no scope for moral behavior or ethical judgment. The foundational amorality of the plebeian worldview is consistent with atheistic modernism. Its orthodoxy has forced modern thought to become absorbed in deflecting criticism rather than philosophically evaluating its foundational assumptions.

Ideology strives to make life meaningful by fixing on one facet of experience and turning it into the fulcrum by which meaning is created. Marxist socialism portrays meaning as being created in the distribution of resources and services. Positive meaning results in the establishment of equitable distribution; negative meaning is the consequence of inequitable distribution. Private property is perceived as a hindrance to equitable distribution, and its abolishment is the first step toward justice. Those who have lived in the socialist world know the terrible hypocrisy endemic to such truncated explanation. To believe it, one must ignore other dimensions of human existence. Ideology enforces an orthodoxy more terrible than anything previously generated by the human imagination because it demands that we bracket out inconvenient truths.

What ideology can least tolerate is mystery, ambiguity, or any suggestion that human destiny is transcendent (beyond the confines of material time and space and, therefore, easy explanation). If human destiny is clothed in mystery, it lies outside the compass of human interpretation and can only be grasped through revelation or via knowledge that arrives from outside the parameters of human existence. A transcendent source of real knowledge places the source outside the reach of those aspiring directors of human destiny, consequently undermining any concocted justification for their authority.

Modern plebeianism is the behaviorial consequence of modernity's anthropology; in its first impulse to explanation, it gave a jump-start to ethnogenesis. It did not matter that neither Goethe nor Herder promoted the idea of the nation-state and actually attempted to incorporate the idea of national culture into a higher moral project. Because Herder believed that culture would lead to humanitarianism, he was adamant and vigorous in his oppposition to both national chauvinism and racism. He wrote that each nation must be considered exclusively within the context of what it is and has.

Instead of breeding tolerance, however, the new humanitarianism bred relativism. Instead of learning to appreciate non-European culture, it led both Herder and Goethe to a kind of cultural self-hate that we discovered earlier in primitivism. Herder wrote that "least of all is European culture the measure of general

human goodness and value; it is either a false standard or no standard at all."[8]
Goethe promoted the idea that a higher culture throughout human society, both
Western and non-Western, contributed artifacts and set standards that established
a "world" civilization.

The fact that the eighteenth-century European nobility did constitute something of an Pan-European or international culture with a shared language—French
—probably convinced these two parvenu products of the middle classes that sophisticated, humanitarian world culture was a real possibility and represented the
true hope of the future. Such a culture was, of course, restrictive, exclusive, hier-
archical, and elitist; yet none of these conditions were perceived as inherently evil
if they produced in combination a highly civil order. Herder, Goethe, and other
intellectual leaders during their generation were comfortable with Socrates' view
that only the few really understood and exhibited virtue. The great Immanuel
Kant asserted in his essay "What Is Enlightenment," that the majority of humankind choose out of a natural lethargy to remain immature and nonautonomous
beings governed by the prescriptions of others.

Where these selected few get their understanding of virtue was not quite
clear to these eighteenth century post-Christians. Goethe strived to create a new
vision of humanism freed of the constraints of traditional ethics. So far as one
can determine, that Goethean humanism came out of some inner good sense that
a few exceptional people or geniuses possess. Such geniuses then act as moral
arbiters among their less enlightened fellows, convincing them of what is right
and wrong. The only real power is the arguments and the attractive force of their
higher arguments.

IPHIGENIA: THE GOOD HEART AS MORAL ARBITER

In his drama *Iphigenia auf Tauris*, which Goethe completed while sojourning
in Italy in 1788, he transposes the violent ancient legend of the House of Atreus
into a vehicle to promote his view of a "higher" ethical mandate taken from modern humanitarianism. Agamemnon's daughter, Iphigenia, miraculously escaped
death under her father's sword when a goddess transported her to serve as a priestess
on the island of Tauris. In presenting Iphigenia as a kind of moral oracle, Goethe
makes his strongest case for his belief that woman is the true moral force in society, a vehicle for the promotion of humanitarian values. When her brother, Orestes,
shows up on the island, she is compelled by her honesty to expose him to her
master, King Thoas, appealing to his good will and moral sense not to follow the
laws of his island and execute the intruder.

Orestes is ready to fight for his life. He has no faith in humankind's "better"
nature. Thoas is equally inclined to obey the laws and kill Orestes. Iphigenia
stands between them and argues for humanitarian behavior. Ancient Greek warriors are prompted to take a giant conceptual leap into the ethical world of the late
eighteenth century and refrain from settling a score by force of arms. Their choosing the noninjurious behavior over law and tradition is due in Goethe's play en-

tirely to Iphigenia's intervention. Reluctant though Thoas is not to carry out his duty as king, his admiration for Iphigenia wins the day. Her feminine (i.e., sexual) power over him Goethe equates with moral authority. Thoas desires her; therefore, he obeys her. Her victory is thus less a victory of Goethe's humanitarianism than the triumph of passion and desire.

In writing *Iphigenia*, Goethe failed to note that Christianity intervenes between his time and Iphigenia's. His oversight was due to his habitual dismissal of Christianity. The humanitarian views he has his character articulate actually spring from insights neither acquired by the savage Greek milieu nor generated by Goethe's own second half of the eighteenth century. Iphigenia urges two warriors to act as though they believe in an ethos about which neither she nor they historically would have had any knowledge. It was long after the age of the Trojan heroes that even Socrates appeared on the scene with his admittedly incomplete knowledge of the Good. The play *Iphigenia* is another Goethean opportunity to show the solitary ego displaying its moral superiority, dazzling or persuading other characters in the fiction while appealing to the sentiments of the reader.

Goethe promoted a titanism in which the hero is ruled by the passions of the human heart. Herder portrayed the passional drive as leading the hero into relationships, families, and nations. Herder pictures the nation as the corporate ego, governed by natural passion, with reason operating to convince its members that humanitarian behavior is best. It was up to the next generation to connect the nation with the state, for neither Herder nor Goethe had much use for the latter. As Napoleonic titanism exploded over Germany, younger people began to recognize that the nation—no matter how great its culture—cannot become a mature political actor or an autonomous unit without harnessing the mechanisms of force and government for its use. The nation can only become the natural embodiment of a reincarnated civitas when its will is manifest in the state.

FAUST AND THE NATION-STATE

In spite of the fact that neither Herder nor Goethe were believers in the state, *Faust* is the archetype that makes nationalist behavior possible. The nation-state could not be envisaged without the anthropology of the human heart developed by these eighteenth-century sentimentalists. Faust trusts in the insatiable drive of his appetite and values his compulsion to pursue the objects of his desire whatever the cost (to others). He is willing to engage the force of magic (technology is its modern equivalent) and the help of the devil in the pursuit of satisfaction. In spite of the mischief Faust works, it is never clear either in the work itself or in its author's comments that his behavior is wrong, and his ruthless quest for the tools of coercion and force presage the willingness with which future generations would embrace the state.

Goethe was fortunate. He came along at a time when his private propensities corresponded to a perceived public need. There was a growing consensus in

Europe that the old order was no longer binding, its sanctions no longer real. People were tired of the absolutist arrogance of their princes and the collusion of the church authorities. Spokesmen for the new morality of the human heart appeared as harbingers of a new and wonderful freedom, especially when they spoke with the genius of a Goethe.

NOTES

1. "Schwager Kronos" is actually a more ambiguous reference than I have indicated, for "Schwager" means "brother-in-law," the address one likely used in places for the coachman, while with Kronos Goethe was not thinking about Zeus' father but, perhaps, of Chronos or time.

2. There are, on the other hand, a number of new works protesting the tradition. Michael Morton, *The Critical Turn: Studies in Kant, Herder, Wittgenstein, and Contemporary Theory* (Detroit: Wayne State University Press, 1993), is the most comprehensive critique and well worth reading.

3. *Faust,* Der Tragödie, Erster Teil, Nacht, Lines 354–59, 370-373.

4. John Schaeffer, *Sensus Communis. Vico, Rhetoric and the Limits of Relativism.* Durham, N.C.: Duke, 1990.

5. Agneta Johannsen argues in "Applied Anthropology and Post Modernist Ethnography" that postmodern leadership and authority can only be established once the candidate has demonstrated certain antihegemonial credentials that prove an opposition to authority. See *Human Organization* 51 (1992), No. 1, 76.

6. Jost Hermann, *Interpretive Synthesis. The Task of Literary Scholarship.* New York: Fredrick Ungar, 1975, 4: "For the serious student, the capacity of literature to point to the future is its greatest strength."

7. Stephen McKnight's work and his excellent bibliography have been cited earlier. Eric Voegelin has also done pioneering work on the subject. A good commentary on Voegelin, whose writings are vast, can be found in Barry Cooper, *The Political Theory of Eric Voegelin.* Toronto Studies in Theology. Vol 27. Queenston, 1986.

8. Rolf Geisler, ed., *Humanität.* Frankfurt am Main: Verlag Moritz Diesterweg, 1969. J. G. Herder, "Briefe zur Beförderung der Humanität," p. 39.

6

THE MARRIAGE OF NATION
AND STATE

Goethe-Herder & Co. created a new concept of the sacred with their notion that culture coheres first to a particular language. They were naturally most interested in transcendent culture, however, not ethnocentric culture. Goethe envisaged a world culture that consisted of the highest aesthetic products of the human imagination. It was to be a temple of the human spirit. German patriots had, for their part, other ideas. They took the concept and used it in their fight against Napoleon and French dominance. Instead of the glue that was to bind humanity, the concept became the stickum for German resistance.

There were those who desperately sought some rallying cause they could use to mobilize a great resistance to the force of Napoleon's authority. Among these were remnants of the nobility in the many vanquished principalities throughout Central Europe, Prussian Junkers, sundry petty nobilities from the Austrian states, and the middle class, educated youth, among them students who were thrown out of the classroom as Napoleon shut down their universities. The patriots were disparate types from many backgrounds who found themselves gathered under a single banner: hostility to Napoleon. The chief impetus for a patriotic propaganda front was given by an activist faction of the Prussian cabinet led by Baron Heinrich Friedrich Karl vom und zum Stein. During an intensely productive period between 1807 and 1814, writers joined theologians, actors, political figures, and soldiers to promote the idea of a unified German nation freed of Napoleon.

Having been schooled on the Enlightenment and the thought of Herderian anthropology, most patriots accepted as a matter of course the idea of the supremacy of the artifacts and products of culture: literature, modern critical philosophy, art, and music. Convincing larger groups of the population was, nevertheless, no easy task. The peoples of Central Europe had by long habit, tradition, and the police force of their princes been compelled to confine themselves to the domestic and vocational spheres. They were not a population likely to move rapidly into the public area of politics and open debate. Since they were also accustomed to hearing their French-speaking elites talk of their own German dialects with contempt, it was no easy task to convince them that their cultural products were of any universal value, much less cause to risk life and limb in opposing established authority.

Vehement expression was a necessary part of the cause of persuading the inhabitants of German-speaking territories that being German was a state not only worth claiming but worth defending against non-German outsiders. Since propaganda is a form of vehement expression that resorts to hyperbole and distortion of previously coherent ideas, it is little wonder that the Herderian anthropology underwent certain significant changes as the patriots adapted it to their own uses. While the universalist ideals had most engaged Herder's generation, the patriots appropriated the idea of ethnocultural singularity to their cause. It was no longer a world-caliber product that divinized cultural acts; with the patriots virtue lay in the fact that the literature, art, music, and even science and philosophy were peculiarly *German*.

Thus did the patriots begin a long campaign to move people's hearts by proclaiming the urgent necessity and holy duty of defending German culture against French (or any other external) onslaught. An obverse ideal to the Herderian was achieved: No longer was the universal Desire of anthropos to be worshipped at the altar of great works like *Faust*; rather was the integrity of the artifact, *Faust*, to be defended as a constituent of *German* culture. The new patriot would no longer seek to achieve that level of critical intelligence and transcendent cultural product the men of Goethe's time at their best sought. A new, German patriotism split humanity between the good (us) and the evil (them), converting universalist aspirations to particularist neurosis, abjuring critical intelligence and erecting a chauvinist particularism to replace it.

It would be a mistake to paint the canvas of the age in bold nationalist colors alone, however, for many forces were engaged in a fierce rivalry for what we have come to term power (i.e., authority over the domain of human behavior). Nobody contends for an authority to command squirrels, rabbits, and other game; neither do human beings compete with one another to master climate, weather, and the forces of nature. Wherever we succeed in establishing dominion, the primary use of authority is to enforce human behavior; our control over anything else is ancillary to that purpose. The emergence of nationalist patriotism was connected to the political aspirations of a reformist group of actors tied to the Prussian court. These men sought to bolster Prussian strength against the French gigantua by establishing a Prussian-led German coalition. Stein realized that, in order to create a political counterbalance to French power, society in German-speaking Central Europe would need first to be changed and authority redefined.

The issue of establishing an acceptable and viable national authority remained nevertheless undecided in Central Europe until Bismarck orchestrated the establishment of the Second German Empire in 1872. In some respects, it was somewhat like the state Stein and his supporters had envisioned; it was also unlike their vision. The generation that had participated in creating the myth of the German nation-state had, at any rate, disappeared from the scene before Bismarck's successes and would hardly have recognized in that apparently conservative Junker an ally and cosympathizer. Indeed, Bismarck was not of their ilk. The Germany he created was, like most authority in the modern age and the West, grounded in an ill-articulated hodgepodge of justifications bound by a rather fuzzy sense of national destiny.

There was, on the one hand, a presumably nationalized and, therefore, domesticated nobility centered in the person of the emperor and, yet, in no way resembling the ancient nobility in affection, function, or habit of mind. The nobility had rather been co-opted to the purposes of the modern, capitalist state even though it still differed from other elites by being incorporated in a constitutional persona (i.e., the emperor and one part of the bicameral legislature) with juristic definition. Most of the patriotic writers addressed themselves in their fulminations to the upper classes, the nobility, and the educated bourgeoisie. The predominant notion appeared to be that if the elites are converted to a cause, then the rest of a population will follow. There was the additional constraint that a writer writes for the readers he or she knows and understands.

First and last, these propagandists promoted the idea that there is nothing more sacred than the *Volk* or people, who in the patriotic calculus constitute the real body politic and whose collective will provide the only justification for any exercise of political authority. It can be argued that such a notion is of French origin, and certainly it belongs to the complex of ideas articulated to justify the French Revolution. The fundamental principle of popular sovereignty had been concisely stated less than a century earlier in the American *Declaration of Independence*. Since that time a Western consensus had been duly established, and even those opposed to the view had come to accept the inevitability of its correctness and justice.

Whether the view of popular sovereignty were English, French, or German in origin is of less importance here than the fact that it had become an acceptable way of thinking about political society in Western Europe and its cultural appendages. Both those striving to establish popular sovereignty and those opposing it were agreed that it was the inevitable course of history. Any political order that deviated from the popular will was, therefore, perceived as being usurped. Even princes saw their own justification in their sacrifical service to the national state; that is, at least, what they told the world. Having told the world, their actual functional significance was eventually subsumed in the national purpose. They were henceforth German first and princes second.

Germany was not the only European state that chose to preserve some relics of its institutional past. Even at the end of that revolutionary century, monarchs still sat on thrones throughout the continent; they had, furthermore, not only become adept at articulating nationalist pieties but participated—when they were allowed to participate at all—in designing a nationalist polity. Ethnogenesis co-opted ever larger areas of the body politic as the nineteenth-century drew to a close. The authority of the church was subsumed by the hegemonial claims of the national state as well, so the twentieth century opened with the national state the unchallenged sovereign power in the world. Things have not changed much since, the emergence of the European Union notwithstanding.

THE HEGEMONY OF THE NATIONAL STATE

It was certainly never the intent of Herder's generation to prepare the way for the ascendence of the state to sole authority over human affairs. The men of that day despised the state, which they associated with princely authoritarianism. It was they who formulated the Enlightenment principle of individualism, who celebrated the individual's quest for independence from (unreasonable?) external constraint in works like *Faust*. Neither did the nationalists see the dangers in their devotion to ethnolinguistic culture. Events pressed on them too hard, so they were little inclined to devote their time to long-range planning and quiet contemplation of the future. They saw it as their business to convince enough people of the justice of their cause to make a difference. They succeeded well enough, but in some ways they never could have anticipated. Their initial success was part of the larger European effort to bring down Napoleon. Their hope of creating a German nation-state, however, had to be put on hold while antinationalist forces under Metternich dominated the scene from about 1819 until at least 1848.

One might simply say that a convergence of circumstances and interests helped to invest the notion (many prefer to call it the myth) of the nation-state, which had become a bureaucratic-police-military leviathan with a virtually unlimited warrant to aggrandize itself over and against other existing authority centers. When patriotic nationalists succeeded in identifying the state with the national *Volk*, a connection was made that would prove virtually impossible to undo, even if the Restauration under Metternich did inhibit its political expression for decades, at least in Central Europe. Meaningful social groups were identified with a particular language and its culture; they were, furthermore, viewed as being located by destiny in a certain place on earth. The political elites were subsequently portrayed as having acceded to dominion as nationalist representatives, owing their authority to the national Volk. How these representatives came into office is a tactical question that differs with each people and in every state.

Regardless how they are recruited, those acting with authority (i.e., elites) henceforth did so as agents of the nation. The integrity of authority is determined by the most convincing intepretation of the people's will. As long as the individuals holding office act in apparent congruence with that will, their authority is accepted as valid by the majority of those whom they govern. The mechanism can be summed up as follows: (1) ethnoculture is the decisive instrument of national self-definition and redefines the domestic inhabitants within a realm, who subsequently become either nationals or aliens; (2) the ethnocultural nation perceives external neighbors as aliens; (3) it is on behalf of the perceived need for defense (i.e., protection and promotion of the purity/integrity of national culture against alien forces) that state bureaucracy and police establishments are justified; and (4) the function of the state is, therefore, to regulate and (where possible) control the alien elements within and without; the consequence is an escalation of conflict and a restless quest for dominion which ostensibly, especially in its relentless subjugation of aliens, aims at producing harmony.

The quest for ethnolinguistic purity or integrity requires an instrument of forceful authority; thus the state is appropriated to the uses of the nation to achieve a projected state of harmony that is understood as an absence of conflict (i.e., absence of aliens). In post-1990 Europe, for instance, the ethnogenies peculiar to Magyars, Slovaks, Czechs, Poles, Romanians, and others began once again to play a major role in delineating the emerging contours of the new or newly reemergent nations of the former Soviet bloc. These developments are a continuation of a tradition initiated in Germany during the first decade of the nineteenth-century and begun in particular through the appearance of *Deutsches Volkstum* (1808–1810) by F. L. Jahn (1778–1852). If the movement failed in 1819 to reach fruition in the establishment of a German nation-state, the ideas were even then already spreading to Slav populations to the east.

Jahn's work had a more far-reaching effect than that of more systematic patriots because he did not write for an elite readership but aimed rather at a more popular forum. Although his title resists translation, it is clear that Volk connotes people, nation, race, or even the attribute "folkish" (which itself is circumventiously taken from the German). The suffix *tum* serves much like English "hood," as in knighthood, so that the work purports to explicate a particular kind of "peoplehood," namely German peoplehood. It is about the distinctive character, origins, and history of the German people. The development of an ethnogeny is essential to the first stage of ethnogenesis, though it does not necessarily need to be written out, and Jahn's work is exemplary for the whole process of Western ethnogenesis.

An ethnogeny can precede a general belief in the nation, as the founding documents of the United States actually did, or it can be a summing up of much that is generally shared and already believed by certain groups that see themselves as harbingers of national unity and culture. In Jahn's case, there was an existing readership reasonably acquainted with the general ideas of his thesis of national destiny. He certainly shared with a substantial and, perhaps, growing number of people a sense of urgency about the need to better formulate what nation means. In Jahn's case, of course, the question was what *German* nation means, who is German, who is not, and how that is to be determined. He sought to establish the ground rules of nationalism (i.e., the ethnogeny) in his work.

Since an articulated ethnogeny represents a kind of elite consensus, the opinion of leading patriots, it is important to understand that Jahn was not alone in holding his ideas. There is a correspondence in what he writes with public statements made by J. G. Fichte (1762–1814) and other patriots. Fichte argued, for instance, that loyalty to one's nation or, as he put it, love of Fatherland (i.e., country) is more important than obedience to any state. Love of country should even determine one's relation to a state. Finally, the idea was promoted among this company that only a state which truly embodied the needs and interest of the Fatherland could be worthy of allegiance.

The connection between nation and state was, in short, made by thinkers and propagandists among whom were numbered both Fichte and Jahn. It was especially in his *Addresses to the German Nation*, which Fichte delivered under the nose of the French occupation of Berlin during the autumn of 1807 and winter of 1808, that he developed his view that "the significance of *Volk* and *Vaterland*. . .as container and guarantee of earthly eternity. . .is much greater than that of the state." The state and the societal order are, he adds, only the "means, condition, and structure of that which the *Vaterland* really desires, the blossoming of the eternal and divine in the world." [1]

If one substitutes the word *nation* for Fichte's *Vaterland*, the principle of popular sovereignty is already in circulation, and had, in fact, actually been developed and used earlier in the preamble to the Constitution of the United States to justify its act of government-creation. The state and all else is conceived as subservient to and guided by the will of the nation and no longer is seen as the embodiment of the will of the crown or sovereign. Sovereignty (i.e. authority to use force) is transferred to the nation. Fichte makes the explicit connection when he delares that "love of country must govern the state." If we are familiar with these ideas today, we are less cognizant of their recent vintage.

Vaterlandsliebe (i.e., Love of country) had been used in prior works, such as Thomas Abbt's *Death in the Service of the Fatherland* (1761), but those works had expressed a more parochial sense of patriotism. Abbt wrote his text when he was trying to get a job with the Prussian government and hoped to make himself appear a potentially loyal subject of a state in which he, having been born elsewhere, was actually in the modern nationalist sense an alien.[2] *Vaterlandsliebe* is a moral imperative that calls for one's primary devotion to be to one's nation; the state is merely its instrument in the world. When the state is governed by national interest, the objections of Herder's generation are canceled and a new justification for political authority is in place that is based on a thoroughly articulated ethnogeny, which in essence replaces the original anthropology. When we think of Jahn's work, we must remember that Napoleon was not removed from the scene until 1815, which was roughly half a decade away. The hope that the nation would ever successfully come into authority was still a long shot; its triumph was far from being an established fact. Neither was the apparent success of popular sovereignty across the Atlantic in the United States any guarantee of ultimate success at home.

It also sometimes escaped notice that the American success was not grounded in the same worldview as ethnogenesis in Europe. In the first place, American life was, though influenced in some ways by the British Enlightenment, not determined by the fundamentally populist concept of nation that took shape in Germany and then across the continent. The American mind was still tempered by a respect for universal principles and much farther from being persuaded by principles of ethnocentristic singularity. In spite of later historical presentations to the contrary, it was not possible for an American to speak of a clear sense of a specific and clearly delineated national people with certain attributes described— and prescribed—in an ethnologically coherent fashion. Neither was there a sense of ethnoculture as a visible and real manifestation of a national spirit. The climate of ideas was very different from that of Central Europe, where the humanitarianism of Herder was being telescoped first into Fichte's belief that German patriotism could lead to world citizenship and, finally, into Jahn's exclusivist chauvinism.

In America, the population was mixed rather early and consisted not only of numerous groups of British origin who often were alien to one another, but also distinctly non-British elements, such as Germans, Dutch, Spanish, French, Indians, and Africans, not to mention the regional identities that emerged with New Englanders, Virginians, and eventually Southerners. These diverse peoples were both present and important and presented a population profile that prohibited any effective ethnogenesis in the European sense. There was not only a good deal of ethnic cohesion within these groups; they added to the broad American picture of multiple authority centers.

It might also be said that the American justification of order was more theocentric than was that grounded in the eighteenth-century Herderian anthropology. The Declaration of Independence appeals to a God-creator as the source of natural "rights," which have little if anything to do with ethnolinguistic notions of culture this is a far cry from appeals made to national culture. American authority is founded on the warrant of God-given rights that defy ethnic specificity. This is not to say that the United States has not been the scene of nativist movements; it is merely that such movements lack any constitutional sanction.

There is, moreover, nothing in the American mind equivalent to the profound sense of ethnic identity experienced by many nations in Europe. The American often only discovers while living abroad (among foreigners, as the ethnocentric person might regard it) that he or she shares something beyond articulated rights with compatriots. I recall numerous discussions with American students who, in the process of recognizing one another and entering into eager and sometimes homesick discussions, were completely surprised to identify something peculiarly American in their shared experiences, something not readily accessible to explanation. It is not a state of mind that is valued at home, except, perhaps, within a regional culture that did experience an ethnogenetic moment, such as the South, and that has cultivated a distinct form of American English.

The experience of shared identity is part and parcel of the everyday experience of millions of Europeans. They are often reminded in their daily encounters of their membership in a particular ethnolinguistic group. Germans are certainly not the only people with a deep faith in what they share with other Germans. Europe is a honeycomb of peoples tied to particular places, dialects, customs, and history. Nobody waxes more mystical about ethnolinguistic differences, for instance, than Magyar speakers, who literally treasure their own unique distinctions. More than once I have listened to Magyar speakers making extravagant claims about the utter inaccessibility of their Hungarian-ness to outsiders and non-Magyar speakers. I have heard them declare, for instance, that it is impossible for non-Hungarian speakers ever to understand the essence of their experience. There is surely no more extreme particularism than that, and it brings to mind the slogans my own fellow Southerners sometimes emblazon on their T-shirts: "American by birth, Southern by the grace of God."

RIVAL FEARS: OBLITERATION VERSUS UTTER EXCLUSIVITY

Nationalism draws on atavistic moments of the human mind. There is the soaring pride and esprit of belonging to an impenetrably esoteric club in which the very best matters are reserved only for members; but there is also the terrible fear that, precisely because the secret language is inaccessible to outsiders, the common tongue will be obliterated and lost when the group dissolves and all memory vanishes. Since others are excluded from sympathy, they will in turn have no compassion and give no quarter in the battle of life. Fear and aggression are two facets of the same consolidating experience: Ranks are shut even tighter to protect against those who cannot understand and who, therefore, cannot empathize. If it is impossible for a non-Magyar speaker to access the real Magyar experience, then Hungarians cannot expect to find real friends anywhere else.

Ethnogenesis draws on the kind of atavism that is grounded in real historic community—but with a decisive twist. Instead of portraying exclusionary community as secondary to more universally shared human attributes and interests, nationalist apologists view it as the pivotal or foundational value on which the lever of civilization is balanced. Since it is the difference and not the commonality that is highlighted, the thrust of ethnogenesis is divisive and, therefore, conflict generative. Even when nation-states join in alliances, they do so in deep suspicion of one another. No so-called realist nationalist has ever denied that the basis for any alliance is national self-interest.

The difference in the American and the European concepts of popular sovereignty is expressed in practical matters. In Europe, each nationality reserves its spiritual and intellectual offices, as well as its political offices, for its nationals. It is as unthinkable, for instance, that a non-German could become a professor in Germany as that a non-native could hold high political office. It is not uncommon, on the other hand, to find foreign-born professors at every American college and university. Foreign-born pundits are certainly welcomed spokesmen in the American media, and the United States has recently had in Henry Kissinger a foreign-born Secretary of State with a rather distinct German accent.

The fear of obliteration surely was present in the minds of German patriots during the first decade of the nineteenth century. Napoleon's impact on his contemporaries is difficult to reconstruct, much less to grasp imaginatively. If one remembers the somewhat hysterical portrayals of the murderous but petty despot Saddam Hussein during Operation Desert Storm and compares his relative impotence to the effective force of French arms when guided by Napoleon's incomparable genius, then one might begin to understand the fear, anger, and frustration of Europeans confronted with the irresistible might of France. A sense of acute urgency drove the best minds in Europe to look for some cohesive force mighty enough to withstand French hegemonial ambitions.

The groundwork had been done by Herder's generation. Political authority had been detached from divine sanction. It was incumbent on a new, distressed generation to invent a new, immanent political sanction in the idea of nation. Napoleon advanced the national idea himself when he crowned himself Emperor

of the French. After that there was little doubt that French encroachments constituted French conquests and could no longer be interpreted as advances in a European revolution. Europeans everywhere began to understand Napoleon's triumphs
no longer as a crusade to create a Pan-European realm governed by Enlightenment principles. Opposition to Napoleon gathered on both a growing national
and a European basis.

"FATHER" JAHN: THE AUTHOR OF AN EXEMPLARY ETHNOGENY

Ethnogenies are by no means always written, much less published. Sometimes the consensus necessary for the establishment of an ethnogeny and the consequent national identity is itself problematic. Sometimes, as in the case of Switzerland, it is only barely present.[3] In Germany as in Switzerland and, subsequently, other places, the real internal tension grew in the disparity between the
elites, who urged the creation of national identity and the larger populations which
clung to their local traditions and life. It was no easy task to convince the multi-
tude of different types of people and groups in Central Europe that they were all
German. In some cases, German nationalist spokesmen had to work against the
efforts of regional elites to build their own identity. The Bavarian campaign to
create a distinct subnational identity among its subjects enjoyed signal success
and placed being Bavarian in direct opposition to the German identity toward
which national patriots strived.

There were cohesive linguistic groups in existence and bound to particular
homelands throughout the Germanies. These groups cohered around shared dia-
lect, folkways, dress, cuisine, and distinct architectural styles. They included the
remnants, in some cases, of ancient tribes like the Swabians, Franks, and Saxons.
Their spoken languages were, in some cases, not even mutually comprehensible.
Frisians inhabiting the North Sea coasts spoke a variety of language that could
not be understood by other non-Low German speakers. Swabians, Bavarians,
and Allemanic-speaking Swiss would find it often impossible to make themselves
understood in Berlin. Persuading these disparate peoples that they had much in
common, or that it might be in their interest to discover a commonality was a
daunting job.

The new theory of intertextuality that has rejuvenated influence studies in
literature encourages us to be mindful of the complexity of our conceptual inter-
dependence. We accept, digest, and use as our own ideas and beliefs that come
virtually intact from sources outside ourselves, making them our own and seldom
mindful of their original source. Jahn's German ethnogeny was prepared and
cooked in the kitchen of the opinion-forming elites and consisted of 80 percent
indoctrination. Otto W. Johnston has indeed shown that his material closely resembles not only Fichte's but often reflects the intent of the official policies promoted by the activist faction led by Baron vom und zum Stein, Wilhelm von
Humboldt, and others.[4] The existence of a reading public, though at the time
miniscule compared to the size of the reading public today, played (as Benedict

Anderson first pointed out) an important part in publishing the terms of the national ethnogeny. It was through the print medium that members of both the political and interpretive elites propagated the idea of nation, explaining to their various publics what it meant to be German, describing the attributes, and prescribing the behavior. The campaign to promote the German ethnogeny constituted a social, political, and moral agenda and was the first coordinated attempt to create a modern faith system with a dimension that included religious pagentry and symbols.[5]

Johann Ludwig Christow Jahn was an unlikely candidate for any heavy responsibility, but it is not insignificant that he, like so many of the nationalist elites, was the son of a clergyman. His antics after the initial failure of the nationalist movement of 1819 led to a castigating postmortem. Jahn has been taken to task by critics during and since World War II who connect him with the morbid traditions that found their deadend in Hitler.[6] Jahn was born on August 11, 1778, just about the time young Goethe had become deeply involved in the administration of the little duchy of Saxon-Weimar. The second child of a Protestant pastor, Jahn was spoiled and given a great deal of freedom. He developed prodigious athletic prowess and was a roustabout and ruffian. His parents' forebearance and patience enabled him to get something of an education in spite of being expelled from virtually every school he attended. As a young man, he was the sort of muscular outdoor male who appeals to boys as a role model. After sporadic attendance at the university, he found that the job he did best was as a coach-teacher-mentor of boys.[7]

Jahn might not have been able to pass the Prussian examinations for teacher certification, but he began to develop a particular teaching style that depended on his ability to evince intense loyalty and admiration among his pupils. Soon he won over sponsors among those who admired a rough-and-tumble teacher-mentor and sympathized with his nationalist objectives. What Jahn taught was the call to rough-hewn "German" virtues. He mixed his appeal with a love for athletics and developed a whole course of gymnastics and track and field sports he called *Turnen*, a word he claimed was taken from the medieval and knightly sport of tournaments. It was because of Jahn that German patriotism was bound closely with a cult of physical fitness. His athletic associations provided a network of patriotic organizations whose effectiveness in spreading the nationalist gospel cannot easily be overestimated.[8]

Later Jahn began to wear his "ancient German" suit, a self-designed outfit that was suited for strenuous athletics. His "old German exercises" were developed into a systematic fitness curriculum. Jahn is thus something of the precursor of the modern physical fitness center because it was he who developed structured exercises and accomodating machines. He was much more than a coach and bodybuilder, however, for his fitness program had an ambitious spiritual dimension: the liberation and sanctification of the German nation. Young atheletes, it was assumed, make good soldiers in the cause against Napoleon. Building societies of *Turner* was a way to develop a cadre of potential soldiers, thereby circumventing the restrictions placed on Prussia by Napoleon at the Peace of Tilsit.[9]

Jahn's ultimate effectiveness in the cause went beyond his charisma and physical prowess, however, for the man could write. He could write, moreover, for a readership that was not being effectively reached by the patriot-intellectuals: The middle and lower-middle classes. The very flaws in his work that have called up derision from scholars ever since contributed to his effectiveness as a purveyor of popularized tracts of nationalism.

What Jahn wrote was a treatise on German ethnoculture he called *Deutsches Volkstum*. Jahn's work attempts to describe what Germanhood, or German ethnocultural identity, really means and then to prescribe how it should be further developed into a full-blown nationalism. He claimed to have written the text in more systematic form in 1806, along with another work entitled *Denkbuch füer Deutsche* (A Thoughtful Book for Germans).[10] The text he made available was presumably something he put together as a hasty reconstruction of the better work lost, as he implied, for the sake of pushing the nationalist idea during a time of crisis. Whether or not the story is true, it is an ingenuous excuse for a work that falls short of more stringent scholarly standards.

In one respect, Jahn's work anticipates the preoccupations of modern social anthropology. He is at pains to create an ethnogeny for the German nation (i.e., a coherent explanation of the folkways, customs, and traditions that make things German unique—only Jahn accomplishes his task less through empirical observation than invention). His work is really a political program. The reliability of the ethnographic and historical claims he makes are as subject to doubt as the similar claims he made for the authenticity of his "ancient German" costume and the genuine antiquity of his curriculum of fitness exercises. The work struck, nevertheless, a resonant chord among readers and had enormous influence on both his contemporaries and successors.

The significance of Jahn's *Deutsches Volkstum* has been generally overlooked or ignored because of Jahn's identification with the radical elements among the nationalists, but also because of a more unsavory behavior after he was later marginalized. He was not only branded a hopeless crackpot, he became a strident antisemite. Jahn's credibility was thus permanently undermined. For our purposes, on the other hand, Jahn can be regarded as the instrument through which a comprehensible ethnogeny took shape and infected the public imagination. His notions of physical fitness also provide a literal (or physical) analogue to Goethe's notion of robust spiritual (i.e., artistic and cultural) achievement, which is one of the chief criteria for a culture becoming worthy of being world class. While Goethe was concerned with rising above particularist interests, the contrary was true of Jahn.

Neither did Jahn waste any narrative space in establishing his agenda and tying it to the great poet. Goethe was already on his way to becoming the national poet and icon of German culture, so introducing the work with a quote from *Hermann und Dorothea* obviously seemed appropriate to Jahn even if he did not really share or, perhaps, understand Goethe's worldview.[11] In the passage the reader is called to resist humankind's tendency during "uncertain times to vacillate." Whatever Goethe may have meant by that, Jahn believed steadfastness to be a specifically German virtue. Furthermore, he invoked the subjectivist perspective when he wrote that he who steadfastly resists can create "a world in himself. It is not right for Germans to promote terrible movements nor to waver here and yon. *This is our charge!* Thus let us articulate and assert it!" In this phrase Jahn combines virtue with the noninjurious ethic of humanitarianism associated with Herder and Goethe.

If we take the passage from Goethe out of context, the lines quoted appear to promote a mixture of notions important to the idea of nation but also still connected to the ideal of humanitarianism characteristic of the Herderian anthropology. The text promotes, as a matter of fact, a new kind of political sanction that has nothing to do with the Herderian ideal. A *we* is postulated as opposing a *them*, and the theme of the autonomous ego opposing a corrupt world is invoked. It is we, the authentic (Germans), who want to survive, who want to hold fast to our treasured possessions. If the line "he who perseveres can create a world in himself" has obvious subjectivist resonance, the new ideal is rather a Faustian hero, daring to strive against reality and (evil) external interference to achieve desire.

Jahn protests, nevertheless, that he is dovetailing the idea of nation with Goethe's promotion of a new humanism even though it becomes clear that his nationalist vision is ethically far removed from Goethe's own elitist cosmopolitanism. In that light, Jahn's claim that the cultivation of Germanhood is tantamount to advancing civilization becomes doubtful. He is actually promoting something quite different, a contrived tribalism that excludes considerations of universal humanism. His self-presentation as a harbinger of a new path to humanism should be considered a strategy designed to disarm the reader. His real agenda is quite a different matter.

NOTES

1. "Vaterlandsliebe," excerpted from *Was ein Volk sei, in der höheren Bedeutung des worts* [sic], *und was Vaterlandsliebe*, appearing in *Reden an die deutsche Nation*, Fritz Medicus, ed. 8th Address. Hamburg: Meiner, 1955.

2. The Austrian counterpart to Abbt's work is Joseph von Sonnenfel's *On the Love of the Fatherland* (1771).

3. John Bendix, "Switzerland's 700th Anniversary: The Politics of Negotiating a Cultural Display," *Canadian Review of Studies in Nationalism* XXI (1994) Nos. 1–2, 33: "The inability of the Swiss to agree on a national identity has been ascribed to the linguistic and religious cleavages that divide the country. While such cleavages continue to play a role, there is a more important political factor at work: the power of elites to shape national identity and the reluctance of citizens who cling to local or regional identities to agree with the identity with which they are presented." Carol Schmid, *Conflict and Consensus in Switzerland* (1981), is cited in the passage.

4. I am indebted to Otto W. Johnston's study, *"The Extremist: Friedrich Ludwig Jahn,"* in his *The Myth of a Nation: Literature and Politics in Prussia under Napoleon.* Studies in German Literature, Linguistics, and Culture, volume 32. Columbia, S.C.: Camden House, 1989, 129-142.

5. Johnston, footnote 1, compares Humboldt's plan to establish elementary, district, and "scholarly" schools with Jahn's call for community, district, and "schools of the margraviate" (p. 134).

6. Peter Vierreck recognized the elements exploited by the National Socialists in Jahn's work and reported them in his *Metapolitics: from the Romantics to Hitler* (1941).

7. Ernst Frank, *Friedrich Ludwig Jahn. Ein moderner Rebell.* Heusenstamm: Orion, 1972. Frank's biography is written from a German-nationalist perspective.

8. Jahn published *Die Deutsche Turnkunst zur Einrichtung der Turnplätze* with his partner Ernst Eiselen in 1816 and cited the works of several predecessors, including J. C. F. Guts Muths *Gymnastik für die Jugend* (1796). A facsimile edition was subsidized by German Turner organizations in 1961. Otto Johnston writes that "a physical education center was nothing new in Germany. As early as 1774 J. B. Basedow had proclaimed the benefits of physical fitness. In 1784 Christian Salzmann had founded a gymnastic facility at Schnepfenthal in Thuringia. By 1793 Johann Gutsmuths could describe the principles of athletic training...and in 1794 and 1795 Gerhard Ulrich Vieth published his three volume *Attempt at an Encyclopedia of Physical Exercise*" (p. 138).

9. Professor Karl Fink (Saint Olaf College) brought to my attention a paper recently delivered on Jahn's Turner movement and its close connection with the German National Movement by Antje Knoop of the Bildungswissenschaftliche Hochschule Flensburg in Germany. In her paper Knoop relies on the extensive bibliography in Dieter Duding's 1984 study, *Organisierter gesellschaftlicher Nationalismus in Deutschland (1808–1847). Bedeutung und Funktion der Turner-und Sängervereine für die deutsche Nationalbewegung.*

10. The text used in this study is available in a more recent edition published in 1991 by Aufbau-Verlag in Berlin/Weimar. Jahn's works were edited and his first biography written by Dr. Carl Euler (1855–1887). Jahn produced an autobiographical narrative in *Denknisse eines Deutschen oder Fahrten des Alten im Bart* (1835).

11. Nancy Birch Wagner offers the most recent study of Goethe's influence as cultural icon of the nation in her study, *Goethe as Cultural Icon. Intertextual Encounters with Stifter and Fontane.* North American Studies in Nineteenth-Century German Literature, volume 17. New York: Peter Lang, 1994.

7

JAHN'S ETHNOGENY AND THE SACRALIZATON OF GERMANHOOD

Perhaps Jahn misused Goethe to promote a cause for which the sage of Weimar would hardly have been in sympathy; nevertheless, the stage was set for him and his fellow patriots to provide a new justification for the exercise of authority in the affairs of the world.[1] The first readers of his book must have moved with some fear and trembling from the introductory quote into a celebratory description of German *Volkstum* (peoplehood) as a joyous brotherhood in which Germans live "heart to heart." Fear of otherness is a second theme sounded almost immediately and already implied in Jahn's use of the quote from Goethe. The idea is that external influence brings ruin because it contaminates the pure body of German culture. A stalwart and virtuous in-group is depicted as holding its own against the nasty assaults of the outside world.

Jahn's ethnogeny is built on the anthropology of the human heart—only with an exclusionary modification: he ties it to a belief in the autonomy of the (authentically German) human heart, urging that the authentic and independent (German) heart keep itself pure from "foreign" or external customs and ideas, which are assumed to be corrupt. Anything of value in non-German culture, at the same time, can, he insists, be easily recognized and appropriated by the perceptive German heart, making it oddly unnecessary to consort intimately with foreign elements or other nations. It is like saying that we appreciate other nations so much that we want as little as possible to do with them. National integrity is tied to the idea of chasteness, which in turn denotes lack of foreign contact, which, again, signifies blemish or contamination. All of these qualities prepare the way for a politics that seeks to achieve either splendid isolation or an autonomy based on hegemony.

After the East German state collapsed in 1989, I found the residue of such a fear of the foreign expressed in an interview with a former East German policeman. Sitting in his apartment one afternoon, his surprise and bewilderment at being in the presence of an outsider was still tangible. He told us that two months earlier such a meeting would have been impossible; that even a rumored brush with an outsider was enough to stir official action against the supposed miscreant. One need not have actually visited with a stranger. A casual smile, nod, or greeting would have been enough. Even having an automobile with a foreign tag parked in front of one's apartment could set off the process.

Any act that could even remotely have been interpreted as consorting with Westerners was viewed in the East German context to have defiled the integrity of socialist solidarity against the corrupt West. It is interesting how much socialist habits of mind reflect the same fundamental attitudes as those animating the nationalist. A belief in the absolute goodness of purity—interpreted as unquestioned loyalty—provided a litmus test for what was right in the Communist world. As we shall see in Chapter 10, which examines the development of an American socialist during the first forty years of the nineteenth century, other parallels can also be traced. The exclusionary assumptions underlying the modern justification of authority and borne in the fundamental worldview developed by Herder and his generation are transferrable to other ideologies.

In attacking the corporatist society of traditional Europe, a society in which privilege and authority were assigned by rank, Jahn treats another theme that actually had troubled Goethe and his generation. While Goethe viewed the feudal estate as representative of an intolerable oligarchic system, Jahn reinterpreted it as a stage of extreme social decline and corruption of the *Volksgeist* (spirit of the people). Others of Jahn's generation offered similiar interpretations. Joseph Goerres argued, for instance, in his introduction to the *teutschen Volksbücher* (1807) (German folk stories), that the higher classes, by separating themselves from the "spirit of the people," rejected the very essence of nature (viz., Germanhood). "In every human being," Goerres wrote, "exists every social rank, class, or estate." The nobleman hides the peasant behind an affected elegance; most importantly, "we finally recognize the authentic inner spirit of the German people just as the older painters depicted it: calm, simple, quiet, self-sufficient, honest, less moved by sensuous depth but therefore more directed towards higher ideals."

Part of the impulse to provide a patriotic code of dress that applies to everyone equally, as occurred first in revolutionary France and then among German patriots, can be traced to the desire to eliminate outward symbols of rank in apparel, hair dressing, jewelry, etc. Jahn's old German outfit was a part of the trend toward democratic clothing styles. The association of "genuine" or patriotic modes with the peasant style of behavior and dress has its linguistic analogue in the rich use of organic metaphor that one finds in Jahn, Goerres, and other patriotic writers in describing the spirit of the people. Earthy metaphor points to the Herderian view that the nation is an organic or natural phenomenon that takes precedence over the artifices of corrupt society. *Volk* is likened, for instance, to the flow of a river.

An inner necessity of purity (pure water, pure springs) is depicted as pressing toward perfect homogeneity. Thus is the elimination of foreign influence a principal mandate in the emerging nationalist code, and its redemptive movement is articulated in terms of moral principles, as Jahn states in his *Volkstum*: "the purer a people, the better." (p. 34). Jahn goes even further. The purer a people, the more the world advances toward the ultimate fulfillment of history. As Friedrich Schiller put it in his essay, "German Greatness," (1797), "Each Volk has its day in history, but the day of the German is the harvest of time as a whole."

Jahn's folksy beard and dress, for all their questionable historical authenticity, were designed to recall for a new generation the myth of aboriginal virtue while obviating symbols of the older, aristocratic order. Fichte put it similarly in his Seventh *Address to the German Nation*:

The true criterion [of Germanhood] is this: do you believe in something absolutely primary and original in man himself, in freedom, in endless improvement, in the eternal progress of our race.... [All such] are original men; they are, when considered as a people, an original people, the people simply, Germans.[2]

Fichte's reach, though seemingly universalist, is actually particularist and exclusionary. Even if a non-German reader identifies with the ideals set forth, he or she would be unable to qualify as German. The rhetoric is designed to promote the notion that Germans are the most aboriginal people who have, at the same time, an exclusive claim to other virtues expressed. An identity is made between being German and being authentically human.

The identification of ethnic purity with being authentically human is a constituent of every ethnogeny with which I am acquainted. The parallel claim to both universality and exlusionary uniqueness is indeed a masterful piece of sophism that draws on the emotive force of ethical ideas deeply ingrained in the Western imagination. It is through such an appeal that the nationalist patriot connects a strong sense of the hallowed or sacred to the new idea of political nation, working a sanctification that, furthermore, endows *nation* with an inviolable character. Since nation becomes inviolable, it is secure from criticism, as well as from other intrusions on its integrity. There is good reason to argue that nationalism is not an ideology because it does not resort foremost to rational explanation but appeals rather to strategies of emotional sanctification. Unlike their socialist counterparts, advocates of nationalism are more interested in providing a ritual system of sacralization in which the nation becomes hallowed. Its integrity is, in other words, established beyond reason.

The very concept of patriot is endowed with meaning because the nationalist patriot is depicted as custodian of national culture and language. Since Americans are much less likely to view themselves as custodians of a language culture in the way an English or French person might, the notion of patriotism as a sacred duty is more conflicted in the United States. Americans seldom interpret patriotism as their chief defining duty and are much more likely than their European cousins to regard individualistic destiny as their primary concern. Since the American's sense of destiny is not irrevocably tied to a national community, he or she also is not imbued with the same urgent sense of the moral dichotomies between the domestic and the foreign which the European experiences as a matter of course. Americans (i.e., citizens of the United States) incline to be relatively more hospitable to the foreign.

All of this is not to say that Americans are innoculated against the national idea but only to highlight certain differences in order more clearly to define the character of modern nationalism. There are significant parallels in the structure of the American imagination. We have, for instance, observed the part played by the Romanticist search for aboriginal virtue in the development of the national idea. In fact, the same quest is an important theme in American thought, though its objective is usually individual rather than collective redemption. The source of the correspondence between the American and the European mind may be sought in the kinship between liberalism and nationalism, which we will take up in the next chapter.

NATIONALISM AND THE MODERN CONCEPT OF SCHOLARSHIP

The vocation of the Romantic nationalist did not become any easier in the years after Napoleon. The establishment of "original" German culture was not to be achieved without sacrifice. Conceiving himself as living in a world of corruption, the Germanophile needed to work like Jahn to unearth the primeval culture at its original point, much as does the archaeologist or, for that matter, the cosmologist, excavating to get to the bottom of things. Incalculable energy and resources have been spent in a number of areas ever since in an attempt to find the authentic moment of creation. Having arrived at the source, one presumably would fully understand the destiny of humankind, the nation, the individual, or even the universe.

Excavations in quest of the aboriginal moment do not inevitably have something to do with texts. Astronomers work with telescopes. They work on excavation of successive time layers in the cosmos. Anthropologists fan out into primitive regions to excavate the lives of living primitivist tribes. Except for cosmology, which is concerned with the origins of creation, these disciplines began with a faith that such excavations reveal something of our own essential nature by showing how we might have been living had we not been corrupted by modern civilization. Archaeologists dig ever deeper, turning up artifacts of successive levels of civilization. They subsequently create texts to explain the artifacts they uncover.

Historians and philologists, on the other hand, excavate texts, digging them up out of archives and attics in order, in a paraphrase taken from the father of modern empirical history, Leopold Ranke, to tell it like it was. If telling it like it was has been perceived as a *de facto* moral act, it is because it is assumed that one can recover the most valuable insights in the documentation of actual events. Through such insights it becomes possible not only to transfer an accurate knowledge of past behavior but through that transfer to affect the present. The mission of these scholars has been didactic; even when denying it, science and scholarship have been animated by moral purpose and have sought to provide contemporary society with guidance.

Recent discussion in the academy has been centered on uncovering the moral (and the political) character of modern scholarship—exposing its animating spirit, as it were. The moral objective of the area that is becoming known as cultural studies is to restore the delicate balancing act in any truth-gathering behavior (i.e., to assure an instrumental and corrective awareness of the self-interest inherent in even the most altruistic human enterprise while, at the same time, avoiding stifling it). Cultural studies seek to elucidate texts within the historical contexts in which they were created because their practitioners believe (like the good heirs of Romanticism they are) deeply in the edifying nature of exegesis—even when they are professed nihilists!

Within the context of modernity's anthropology, it is in the transfer of knowledge of a better, precorrupt past that the present can be redeemed from its meaninglessness and the balance restored in a better future. It is within this modern context that scholarship has been assigned an unprecedented value as a redemptive labor. Time and space become the media through which the redemptive work is carried out by the good scholar-soldiers who are, in one fashion or another, devoted to modernity's "truth" that we must be rescued from the insignificance of our present. One of the most interesting facets of new cultural studies is their focus on the dynamics through which rival elites use modernity's anthropology to advance their own interests.

DECONSTRUCTION AS A PRELUDE TO OBJECTIVITY

The study in this book is a kind of excavation, as well, which fits into the new branch of cultural studies; yet it violates certain basic tenets of modernity. On the one hand, I am uncovering the past in an effort to redeem the present, but not because I believe the specific past with which I am dealing here contains an aboriginal purity that society needs to recover. Quite the contrary, for I am arguing that the past in which modernity was constructed contains certain mistakes that underlie the unaffirmable justifications for authority that have prevailed in the modern world. The modern justifications constitute a kind of orthodoxy of modernity that has locked the modern era in service to three prescriptive ideologies incapable of standing the tests of real conditions or adjusting to the exigencies of human nature. These three ideological configurations include nationalism, liberalism, and socialism.

If one approaches my study globally, there appear to be distinct parallels between it and the paradigm of modernity's anthropology. Surely, there is an assumption here that the present is errant or corrupt (or both); furthermore, there is an implication that value lies elsewhere, waiting to be rediscovered by the valiant quester after truth, the maverick, or the scholar-scientist. I have obviously placed myself in the position of the scholar-quester who seeks to engage the reader in his or her project of discovery. I take it for granted that the present is dysfunctional, and I invoke more than once the spectacle of atrocities, escalation of public violence, and the spreading lethal environment as evidence. The consequence of modernity is depicted as culminating in the unparalleled genocides committed from 1936 to the present in places as far afield from one another as Germany from China, or the former Soviet Union from Rwanda. The defining events of modernity are destructive, and its history is littered with memorials to the failure of authority in the modern world. Sometimes it seems to me that this final failure is encapsulated in the ritual celebration of Civil War battlefields in the United States, for this activity encompasses every facet and every dimension of human experience.

In addition to being an indictment of both the present and its affiliated past since the advent of modernity, I suggest the existence of an aboriginal value that is seated in a premodern and theocentric age. My portrait of this more felicitous age is captured in chapter 3, which is concerned with the world that modernity spurned. My somewhat guarded appeal to a premodern, traditional world is the inverse of Roussean primitivism, however, because it emphasizes the moral importance to civilization not of nature but of the extranatural (i.e., transcendent) agency. It is at this point that I must take leave of the modern paradigm, for there is no reasonable hope of restoring the order of traditional Europe, even if it were desirable. The discovery of a certain aboriginal virtue cannot be transferred across three centuries or more to transform the present.

The present work is consequently not a prescription or a program; it contains no transformatory agenda. To claim that this study is disinterested is, at the same time, a patent falsification of my intention since I cannot help being involved and caring. My involvement in the events of my age and my concern for the character and consequences of human behavior are the motors that drive the assessment presented in these pages. But I am neither ideologue nor prophet; I do not profess to know the answers. Looking behind my intent to assess, one would doubtless come upon my own belief that critical work does carry a certain didactic import even when solutions are not overtly prescribed and advocated. Like the liberal with whom we will deal in the next chapter, K. A. Varnhagen von Ense, I believe that critical study is a helpful guidepost for action and an admonishment to change if it honestly assesses the failures and illusions that confound us in our time. The interpretation of texts is a behavior through which existence achieves a spectrum of intelligibility, thereby delivering us from blindness about and ignorance of the meaning of how we live. It is first and last a moral enterprise.

It is impossible for me to become a partisan of some program, plan, or ideology because the fundamental error in modernity is, I believe, the assumption that human nature can will its own government. The understanding that can be rescued from the oblivion of a dead past concerns a truth that modernity has chosen to deny—but that traditional humankind knew well. The justifications we study here by focusing on the work and career of certain individuals are our texts. They constitute a complex and devious attempt to justify what cannot be reconciled to the conditions of human existence. Any individual who searches the boundaries of human capacity must be struck first by its severe limits and the vast areas of the world utterly beyond its control or influence, including its own immediate human sphere. Although this is an insight that has not escaped many moderns, it is, at the same time, no reason to despair.

There is a folly in the very notion of that amorphous configuration we have come to call modern consciousness: It is glued together by a constant faith in self-government or an assertion of human autonomy that is not congruent with human experience and consequently leaves us vacillating between elation and despair. My program cannot go beyond the hope that an assessment of the modern state will edify us and improve our behavior by pointing to acts that do not warrant repeating. If we subsequently refuse to be drawn into the entanglements that have made a mockery of the very liberty to which we have been presumably pledged, that is enough gain.

THE GOVERNMENT SHALL BE UPON HIS SHOULDERS

In anthropocentric modernism, as we have already observed, the burden of government is seated in the anthropological motor of our ethos, in human nature. Jahn's contribution is to locate the aboriginal seat of human nature in ethnolinguistic culture. Since he retained only a vestigial concern for humanity's universality, Jahn managed with little more than a cursory nod in Herder's direction to proceed with the construction of a new exclusionary authority. His work is, nevertheless, consistent with the dogma of modernity, for his narrative is informed by a strong belief that the human imagination wills its government.

In the introductory remarks of *Volkstum,* Jahn maintains that his historical research had led him to seek out the earliest evidence for the emergence of a specifically German sensibility. He assumes the pose of a historian and scholar, claiming to have written more substantial research works that were lost in the confusion of the war with Napoleon. His strategy is to establish credentials both as scholar and patriot: He did his homework, but it was lost while he dedicated himself to the patriotic struggle. Now he has returned, he claims, urged by popular demand. If his present work proves to be less systematic than one would expect, the reader is urged to remember his patriotism and the sacrifice of service in time of war that caused him to lose his major work.

Jahn has an agenda. He wants to turn the motley inhabitants of a rather amorphous territory into Germans. He is confronted with serious problems, which he meets with a detailed program of recommendations on government and education. Like every nationalist advocate since, Jahn is concerned with turning people into Germans. The Italian nationalist Massimo d'Azeglio put it simply when he declared, "We have made Italy; now we must make Italians."[3] The difference in 1809 was that nobody had yet made Germany. Jahn and his fellow sympathizers hoped first to make Germans who would then demand that Germany be created.

The nationalist agenda is not for outsider consumption, as Jahn makes plain at the beginning of his work. The non-German can misconstrue, Jahn suggests, what he or she reads as exclusionary chauvinism. True German ethnological explanations are not chauvinistic, according to Jahn, because authentic Germans respect the cultural product of other peoples. Jahn mixes such paradoxical assertions with bold declarations of his personal honesty and reliability. If the reader will trust him, he assures us, his treatise will make sense. He paints a picture of himself as the embodiment of the rough-hewn, simple, and honest German he preaches to others.

Jahn weaves into his narratives a mixture of naive candidness, homespun proverbs, and agricultural metaphor. He manages also to write a prose that affects us directly, that comes across as a straightforward, clear narrative — and this is no mean achievement for a German. What he avoids is the turgid erudition typical of so much German writing. In the process, he takes Herder's humanitarian anthropology and combines it with Romantic ideas of organic community, pairing its universal application and bringing it into congruence with the requirements of an exclusionary national community. The underlying worldview is pantheistic. The animating source of behavior is nature — human nature or, more specifically, a particular human nature, a German nature. The animating source is revealed in history. History is the record of national achievement, the source of national identity. Jahn establishes a consistent identification with the entities of nature, world, history, nation, and people. There are "three holy revelations of humanity: Nature, Reason, and History," he writes.

Jahn establishes his authority as prophet when he steps forward narratively and develops that persona for himself. He can, he writes, decipher the secret codes of nature, consequently gaining an understanding of world history. The glory of humankind is its multiplicity, its diversity; he writes, "only Tammerlane, whose daily work was extermination. . ., wanted to tolerate only a single people, a single language, and a single religion on earth".[4] What stands in the way of a full appreciation of diversity is the German inferiority complex, Jahn believes, urging his reader to note that, if the world is made of diverse cultures, with each culture having unique value for human civilization, then German civilization is also valuable.

JAHN'S VERSION OF NATURAL EUROPEAN REALMS

Once he establishes the value of German culture, Jahn proceeds to part I of *Volkstum*, "The Natural Division of Territories," in which he criticizes the fragmentary nature of the political organization of the German-speaking Europe he knew. He hypothesizes certain natural divisions within Europe which, once they were truly recognized, would enable its peoples to live in cooperative peace. He analyzes these geopolitical and cultural divisions and concludes that nature and human society have created nine natural realms:

1. The Iberian peninsula

2. The Western Alplands

3. The Southern Alplands

4. The Northern Alplands

5. The Carpathians

6. The Danube regions

7. Greece

8. The Scandinavian peninsula

9. Britain

Were Europe to organize itself into state systems congruent with these natural realms, it would establish conditions of friendly coexistence and eliminate the causes of conflict, rivalry, and friction in the interrelations of its peoples.[5] Most of Europe's wars had been fought, Jahn believed, to maintain unnatural structures. The future lay in waging *holy* wars to establish a natural structure.[6]

"Luckily," he writes, "there are only two places where nature has marked the borders" between the nine natural states less clearly: (1) between the Carpathians and the Volga River to the east, and (2) between the western and northern Alpine countries (i.e., the Germanies, Lowlands, and France). Jahn believes that the problems with the second of the aforementioned places can be naturally resolved if one accepts the natural border beginning in the Swiss Jura and falling north along the Rhine to the North Sea.

The territory Jahn staked out as the natural realm of the Germans includes some of the Western territories of present-day Poland, much of the Federal Republic of Germany, and, perhaps, the larger part of Holland. It does not include, on the other hand, the territory south of the Rhine which does belong to Germany today. His program for Germany hardly provided an agenda for aggressive conquest and was not inconsistent with the plans of other Romantic nationalists of the period, including in its expanse only the states in which people resided who spoke a form of German or Western Germanic.

Having first introduced the reader to the idea that peoples (*Völker*) are both a natural and a constructive human configuration, Jahn proceeds to establish the parameters of a reasonably acceptable homeland for Germans; only then does he proceed to deal with the subject of government in part II of the *Volkstum*, "Consistent Internal Administration of the State." Indeed, in his discussion of governmental structure and administration, he does not depart much from existing realities. The system he outlines is a monarchist bureaucracy that endows the king with powers to appoint a cabinet at the imperial level, while the administration of the provinces is left to a cadre of professional officials.

Jahn enumerates a complex civil service for the administration of agriculture, forestry, commerce, health care, mining, construction, industry, police, and education. These departments consume his entire interest while he proceeds to discuss in more detail the character and administration of each. In a separate chapter he is also attentive to the judiciary, tax authority, and education. Education requires a total of fourteen pages and is treated at even greater length later in a special chapter devoted solely to it. The judiciary takes the space of only two pages, while the question of tax administration is four pages long.

In his analysis of the uses of education, Jahn insists that the limited education targeted in bourgeois society to "secure private property" must give way to a general education aimed at creating both nationals and citizens fully cognizant of their rights and civic duties. He reserves special criticism for the universities, which he believes are needlessly isolated from practical affairs. His agenda in university reform would make university research applicable to actual problems and would include the forced retirement of faculty that fell short of such a goal. Jahn's perspective as a grammar school teacher is clear in his program, for he is primarily interested in educating people by beginning "down under" (*von unten*). He discards the elitism of his predecessors, Goethe and Herder, and urges the nationalist movement toward a concern with educating the common person. Education is to be extended to include all members of the ethnocultural body.

The focus shifts with Jahn and other Romantic nationalists and is no longer on the genius-titan. With the inception of ethnocultural nationalism, it was not the autonomous Faust but the ethnocultural body, the *Volk*, that came to count in the progressivist scheme. The character of conservatism also radically changed in response to the new democratic-nationalist ideal. Conservatives were no longer aristocrats but middle-class cultural elitists who remained true to the Herderian vision of the Protean hero. As the century passed, that hero took on the character of the Great Artist. Conservatives borrowed the image of Goethe and posthumously elevated him to the position of reigning *Dichterfürst* (Poet Prince).

The new conservative view has been expressed in the works of writers such as Thomas Mann and is centered in the ideal of the *Kulturträger* (bearer of culture), or the creative individual who articulates the best potential of national culture. The new ideal is a person who acts as a cheerleader for national culture, producing artifacts and texts admirable enough to capture world attention in the spirit of Goethe's concept of world literature. Such an ideal does not, however, reflect Jahn's intention and emerged in successive intellectual generations. There is little reason to doubt that within the new conservatism there lurked the rudimentary outlines of a *Führer*, a titan who would claim to speak for and to guide the nation—a bearer of both culture and politics; at the same time, those partisan to the notion of the great person of culture would have hardly been able to imagine a monster like Hitler.

In defining what Germanhood means, Jahn describes "German" qualities. All Germans are animated, for instance, by a dynamic striving toward articulation (through cultural product) that cannot be hemmed in by the "surrounding chain of states":

Human beings don't allow themselves to be poked in like herrings, or herded into a pen. . . . Living side by side does not necessarily afford any true union. The process of existential bonding, the quiet, confidential manner in which people become accustomed to one another and in which mutual love and trusting integration become a reality, all that is what forms a people, preserves and sustains its national culture and life.[7]

If the common Romanticist theme of the sole authenticity of organic social growth is foregrounded in Jahn's narratives, it is used to subvert rather than to sustain the ancient order. By harkening to a hypothetical original order, Jahn animated his myth while, at the same time, opposing the real order of society in which he lived. Instead of rejecting the notion of the state, he integrated it into his vision of nation:

A state is nothing without a people/nation, a soulless artifice; a people/nation is nothing without a state, a bodiless, airy affair like the superficial gypsies and Jews. State and people/nation in one creates a realm (*Reich*) whose power to maintain itself is found in the ethno-linguistic culture (*Volkstum*).[8]

The state is the fundamental "framework of the nation" (p. 33); it is permanent and static, though also dynamic and changing positively as long as the essential condition of ethnonational purity is maintained.

The rogues gallery of the national idea includes not only those who permit themselves to be mixed with other races and cultures and, therefore, corrupted, but others like Jews and gypsies, who have no homeland. These categories are gathered into the Other, the "them." Those peoples who have permitted themselves to be corrupted include, according to Jahn, the Arabs of North Africa, the Walloons of Belgium, the Turks, and the Greeks. At the end of the long century begun with Jahn, one Jewish response to the occasionally aggressive antisemitism of the nationalists was Zionism, an ethnogenetic remedy being sought in the establishment of a Jewish state in Palestine.

A postulated state of self-hate on the part of the projected nation is another element in the founding stages of ethnogenesis. Germans were said to feel inferior, to despise their own ethnoculture. For some time, France had been the great culture Europeans had sought to emulate, and French had been the language of civilization. Jahn believed no doubt rightly that Germans also found their current (dependent) political status denigrating, though the common German person had always been subject to one lord or another, most of whom—at least in human memory—had spoken better French than German.

Self-respect could, therefore, only come when members of the same ethnolinguistic culture constituted the government of their nation. One of the first precepts of ethno-linguistic nationalism comes into view here: the absolute demand that those in authority be native speakers of the national language. In more recent years we have seen, for instance, how Slovaks took as an excuse for claiming their independence that chief government officials in Prague spoke only Czech. In South Florida resentment on the part of Anglophone Americans to the widespread use of Spanish represents a cause for escalating anger. The examples could easily be multiplied and include the movement now afoot in the United States to legislate English into a position of exclusive authority.

Jahn formulates the principle of linguistic chauvinism in part III of the IX section of *Volkstum*. He initiates his remarks by quoting from Justus Moser's work, "On the German National Spirit," beginning with the declaration that "we are one people with one name and one language" and ending with the conclusion that Germans are actually a "deplorable people" because their lack of unity had made them history's victims. Since they had been unable to create a true nation-state, they had been exposed to ruthless exploitation by their neighbors. The underlying text in Jahn's complaints is the anxiety stirred by his fear that a standard German language did not exist with sufficient authority to assure a national dialogue. Whom does he blame? Existing elites are the culprits; it is they, according to Jahn and many of his generation, who failed so signally to provide the structures necessary to ethnogenesis. In the process, he and his cohorts conveniently forgot that existing elites at the time hardly viewed the prospect of nationalism hospitably.

It was such passages that raised myths of victimization which eventually became so important a facet of ethnogenesis. Germans were victimized by their own elites and then by the foreign elites of France. Since then, nationalist patriots have continued to insist on myths of their own national victimization. We are familiar, for instance, with the story of Irish victimization by a ruthless British power. Similar examples can be found throughout the world community. Nationalities lay greedy claim to being victimized by somebody. Slovaks claim to have been victimized by Czechs, Hungarians insist on their victimization at the hands of Romanians, Slovaks, and Russians, while they, in turn, were the culprits who the other groups claim had victimized them! To the south, Croatians were victimized by Serbs—and so on, ad infinitum.

Dozens of tiny nationalities have since declared themselves victimized by the United States, Russia, Britain, France, and other erstwhile hegemonial powers. Within states, domestic ethnicity is expressed, as with American blacks and native Americans, through a strong sense of having been victimized by the majority group. One of the most important initial stages in ethnogenesis is for the emerging group to locate a point in its history when some external force abused its members. A strong sense of moral indignation, an undercurrent of resentment and anger, and a desire for revenge all appear to be prerequisites of ethnogenesis. The process of national self-definition depends on it and cannot proceed without the poisonous fumes from such a fuel.

The self-loathing that comes from a state of victimhood makes self-improvement an imperative moral act. Those who despise their present condition must change or perish. The myth of the German *Sonderweg* (special destiny) begins with just such a dictum but has since become an important lense through which not only the Germans understand themselves but by which others are taught to "understand" Germany's needs. Germany's uniqueness was due, Jahn urges his reader to believe, not really to its geopolitical position but more certainly also to its special victimization status: a divided and vulnerable people squeezed in between rival and ruthless great powers.

The concept of the German *Sonderweg* became a standard component in formulating German policy and was used to justify polity during much of the nineteenth and twentieth centuries. In our own postwar age, when multicultural understanding becomes a mandate for ill-judged relativism, Anglophone historians have taken to explaining Germany to their readers in the same terms. It is only recently that certain German historians have sought to refute the notion of Germany's special destiny as a unique intermediary between Western and Eastern European civilization and called for a more honest evaluation of the country's role in world affairs.[9]

The first objective of ethnogenesis is to recover a lost integrity and self-respect in a process that involves change from the indefinite and nebulous idea of a people to a real, independent nation-state. The next stage, sometimes articulated and sometimes merely implied, is hegemonial and is expressed as the imperialistic desire to bring all of European civilization, perhaps even larger areas of the globe, up to the higher level of (German) culture. The latter objective poses as a humanitarian enterprise, but it is really a campaign for dominion and cannot be attempted until the nation-state becomes an effective force. It is only in the concentrated power of the state that the nation can enforce its cultural agenda on others. Jahn wrote that "the striving for unity is a beautiful gift to humanity, one God, one fatherland, one house, one love." And the desire for unity is the first sign of self-consciousness in the beginning of a people."[10] Mobilization of a general population is viewed as a necessity, but it requires tying "general civil rights" to the establishment of a state capable of protecting and promoting humanitarian values: "There are no civil duties without civil rights. All servitude ends.... Civil liberty creates health and happiness".[11] Such benefits and gifts are to be reserved for members of the ethnocultural nation.

Jahn's work shows how European political constellations would change once the new ideologies dominated the political scene. During Goethe's time, just a generation earlier, the aristocratic-universalist order was viewed as the conservative force. The ideology of nationalism introduces a new political spectrum in which one kind of conservatism comes to mean effecting and conserving national purity through the vigorous promotion of national culture. Jahn develops the theme of national purity further in a chapter he entitled "Banning Foreignness" (*Verbannung der Ausländerei*). In the aforementioned chapter, it is clear that everything bad derives from that which does not belong to the pure ethnocultural body. Skewing the anthropology he inherited from his great predecessors, Jahn writes that, "in the most important moments of life, it is seldom the mind but even more frequently the heart that serves as the protector of humankind."[12]

Jahn's agenda is authoritarian because it prescribes a national program and takes its validity for granted. Jahn also rejects any significant role within national culture for critical debate. Education is described, by and large, as a process of indoctrination. If we return to the debate between Socrates and Protagoras, we will recall who argued against expedience as a governing ethic. Jahn displays no compunction for promoting expedience because his real agenda is to wield first a power out of nothing (i.e., a hypothetical German nation) that is capable of establishing dominion.

THE OTHER HUMAN SPHERES INCLUDED IN JAHN'S PROGRAM

Jahn is not only concerned with matters generally touching on politics; recreation falls under his purview. He sets out which holidays should be celebrated and how people should be buried, what sorts of monuments should be built and where, what books should be tolerated, and how domestic life should be arranged. There is no area of life that escapes his didactic muse. In his drive to build a comprehensive ethnogeny, he shows us the mechanisms of the totalitarian mind. It is a disturbing revelation. The objective is to synchronize the national body through a process of disciplined training and education that can leave nothing to chance. Faust becomes Big Brother.

The agenda Jahn sets includes a systematic promotion of a standard language (*Hochdeutsch*), establishment of standard weights and measures, and then more ominously the inculcation of a national *Ton*, a German word that connotes manners, etiquette, and general behavior. A *Ton* is to be inculcated in the people via *Tonangeber*, or fashion-setters. Jahn does not say how these fashion-setters are appointed; they appear, nevertheless, as harbingers of our own conformist and media-orchestrated world but hardly suggest the fascist totalitarian drive to *Gleichschaltung*.

Jahn's insistence that the program of education be guided from a central location, a national capital where the machinery of state is seated, sets another durable precedent for ethnogenesis' centralist orientation. While urging centralist manipulation, Jahn does not perceive that he is contradicting his own teaching about the vitality of national culture and the people themselves. Even when guided from above, the people "down below" are still for Jahn the real impetus for social and political action. Never mind the bureaucratic authorities and the trend-setters governing them from a distant capital. In spite of his emphasis on the *Volk* as the wellspring of nation, Jahn's treatise emphasizes a program of systematic indoctrination that requires centralist coordination.

Jahn declares at the outset that "the Fatherland cannot exist without virtue, virtue cannot exist without citizens! You will have all of that if you educate your citizens." First priority is assigned to inculcating the children with an appreciation for and knowledge of the standard language because that language is slated to become the primary vehicle for subsequent indoctrination and control. Jahn claims that the use of other languages damages the cognitive ability of children and dilutes their command of their own culture (*Volkstum*); such a cultural dilution is tantamount in his system to sacrificing control of national destiny.

The standardization of orthography and grammar in the national language is of extreme importance to ethnogenesis. Next in priority is the establishment of a canon of texts in the standard language through which the national agenda can be promulgated. The canon is designed to promote an ethnocultural orthodoxy sufficiently "*volkstümlich*" for the cultivation of the child's sense of national identity. As Jahn explains in the eighth chapter, the canon is to be employed to educate the new nationalist citizens to a pride in their language and culture, which is to say to awaken them to a sense of German specificity (viz., another way of translating the adjective "*volkstümlich*" into English).

Literature becomes a tool to effect nationalist consciousness in Jahn's treatise. Although he had begun with a citation from Goethe, his ultimate design is the obverse of Goethe's universalist idea that true "world" literature should embody and promote humanitarian values. Goethe had indeed fallen considerably in the estimation of Jahn's generation, who saw him as an apologist for the old order. Caring nothing for the universalist values of the antecedent generation, the Romantic nationalists were busy constructing exclusionary explanations that would serve authority for the next century and a half. By this time, it hardly surprises one to discover Jahn elucidating the canon with such terms as "Un-German" and "*unvolkstümlich*," terms that, moreover, describe works to be excluded because they are presumably less accomodating to notions of German national identity.

Jahn's patriotic history is presented as another tool for teaching national consciousnss. It is the genre of "history of the fatherland" that is to be encouraged. Such study is to be integrated into the general curriculum in the national educational system, one of its main functions being to celebrate the spirit and language of the people. In the seventh part of the work, Jahn further explains his purposes by once again stressing the undesirability of "foreignness" (p. 225, VII). Through the introduction of a national dress or costume, regular folk festivals, festive national funerals, and the erection of national monuments, he believes that national identity can be consolidated and integrated even into the visual and spatial experience of a people.

Jahn's frank moralism is his antidote to the rampant immorality of the previous century. Goethe encapsulated (and moralized) the corruption when he created the character of the aspiring amoral titan, Faust, the passionate genius who stood above morals and law. Jahn's generation was tired of corruption and sought to bind behavior to stricter codes, making it also more accountable. The universalist humanitarianism of a Goethe or Herder was seen as inadequately grounded or morally amorphous, providing too much latitude for a careless elite. Jahn places marriage at the center of his plan for national stability, for instance, binding individuals to their role as parents who are to bear the prime responsibility for the training and education of each generation.

Since mutual accountability is essential to the stability of relationships of trust, Jahn vehemently attacks promiscuity and philandering and decisively rejects misogyny. Woman is for Jahn, as much as she was for Goethe, the true moral agent. It is woman who brings to the matrix of communal ties a sense of mutual commitment and responsibility. If woman is abandoned or permitted to err from her role as moral catalyst, the entire structure of ethno-cultural nation is threatened. Woman is depicted as working from a domestic base to assure the cohesion of the social fabric. It is the role of man to assure through the exercise of responsible and forceful authority the continuing cohesion of that base.

TRAVEL AS A MORAL EXERCISE

Travel is another endeavor that Jahn successfully redefines. No longer the pilgrim, nor even the high-born tourist indulging in aesthetic amusement, the traveler becomes a pilgrim seeking the national essence by observing it in all its many forms across the homeland. An inveterate traveler himself, Jahn promoted a kind of nationalist tourism that became one of the hallmarks of German ethnogenesis.

The patriot participates in a program of travels through the native country (*vaterländische Wanderungen*) which acquaint him with the full breadth of what *nation* means. Only by visiting firsthand the many regions and meeting the people did Jahn believe that one could truly grow in Germanness (*Deutschtum*). One can see the antecedents of the modern outdoor organizations devoted to camping and hiking in Jahn's program of patriotic tourism. By the end of the century, thousands of Germans would whistle and sing their way along Germany's growing network of remarkable hiking trails. Today the trail system in Germany is incomparably wellmarked and extensively mapped.

Jahn's treatise is a compendium, in many respects, of ideas circulating at the time. Like any good popularizer, he was extremely sensitive to topical notions and views. His work combines a number of heretofore unhomogenized ideas into a convincing agenda for political and social change, creating a text unique in the early history of ethnogenesis and establishing themes still present in political discussions today.

THE UNEXAMINED ASSUMPTIONS IN ETHNOGENESIS

Jahn breached the gulf between the titanic and elitist individualists. Like his fellow nationalists, Jahn sought to transform the political chaos of Central Europe into a meaningful society in which the inhabitants could speak and act effectively on their own behalf. His purpose was anything but noxious. There are, at the same time, a number of germinal assumptions embedded in the new nationalism that were left unexamined—and possibly for good reason. There were also ideas involved that even Jahn admitted were better left unexamined. Some of these ideas are congruent with the Herderian anthropology and can be set out as follows:

1. The *status quo* is depicted as hopelessly corrupt and not worth saving. Jahn's call is to national renewal, the revival of aboriginal virtue that had long been abandoned.

2. Primitivist assumptions underlie his program. There is an incongruous mixing of hostility toward urban(e) civilization and expressions of faith in centralized authority.

3. Rural peasant or village life is idealized as aboriginal and, therefore, morally superior.

4. The state is deified as the manifestation of the nation; Jahn invests it with sole authority to orchestrate human relations.

Jahn sets out a program of education that can be implemented only through the authority of his centralist state, utilizing the instrument of state bureaucracy. The purpose of the program is to provide the prescriptive indoctrination necessary to produce pliant and supportive members of the national body. National history, which Jahn prescribes as the centerpiece of his educational curriculum, promotes the view that all human effort either contributes to or hinders a national progress toward cultural and political hegemony.

NOTES

1. Interpretations of Goethe's works are numberless. A recent comment that shows how far Jahn is from the original authorial intent can be found in Charlotte M. Craig's "Bourgeois Settled versus Bourgeois Unsettled: Some Observations on the Refugee Problem in Goethe's *Hermann und Dorothea*," *Germanic Notes* 21 (1990), Nos. 1–2, p. 6.

2. Fichte, *Addresses to the German Nation*, ed. George A. Kelly, p. 107. The import of Fichte's lectures is prescriptive, as he points out at the beginning of the chapter when he writes that "at the present time there is little left that is German among the Germans themselves" (p. 92).

3. There exists a strong particularist tradition with ethnogenetic potential in the United States; its history can be traced beginning shortly after independence from Britain in local rebellions and separatist or secessionist movements that culminated in the War Between the States (1861–65). Washington set a precedent for strong federal intervention when he opposed Shays' Rebellion during the winter of 1786–1787. Although particularism is generally met by powerful censorship in the national forum, it is by no means mindless. Defenders of states' rights have provided an eloquent and persuasive body of apologetics and generally view state and regional institutions as the only bulwark to which the individual can resort in the face of federal abuse of power. Such constitutional justifications have been often invoked the past and continue to be mixed with appeals to notions of regional uniqueness. In the *Southern Patriot* (January–February 1995, Vol. 2, No. 1) Dr. Michael Hill argues that "competition among cultural groups seeking the resources to survive and prosper is natural and proper. . . . Our forefathers would be appalled at our hesitation to defend our birthright. We would do well...to remember, even venerate, our proud history. . .Celebrate your Southern roots and cement bonds with those who share your pride. Cultivate. . .your independence of a tyrannous system."

4. Jahn, *Deutsches Volkstum* (Berlin: Aufbau-Verlag, 1991), "2. *Voelker und Staatsscheiden*," pp. 45–48.

5. *Volkstum*, pp. 27–28.

6. Kurt Sontheimer, *"Der historische Sonderweg—Mythos oder Realitaet?,"* Von Deutschlands Republik. Politische Essays. Stuttgart: Deutsche Verlags-Anstalt, 1991.

7. *Volkstum*, p. 29.

8. Ibid., p. 77.

9. Ibid., p. 79.

10. Ibid., p. 231.

11. Ibid., pp. 60–73: Jahn's discussion of education includes a detailed examination of various school types.

12. Ibid., p. 294.

8

THE LIBERAL AS AMBIVALENT NATIONALIST

Rebellious eighteenth-century middle-class intellectuals could not have grasped how their leading thinkers and writers were preparing the way for another kind of state supremacy. Their work to subvert the authority of aristocracy and church turned them, nevertheless, into inadvertent allies of those who would promote the interests of a new kind of government: the nation-state. Once the church and aristocracy were removed, the state bureaucracy and army could be harnessed to the nation; or was the idea of nation just a convenient disguise for the machinations of a new elite who successfully tilted the delicate balance in the tripartite structure of European society? After all, what we have seen is the disturbance of the distribution of authority between governmental, spiritual, and civil realms.

The new elites did not, at the same time, always know who they were or where their interests lay. Ethnogenesis profited more than once, for instance, from the support of those who did not really sympathize with its myths of sacralized national community. When liberals became some of the earliest advocates of nationalism in Germany and staunch supporters of the national idea elsewhere, it was not even the national community that they promoted and cherished; it was liberty. Liberals could never be wholehearted advocates of the idea of nation because they believed with Herder and other forerunners of liberalism in the ethic of universal humanitarianism. Human destiny was for them a progressive movement toward general emancipation, not simply the triumph of a single national people.

The final stage of history, as far as the liberal understanding goes, is a moment of ultimate liberation from all restraints and an arrival at a level of maturity suggested by Kant as ideal. Maturity means that each individual begins to act as a free agent, responsibly and fully cognizant of the importance of noninjurious behavior, striving to fulfill an ideal that fits all human beings and not just persons defined by ethnolinguistic nationality or any other specificity. Liberal support of ethnogenesis had nothing to do with an affinity of ideals. It was the result of a misunderstanding about ultimate goals and concepts of authority. It also represents a tactical moment in the revolutionary history of modernity when liberals and nationalists were joined in their fear and hatred of the *ancien régime*. What they shared was a strong mutual desire to eliminate the traditional order and its theocentric justification at any price.

The true liberal had no fear that his project could be derailed by some rival party. Liberalism was the future. It was history itself. Freed humankind would reject wickedness in any form and turn its energies to generally constructive, humanitarian projects. Since the liberal vision begins with the belief that unfettered humankind returns to its original goodness, the primary goal was to get rid of those fetters. One would accept allies wherever one found them. The liberal had the added assurance that certain living models of a liberal society existed. There was the United States. Its very existence inspired the liberal camp to believe more firmly in the efficacy of liberation. It had not been born in terror, like egalitarian France, but in the character of Washingtonian prudence. There was, of course, the blemish of slavery, but slavery had by no means yet become the shame of Western conscience.

Lying at a considerable distance across the Atlantic, the new world functioned as much as a myth as it was a reality to Europeans. Mythical America, as it was reported in ruminative travelogues like Tocqueville's, played a vital part in shaping the ideas and expectations of European liberals. Liberals held that popular sovereignty, or rule by the people or nation, had been achieved in America and, therefore, offered a viable alternative to the despotic, authoritarian, or aristocratic governments of the European continent. Nationalists appeared to promote the same cause, making agreement with liberals easy in the early decades of the nineteenth century.[1]

THE LIBERAL AND THE ANCIEN RÉGIME

Liberals believed in a secularized version of the Fall. In their view, humankind lost its aboriginal virtue at some moment in the past. There is, however, the hope that it can be restored if only the accumulated restraints of Europe's corrupt order are removed and the individual is freed to return to that original virtue. The destruction of the old order would, in the liberal view, provide a freedom to transform life, to restore humankind to its aboriginal virtue. Adam and Eve were not tossed out of the garden by God. They were expelled by the nasty arrogance of the aristocrat. Get rid of the lord, and human nature is restored.

When the expulsion of all the lords did not lead to a reinstatement of the aboriginal Garden, a new villain had to be found. Out of the liberal came the socialist, who recognized the problem of evil not in human nature but in private property. Without the opportunity or temptation to accumulate, human beings would be free of greed. The liberal quest for the external villain has led moderns on a wild goose chase after the cause of evil. Aristocrats were the ogres in the earliest modern scenario; once they were gone, the capitalists and others given over to private ownership moved up to villain status. Insofar as they were given over to greed (as bourgeois capitalists were by definition), they were not human. The true human being, the authentic Mensch, was free of aristocratic arrogance and capitalist greed alike. The litmus test required the new ideologues to fore-swear a desire for both authority and wealth.

The chief pillar of modernity is placed on a denial of human weakness and consists of a bold assertion of human goodness. Evil is projected upon external agency: dehumanized aristocrats, greedy capitalists, a vicious bureaucracy, or, simply, the "system," a term that encompasses everything beyond the immediate control of the individual. Liberals turn into nationalists when they are fired by the mission of restoring integrity to community through the instrument of state force. They become socialists when they burn so much to eliminate private ownership as the source of greed that they willingly resort to a usurped authority forceful enough to coerce equity. In either transformation, they become the minions of a new tyranny worse than the one they hoped to eliminate.

In order not to be confronted with the failure in their transformations, these devotees of modernity urge a state of permanent transformation, postponing the desired effect to an indefinite future. We coerce appropriate behavior today in order to effect the ideal tomorrow, the modern declares, for people must be re-taught original virtue. The intervening age of corruption must first be overcome. Change, the more radical the better, is the moral imperative of the modern age. The concept of revolution is politicized and becomes that radical change that is to be the governing principle of modern behavior. Revolution is good. Stability is corrupt and evil.

Revolution becomes the new justification and explanation for authority in human affairs; it is elevated to a system of faith to whose articles one must sub-scribe before being certified for any office of authority. As a concept of dyna-mism, revolution provides a scope within which all the forces of passion can be legitimately harnessed to achieve radical upheaval and change. Although the vio-lence of the upheavals is destined to offend the humanitarianism of the original liberal mind, that mind proves incapable of grappling with fundamental causes that lie so deeply buried in liberalism's own ineffable presuppositions: The faith in humankind's goodness is too sacred to challenge. The liberal, the nationalist, and the socialist all view themselves as comrade archaeologists uncovering strip by strip the corrupt overlayers of society in order to return to our original virtue. When the payload of virtue is struck, the world of human nature will be restored and redeemed, and all the intervening violence, suffering, and upheaval will be justified.

LIBERAL QUARRELS WITH NATIONALISM AND CHRISTIANITY

While nationalists were born in liberalism, they proceeded in directions es-sentially alien to the liberal agenda. The devotee of the idea of nation pursues a goal of ending conflict through enforced harmony; the liberal, on the other hand, is most interested in assuring the freedom of entities in open competition. The liberal envisions the world as a space in which independent units—individuals, collectivities, markets—relate in beneficial rivalry to one another. The liberal answer to the "problem" of conflict has not been, as it is with the nationalist, to eradicate it; rather the liberal intends to unleash conflict as a powerful force for good. Whereas the nationalist longs for purity, the liberal dreams of increasing diversity. The liberal imagination conceives the world as a stage on which a kind of dynamic rivalry of autonomous individual entities reigns. The rivalry is good because it produces the constant radical change necessary to move forward to the future.

Underlying all three modern perspectives is the belief that change is a primary good. The liberal seeks to achieve change by unleashing human diversity; the nationalist seeks to enforce it through a process of purification, with the ultimate goal of eliminating diversity. Although these two perspectives are miles apart in their programs, they agree on fundamentals. That which is, that which exists, the *status quo*, is evil and must be overcome at any price. Current authority is corrupt and must be replaced. A dynamic and even revolutionary change is the only mechanism that can work such good in the world, and this is the justification for the authority each of these two perspectives claim over human affairs. Their claims are bound at times to converge in spite of the very different agenda they each represent.

While the nationalist imagination embraces a doctrine of purification and is closed to universalist tenets, the liberal mind is closed on only one subject: Christian religion. The liberal distaste for religion is connected, as we have seen in earlier chapters, with the liberal commitment to human self-direction or its doctrine of human autonomy. The doctrine is indeed a religion in itself with its own articles of faith and the demand of unquestioned obedience characteristic of dogma. The belief in the unfailing felicity of human nature is simply not subject to challenge because it would, in turn, destabilize the ethic of human autonomy (if people are also evil, what benefit could there be in their acting entirely as free and unrestrained agents?). Thus Christianity is anathema to any claim of liberal authority; it places responsibility for evil in human affairs squarely on the moral character of the individual human being, thereby making a mockery of any pretension to human autonomy. Human nature can only achieve goodness, in the Christian scheme, through the intervention of divine agency (i.e., an agency generally called God's grace). One thing the liberal recognized from the start was that the anthropology of modernity and Christianity are in fundamental opposition.

If in Christianity humans are creatures and their freedom is, at least at the operative level, either folly or delusion, no reconciliation is possible between freedom and liberalism. God simply does not figure into the liberal economy. The nationalist has, on the other hand, nothing against Christianity as long as the power of its God is integrated into the nationalist program. The nationalist co-opts the Christian church and transforms it into part of the nation's body. American Protestantism has long exhibited a nationalist syncretism. The American flag is placed up front in churches across the land, usually to the right of the space that once was occupied by the altar. Many devoted American Christians also ardently support the systematic elimination of Christianity from every public stage outside the church proper; this separation has been directed by the federal courts since the 1950s.

The mind of the nationalist has been studied in the person and career of the German enthusiast and physical trainer Jahn. Now we proceed to the case of an exemplary liberal. Karl August Varnhagen von Ense (1784–1858) was six years younger than Jahn and of similar class origin. He came, at the same time, from the western reaches of Germany and was born in the Rhineland, where liberalism was much more likely to exercise an influence over prodigal minds. Varnhagen did not live in authoritarian and monarchical Prussia until he was sixteen. Even then he experienced more the intellectual ferment among the Jewish elite and middle-class intelligentsia than the more characteristic military state that had enabled it to survive in a sea of war.

Varnhagen's father taught briefly at the University of Strasbourg, where his mother's family were natives. His exposure to life in the French-controlled, German-speaking province provided him an opportunity to become fluent in French and to develop an admiration for French culture that never left him. Although baptized a Catholic, Varnhagen inherited, perhaps from his mother's Protestant family, the anti-Catholic rhetoric of the Reformation. His sister, Rosa Marie, was raised in the Protestant faith, and Varnhagen's lifelong view relegated Christianity at best to the backburner of his interest. Whatever Varnhagen did well, he did as a liberal who believed completely in the anthropology of modernity. He counted himself on the side of liberty, diversity, social reform, and institutional secularization.

THE LIBERAL QUEST FOR AESTHETIC CULTURE

We know what Varnhagen would have us know about his childhood and youth, how he was torn from his mother and sister by the upheavals of the French Revolution. After the revolutionary armies had shut down the University of Strasbourg, Varnhagen's father took his son with him on what apparently seemed to the boy an interminably restless nomadic movement from town to town, while his mother and sister stayed behind with her parents. The wanderings of the elder Varnhagen, a physician by profession, probably lasted no more than about six years and were related to the unsettled and revolutionary times, but it seemed a lifetime to the boy, Karl. The family was reunited in 1796 when the father was finally able to settle down to a practice in Hamburg, an old North German port with close ties to England and a tradition of patrician self-government.

His father's early death in 1799 left him, his mother and his sister destitute and utterly dependent on the assistance of a friend, who secured the boy a place at a military school in Berlin, the Pepinière, where cadets were trained to become medical personnel in the Prussian army. Karl Varnhagen's tenure at the school lasted until 1803. In that year, the eighteen year old either left school or was expelled. Somehow he got a tutorial position with a Jewish-Dutch industrialist named Cohen. In Varnhagen's account, it was a happy time for him. His employers gave him a great deal of freedom and permitted him to participate in the exciting intellectual life of their circle. What he reports having taught the two Cohen sons was infused by Roussean ideas and Romantic notions of pedagogy: letting them read what they wanted and otherwise providing a loose and relatively unstructured environment.

The idyllic interlude was spoiled when Cohen's firm fell into bankruptcy and he fled the city. Varnhagen was helped by the Jewish community to find new employment with a banking family in Hamburg. There his introduction to the intellectuality, generosity, and humanity of life in upper-class German Jewry took full effect and permanently molded him. In Hamburg he taught the children of Jakob Hertz, the family patriarch whose late second marriage to a young beauty, Fanny, had produced two children. To these Jewish children Varnhagen brought a knowledge of educated German, providing them with a linguistic means of escaping the confines of their ethnicity.

To his surprise, Varnhagen found that the family encouraged his budding friendship with Jakob senior's young wife, Fanny. The adult sons of Fanny's husband saw Varnhagen realistically as a possible marriage partner for their stepmother once their father was out of the picture. In order to make good husband material, however, Varnhagen needed to be self-supporting. A tutor never earned enough to support a family. The family began, therefore, to finance his attendance at a prep school (*Gymnasium*) where he quickly learned sufficient Latin and Greek to pass entrance exams to the university. The plan was for him to study medicine and follow in his father's footsteps with a practice in Hamburg.

The twenty-one year old matriculated at the University of Halle in the autumn of 1806. His interest in current literature was keen, for, during the three years since he had left the military school in Berlin, he had been ceaselessly involved in literary projects with various friends. Together the young men had kept up with the very latest trends and published literary anthologies of their own. In Halle, Varnhagen attached himself to local literary circles, showing his adeptness at moving into the vicinity of the most important or famous literary personalities. Soon he was sitting at the feet of the great professor of literature, F. A. Wolf, an extraordinary teacher who had reintroduced the study of modern literature at university.

Varnhagen's penchant for meeting the most distinguished people in any particular place also brought him as well into the company of both the Danish natural philosopher, Henrich Steffens, and the great Romanticist theologian, Friedrich Schleiermacher. External events—history—intervened once again, however, when Napoleon dealt Prussia a devastating defeat at Jena. It was in Varnhagen's second semester that the French shut the University down. After that, he had no choice but to look elsewhere. Instead of returning to Hamburg, he chose to go to Berlin, where he would meet his future wife, Rahel Levin.

Never during the period of French conquest of the German states did Varnhagen sympathize with the defeated German princes. He identified himself first as a Rheinlander and second as a citizen of the Republic of Hamburg. The French were generally, in his view, the liberators. Varnhagen could have neither sympathy nor understanding for the despotic state of Prussia. Austria also represented a despised feudal order at the time. There was no way at the time to anticipate the day he would join the Austrian Army to fight Napoleon. Meanwhile, back in Berlin he moved among the intellectual circles often hosted and sponsored by a wealthy Jewish class. It was at such a gathering that he met the most important person in his life, the remarkable Rahel Levin.[2]

Varnhagen was reinforced in his liberal propensities by Rahel, who conceived the world in terms of competing autonomies and for whom conflict was a sign of vital animation. Rahel strove for originality, and she enjoyed and made a social habit of moderate to acute personal confrontation. Her combative frankness was not always welcomed, but the elite usually found it amusing, especially since Rahel was capable of accompanying it with brilliant *bon mots* they could later quote. The enormous social distance between them and her also doubtless innoculated them from the insecurity of indignation. For her part Rahel insisted on being known by her first name and made a cult of sincerity.

What Varnhagen lacked of the liberal disposition before he met Rahel, he learned in her company. Her audacious and agile mind opened the way for her to consider and cultivate diverse views, attitudes, and cultures. It had also enabled her to host a brilliant Romantic salon during the 1790s. As a Jew, Rahel not only had ample experience as an outsider but considered herself a kind of certified maverick. She encouraged Varnhagen as well in his sympathy for dissidents and eccentrics. Somehow the mutual attraction was sustained through considerable up and downs and led finally to marriage. It was a most unlikely combination. Varnhagen's acquaintances were surprised, especially since wedding himself to a Jewess was not the most prudent move a young man on the way up could make. Rahel no longer even had fortune to recommend her.

The couple married about the time that Varnhagen was given a temporary post with the Prussian delegation at the Congress of Vienna in late 1814. They had come a very long way in a very short time—not unlike many others during those unsettled times. Two years before the unexpected triumph, for instance, during the terrible winter of 1812, they had both nearly starved together in her Berlin apartment. Suddenly she found herself the wife of a diplomat. Varnhagen was paid a salary ten times what he had considered adequate just weeks earlier. Their good fortune went beyond anything they had dreamed. At the same time, they would learn again and again how little the liberal truths in which they believed actually held in the world of affairs, where people seldom act in the spirit of goodwill or tolerance and where the presuppositions of humanitarianism are rarely honored in people's behavior.

If Varnhagen had once viewed French encroachments in the territories of German princes as a great emancipatory wave of the future, he went to Vienna in 1814 hoping that Napoleon's downfall would issue in a new period of more representative government and broader political and social enfranchisement in Germany. His job with the Prussian delegation made it his business to promote the interests of Prussia, of course, but he did his best to force those interests into congruence with a more representative and liberal Germany. The truth is, Varnhagen shared the fate of most liberals. He did not possess the authority to exercise any determining influence over events. His being drawn into the charmed circle of official power actually just assured that he would not be able to contribute to any republican opposition to the European Restoration.

Within four short years after the Congress had reestablished a European concert of power, liberals were swept from their largely minor positions of influence throughout Central Europe. Varnhagen was among those who lost their posts. He was recalled from his post in the little duchy of Baden and instructed to report to Washington as emissary to the United States. For all practical purposes, such an assignment was a permanent banishment from the European scene, and he refused to accept it. Varnhagen's nemesis was the eminence grise behind the Restoration, Austrian chancellor Prince Metternich. It would not be the last time the Prince was responsible for keeeping Varnhagen out of public office.

The events that terminated liberal hopes for a generation began when a student named Karl Sand walked into the apartment of the German playwright and Russian agent August von Kotzebue and stabbed him to death. It was all the excuse the nervous princes needed to declare open war on reformist forces throughout Central Europe. Varnhagen generally was consoled for his loss by reminding himself that he was one of many in a fine cause. It is not completely clear, however, that he would have fallen victim to the antiliberal reprisals had he concentrated on his job as Prussian emissary to the Court of Baden in 1819. He had, in fact, spent much of his energy working to promote the cause of a parliamentary constitution in Baden. Once the constitution was in place (in 1818), he became involved in support of an intractable parliamentary opposition that became a thorn in the side of the reigning duke and his government.

When he left Karlsruhe, it was more because he had become *persona non grata* there than that his own government particularly wanted him back in Berlin. Varnhagen was not the sort with whom the foreign secretary could be comfortable. He was known to be brilliant, assertive, and a person inclined to become a nuisance. The functionaries there were not particularly keen on having the troublesome liberal in the ministry. Meeting his enemies head on, Varnhagen refused to report to his new post across the Atlantic. Instead he showed up at the ministry in Berlin to defend himself against any charges. After a loud and quarrelsome session with the foreign secretary, Count Bernstorff, Varnhagen was put "on disposition," a status tantamount to retirement, and told that no formal charges were being lodged against him.

Many months passed with Varnhagen in limbo, uncertain what his position was, his salary suspended. What appeared on the surface to be bad fortune was, however, really a blessing in disguise. Eventually he was granted a relatively generous stipend that was supplemented by periodic work in the ministry, and he found that he had both the means and leisure to write. At the age of thirty-seven, Varnhagen was able to return to his true vocation and devote himself to writing.

German liberals were, on the whole, illequipped to deal with a climate in which self-interest is not governed by civility. They were also political novices. Varnhagen was, for instance, hardly doing his job as Prussian emissary in Baden when he devoted most of his energies to promoting a parliamentary constitution in Baden. Neither had it been especially prudent of him to become so openly involved with the political opposition after the constitution was in place in Baden. Rahel had warned her husband that such behavior would eventually lead to disaster. But when it came to serving the cause of liberal reform, Varnhagen was simply unable to put his own interests first. He believed too much in the cause of representative government and the freedom that he associated with it. He wanted too ardently to play his modest role as a little catalyst in the emancipatory process of history that would lead ultimately to liberty.

THE MIDDLE CLASSES AND THE GERMAN STREITKULTUR

Varnhagen shared his rather desperate social background with many of his fellow second-generation liberals. They were the children of a German professional class kept in marginal circumstances; furthermore, their penurious condition had been made even worse by the Revolution and subsequent Napoleonic wars. They were products of the homes of pastors, teachers, physicians, and middling officialdom, all utterly dependent on the benevolence of petty aristocrats and a system of nepotism that weighed largely against them. Only very few were, like Goethe, the sons of families with moderate commercial wealth. These men were generally ignorant of the culture of politics, foreign to the exercise of authority, and strange to the practical uses of force. Bred to a modest life devoted to private pursuits such as literature, music, and art, they had little notion of how to use authority once they had it.

Lacking access to the political arena, Germans had developed a private culture of fierce partisan debate over theoretical issues. Emphasis is placed on the forceful defense of an ideological position against all comers. Germans call the culture of partisan debate the *deutsche Streitkultur*. Within the "culture," a premium is placed on individuals developing an argument and defending it unyieldingly against all other positions. The object is not to find a level of consensus that makes policy possible, chiefly because Germans could not make policy. The person most admired is the person who emerges as the most forceful and articulate advocate of a position he chooses to defend. Such a person is viewed as having character. He or she is ordinarily described as displaying an appropriate and admirable steadfastness.

In the middle-class *Streitkultur*, men have been loathe to withhold their opinions even when prudence dictated it. Such forthrightness is viewed as honesty. Since the opinions of the middle class for so long lacked any political consequences, individuals were not concerned in argument with the success or failure of its application but rather simply with winning the argument. To stand staunchly in one's position was considered a mark of integrity. In this regard, Varnhagen was a child of his age and nation. While viewing everything from a political perspective, he exhibited a rather consistent lack of political perspicacity. His obtuseness destroyed his public career. It was only due to his considerable talents as critic, historian, and man of letters that he was not shoved into a permanently marginal position.

The periphery is the right spot for the critic, however, who can gain a nice vantage point there. Since Varnhagen's real weapon was his pen, his position after about 1822 turned out to be a convenient place for him to develop his craft as a writer-observer of his society. As he began again to turn out a steady stream of articles, book reviews, and biographies, he demonstrated that the liberal is a much better critic than he or she is an active person of affairs. Varnhagen steadily progressed from erstwhile and fragmentary journalistic work to the more integrated literary production of biography and extensive political comment. He repeated, at the same time, errors that could have ruined him but that, at the same time, show how true he remained to his liberal ideals.

In 1836 Varnhagen undertook to defend the Young Germans, a group of anti-establishment writers, to none other than his nemesis and the gray eminence himself, the Austrian chancellor Prince Metternich. When reading Varnhagen's epistle, Metternich must have smiled grimly. Varnhagen urged on the architect of the post-Napoleonic Restoration the view that "literature has always been an element of opposition that falls into conflict with the state, the church, and morals" and that, nevertheless, deserves protection because it finally triumphs when the world it depicts becomes reality. Varnhagen concluded his epistle with a naive appeal to Metternich to leave the young rebel writers alone. After all, he reminds the Prince, young turks are usually moderated by age and become pillars of society as they grow older, and it is best to be on the side of history, anyway.

The letter shows Varnhagen in the full vulnerability of his liberal good will. Like others of his persuasion, he wanted to believe that the austere power broker and grand seigneur he is addressing thinks and feels like he does, that they share sympathies. A very minor Prussian diplomat forced by his indiscretions into early retirement presumes to offer one of the most powerful men of Europe advice, failing completely to understand how ludicrous he must have appeared to Metternich and how dangerously self-revealing.

Varnhagen was not satisfied with persuading Metternich to forgive and, perhaps, ignore the rebel writers of the Young Germany movement. He also urged Metternich to support his pet project, the founding of an international Goethe society. Unbeknownst to him, the Prince had written concerning Varnhagen's views to his Prussian colleague, Prince Wittgenstein, in Berlin: Varnhagen is an ideologue, and I especially note the association with the Goethe cult that I recognize in Rahel's loyal survivor and to which the new literature is pledged in a way that defies the old poet."[3] As early as 1810 (by Varnhagen's own report), Metternich had the opportunity to hear his views. In that year, Varnhagen had discoursed at a table he shared with Metternich in Paris on the virtues of a free press. During the 1820s, after Varnhagen's dismissal from his post in Baden, Metternich had blocked his reappointment anywhere except to the United States, the latter offer which

Varnhagen refused. The communication in 1836 merely confirmed Metternich's view of him.

THE SENTIMENTALITY OF LIBERALISM

Varnhagen's correspondence with Metternich is worth considering because it exposes both his lack of real influence and authority and a certain unwillingness to accept the realities of authority if it disagreed with certain liberal notions. Since Varnhagen wholly believed in Herder's anthropology (i.e., that humankind in its collective and/or individual form is predisposed to good and destined for "higher things"), he was never fully adequate in dealing with a reality of established interests that conflicted with his own. Like so many liberals before and since, he chose to believe that an appeal to humanitarian sympathies is enough (or should be) to overcome conflicting interests.

Varnhagen obviously believed that, if only he explained to Metternich that the Young Germans were really just youths who would eventually become the staunch leaders of a new order, young men of integrity and sincerity, the persecutions would be suspended. Varnhagen believed that the world could be persuaded to change. A strong appeal to goodwill could, he deeply believed, make a difference. Although he could not have been more wrong, Varnhagen had so completely accepted the orthodoxy of the new anthropology he had inherited from the previous generation that he was unaware, when he spoke of literature changing the world, that he was expressing a fundamental article of his liberal faith and not a fact. Not only did Metternich not share that faith, it constituted the subversive core he was determined to suppress with all his authority.

Varnhagen's perennial inability to gauge these oppositions is an indication of one of the basic flaws in the liberal understanding of the world. The liberal brings to every conflict the expectation that it can be resolved by the sincere exercise of sheer goodwill. Such an attitude is the practical consequence of anthropological relativism, which denies the reality of fundamental oppositions, or what it usually calls "absolutes." Through the prism of such a perspective, conflict is seen and treated as a misunderstanding. The moral relativism to which liberalism subscribes is, as we saw in our earliest chapters, one of the philosophical consequences of monistic pantheism. If the multifaceted world is really an illusion and part of the single body of god/nature, then diversity is an illusory patina that merely disguises the unity of all things. Nothing of any importance can be at stake since conflict is just a misunderstanding. Gentle persuasion should suffice to put everything back into its unitary (and agreeable) condition.

Metternich represented the attitudes and views of old, dynastic Europe. Conflict is real because it arises out of oppositional interests. Meternich correctly assessed Varnhagen's position as subversive. Schooled in the use of authority and force, Metternich was adept at delineating and limiting conflict, using force where necessary to quell potentially dangerous ideas. Metternich's objective was the maintenance of a balance of interests controlled through the agency of a largely benevolent aristocratic oligarchy. In his view, the price of maintaining the desired balance required the limited and special application of force to suppress or eliminate destabilizing interests. As passionately as Varnhagen was committed to the promotion of modernity's liberalism, Metternich was the canny defender of the traditional order. He was, therefore, the natural enemy of modernity's anthropology in either of its two contemporary forms, liberalism and nationalism. Varnhagen had, indeed, no reason not to have recognized the Prince's position.

THE QUALITIES OF THE NEW ORDER

The quality Metternich recognized as intrinsic to the modern anthropology was shared not only by liberalism and nationalism but, as we shall see in the next chapter, also by socialism. Their single effect is to be found in their common hostility to stability and their common cause with urging dissatisfaction and defiance to societal order in its present form. Metternich judged the new faith systems accurately. Varnhagen could teach him nothing. The new world Varnhagen believed literature was creating could bring, in Metternich's view, only unrest, instability, and dissatisfaction, ultimately crowding out any hope of peace.

Napoleon had given Europe a substantial dose of the misery and rampant conflict inherent in the new worldview. In his appetite for power, he was in no way confined to reasonable political objectives. Furthermore, Metternich recognized all too well that the new regime of disturbance and instability had first been prepared by the men of Goethe's time and class and exemplified in the Promethean titan. Varnhagen had argued acceptance of dissenting writers *because* history is presumably proceeding in their direction anyway, and there is nothing anybody can do to stop it; furthermore, he implied that everybody would ultimately share the benefits of a new order and would be well advised to participate in its realization.

Whereas the liberal is convinced that all of history is on the same train to the future, the nationalist believes that some nations are more destined to history than others. From the nationalist perspective, there are circumstances and conditions that select only a few great nations, while all the rest are condemned to little more than accessory roles at best in the process of destiny. These inconsequent nations are fated to impurity and impotence; they lack cohesion, homeland, and/or resources and will subside into obscurity and be lost to the historical drama of great ethnocultural nation-states. The nationalist is thus able to see conflict as real in a way that liberals cannot.

Varnhagen never departed from his liberalism. A liberality of viewpoint and broad sympathy for diverse views remained a hallmark of his life and works. He was a pioneer in introducing the achievements of the new Russian literature to a German reading public that still believed Russian culture to be hopelessly primitive. He supported independence movements outside Germany, especially when they were opposed to German or Prussian and Austrian hegemonial authority, such as was the case in Poland, Bohemia, and Hungary.[4] Ironically, in such cases he lent considerable support once again to ethnogenesis.

The real appeal for the liberal of ethnogenesis and the development of the nation-state lies in the fact that it is the only viable authority system that has developed since the demise of old Europe. Varnhagen and liberals since have been revolted by the chauvinism, racism, and general intolerance that nationalism spawns. They have had, at the same time, no other system to support and find themselves horrified, nevertheless, and impotent in the face of the escalation of violence in the international system. Since 1945, Western liberalism has moved more vigorously to set up community alliances for political and economic reasons. These liberal efforts notwithstanding, the national idea continues to infuse and shape events throughout the world—continues, in other words, to represent the most persuasive form of political authority. Nothing else the liberal imagination has conceived has counteracted the potency of the national idea as an authority system with the force to shape events.

THE LIBERAL ROMANCE WITH SOCIALISM

As the failure both of democratic nationalism and the liberal hopes of building a society in which the individual would find greater scope and autonomy became increasingly apparent, Varnhagen and other hard-core and unrepentant liberals turned more and more to the increasingly radicalized unofficial opposition. He moved from sponsoring and assisting the Young Germans to giving support to anarchists, Communists, and revolutionaries of every stripe. A tradition among the German middle classes was initiated that one could observe during the recent period of active German anarchism and urban terrorism. Some have suggested that Varnhagen really became a Communist sympathizer toward the end, earning the sobriquet among his enemies of the "red" Varnhagen.[5]

NOTES

1. In my article "The *Bruderkrieg* and the Crisis of Constitutional Government: The Treatment of the American Civil War by Georg von Cotta's German War Correspondents, 1861–65," *Schatzkammer der deutschen Sprache, Dichtung und Geschichte* XX (Spring 1994), No. 1, 13–25, I explore the concern of German liberals that Southern secession, if successful, would discredit American constitutionalism.

2. Dieter Kuehn, *Varnhagen und sein später Schmaeher. Über einige Vorurteile Arno Schmidts*. Bielefeld: Aisthesis Verlag, 1994. In "IV. Der glattzüngige Automat," Kuehn presents a rare, unflattering portrait of Rahel as an egotistical person whose tyranny Varnhagen, for unexplained psychological reasons, welcomed: "Zweifellos hatte Varnhagens Festhalten an Rahel (1771–1833) einen starken Zug grotesker Tragik. Sein elementar vorhandener und unablässiger Bedarf an Zuwendung, die damit zusammenhängende leichte Beinflussbarkeit des 'unfertigen, verquaelten, in vielem greisenhaften' jungen Mannes, die Tatsache, dass er sein Vertrauen verschwenden konnte 'bis zur Charakterlosigkeit', all dies führte in der Beziehung zu dieser Frau zu Unterwerfungs-, Opferungs- und Passionsritualen pathologischen Ausmasses" (pp. 65–66).

3. Ludwig Geiger, "Varnhagen's Denkschrift an den Fürsten Metternich über das Junge Deutschland 1836," *Deutsche Revue* XXI (1906). Also discussed in Pickett, *The Unseasonable Democrat: K. A. Varnhagen von Ense (1785-1858)*. Bonn: Bouvier, 1985, p. 76.

4. Pickett, Ibid., p. 75.

5. Varnhagen's later support of independence movements is explored in Werner Greiling, *Varnhagen von Ense. Lebensweg eines Liberalen*. Cologne: Boehlau, 1993, 210ff. The most definitive treatment and a complete bibliography of the research completed during the past twenty years can be found in Ursula Wiedenmann, *Karl August Varnhagen von Ense. Ein Unbequemer in der Biedermeierzeit*. Stuttgart: Metzler, 1994. More information on Varnhagen's contribution to the introduction of Russian literature to Germany can be found in Pickett/Porter, "Varnhagen von Ense and the Reception of Russian Literature in Germany, *Germano-Slavica* (1987), No. 4, 69–78.

9

THE LIBERAL WELCOMES
SOCIALISM INTO THE FAMILY

As early as 1833, in an essay on the significance of Goethe's work published in the memorial edition of Goethe's journal, *Kunst und Alterthum* (Art and Antiquity), Varnhagen pioneered a new field of criticism when he delineated the connections between the new socialist ideology and humanitarianism. They intersected on the issue of the inequitable distribution of goods and property in European society. "Goethe's entire body of writing," Varnhagen asserted, "is a composite picture of global derangement in a world fallen into discord."[1] Unbeknownst to the reader, Varnhagen had written Goethe shortly before his death, proposing his thesis and asking the poet if he had guessed correctly his intentions. The ever-cautious Goethe never answered the inquiry directly, but Varnhagen was not deterred.

Varnhagen continued to be hospitable to socialist ideas long after the death of his wife and companion in 1833. What his liberal mind constantly sought were ideas congenial to his constructivist view of human destiny, particularly ideas that reflected its habitual opposition to the present condition of the world. The future was the thing; all else was disposable, a trial to be managed and tolerated. Although the Darwinian scheme had not achieved complete public articulation, it was certainly present already in the preference of the liberal, socialist, and even nationalist mind for vegetative imagery in depicting the historical process. Old forms had grown up, withered, and died and had been replaced by younger, more vigorous institutions and forms—a sort of germinal selection of the fittest doctrine. Since institutions were viewed as amalgams of human relations, the old, dead, or dying institutions were less authentic and were no longer capable of coping with the weight of human *passion*.

The road to authenticity for the liberal was, however, never a complete break with the past and the traditional world, as it would be for the socialist. Nor have liberals sought somehow to appropriate the past to their own agenda as nationalists have done. There is nothing atavistic in the liberal imagination. One would look far and wide without finding a liberal with primitivist affectations like the "historical" costume à la Jahn. Neither does the liberal imagination attempt to bend and reshape past epochs to suit the programmatic needs of polity. Liberal intersections with both nationalism and socialism have always been momentary, often understood as marriages of convenience, alliances dictated by tactical expedience as much as by enthusiasm. Liberals were, when they remained true to their views, those who came to recognize and oppose the excesses of nationalism as the nineteenth century proceeded on its course of steadily escalating violence. In the aftermath of the Franco-Prussian War, for instance, the French liberal savant, Ernst Renan, attempted to enlist his German brethren in a campaign to discredit nationalism. Never mind that he was rudely rebuffed by none other than David Friedrich Strauss.

Renan attempted in his late works to show how nations are constructs of subjective factors that have nothing to do with shared history or common race. Most telling is Renan's view that the principle of popular sovereignty becomes too easily a doctrine of majority rule—and tyranny.[2] In such circumstances, the door is easily opened to oppression of social, political, and ethnic minorities. Those who do not belong are quickly assigned for reeducation or banishment. If liberals recognize the dangers in the justifications spun out of modernity's anthropology, they are constitutionally incapable of a fundamental criticism, as we have seen, because it would require them to abandon their atheistic anthropocentricism.

Like most imaginations pledged to prescribed fundamentals, liberals have justified their uneasy vacillation by raising their skeptical view of "absolutes" to an article of faith. When liberals speak of unacceptable absolutes, however, they surely do not mean the precepts of heir own worldview but rather any suggestion that human nature is not the final arbiter of reality. Such suggestions liberals attack both as absolutes and, possibly, transcendent references. The latter designation was the worst defamation in the liberal arsenal until contemporary liberals came up with the word *fundamentalists* to apply to anyone who fervently believes in God. In the political forum the term *conservative* is used just as indiscriminately to describe every party that opposes the liberal agenda. Recent American combinations have ingenuously connected these terms and added others to form derisive mouthfuls like "fundamentalist right-wing Christian conservative."

Inasmuch as the liberal mind vacillates, is deliberately skeptical of absolutes, and even sometimes feels ambivalent about the things worth saving or being cast aside, Varnhagen was the archtypal liberal. He could please neither the nationalists nor socialists. Friedrich Engels called him "an utter and cowardly rascal."[3] The nationalists discovered Varnhagen's consistently liberal perspective once again when his niece, Ludmilla Assing, published his papers after his death in 1858. It was at that point that they set to work to ruin him posthumously. The nationalist critic Rudolf Haym managed a devastating postmortem, branding him in the widely read *Prussian Annals* as the symptom of a widespread malady (i.e., liberalism).[4] Haym's view is echoed down the years in the writings of many other commentators, especially those of a conservative or nationalist bent (almost the same thing in postrevolutionary Germany), and, as recent research has shown, his view is not free of antisemitism. In his once widely-read history of the nineteenth century, Heinrich von Treitschke called Varnhagen a malicious gossip-monger. In his definitive work on the *Berliner Romantik* (1921), Josef Nadler portrayed Varnhagen as a "busy show-off and contact seeker."[5]

Varnhagen's posthumous reputation is a kind of seismograph by which we can read the nationalist aggressive tendencies in German society. But he was so thoroughly vilified after his death that the negative portrayal affected the view of those who should have known better. In her biography of Rahel Varnhagen, Hannah Arendt rendered, for instance, a decidedly negative portrait of Varnhagen. The truth is, as Philip Glander noted when he edited Varnhagen's correspondence with the Englishman Richard Monckton Milnes, "Varnhagen was nearly unique among Germans. Much of the misunderstanding he encountered during his lifetime and which caused his reputation to suffer after his death can be traced to a national inability to see in his work the record of history."[6] It was not until the Swiss Germanist, Konrad Feilchenfeldt, presented Varnhagen as a man existentially pledged to a liberal-progressive interpretation of history that his reputation began to recover—a little more than a century after his death.[7]

LIBERAL DISCOMFORT WITH NATIONALISM

The truth is, the liberal has never been at home with the idolatrous extremes of nationalism, anymore than he or she could feel entirely comfortable with the socialist's faith in some future order of society. Liberal humanitarianism was, as we have seen, the brainchild of successful products of the eighteenth-century middle classes, who found themselves recruited into the internationalist and cosmopolitan world of the eighteenth-century European aristocracy. They experienced an operative civility that applied, at least, to all members of the international (viz., European) elite. The destruction of that world in the French Revolution and its aftermath left the next generation with a disjunctive experience of political order at every level.

It was difficult for a post-Napoleonic liberal to imagine an international or pan-European order, though Varnhagen did write about his vision of a new European economic order created by a mass transportation made possible by the railroads. In the meantime, he was confronted at home with a mix of narrow parochialism, petty machinations of reactionary aristocrats, and the strident campaigns of middle-class nationalists. Europe's American cousins were equally driven during the course of the nineteenth century into an experience of disjuncture through the disruptive crisis over slavery, the massive waves of immigration that inundated the country after 1850, the savage Civil War, and, finally, the historically unprecedented continental economic development that followed in the Civil War's wake.

Disrupture was already vivid during the first decade of the nineteenth century in Germany and expressed in the tone of the nationalist boosters, who hoped for a new order of society. Often their assertions reached levels of bathetic atavism. Philosophers of the subjectivist ego, such as Fichte, joined in the fray. In his essay, "Love of Vaterland," he wrote that "who does not understand his immortality cannot love, not even his country because he has no country." Liberty, Fichte insisted, is more important than order—an assertion with which most liberals agreed, though they cringed at the consequences of violence and terror into which the French Revolution collapsed.

An important condition existed that has since been forgotten: These early liberal nationalists believed that liberty led automatically to a higher order of civilization and not into anarchy. They continued to believe it as an article of absolute faith even when they were surrounded by conflict and violence. While they declared themselves friends of liberty and generally believed what they said, what they accomplished was a shift of authority from the old feudal classes to the educated and propertied middle classes. They thought to see the model for such a shift in the liberal societies of England and the United States. Since these examples appeared to be working, striving for the same changes on the continent was viewed as realistic. The fulfillment, happiness, and harmonious community the liberal expected to result from liberty would be the consequence of a liberal sort of person assuming authority.

There were also those prescient enough to anticipate the darker side of the liberal vision. Such minds recognized the limits liberals intended to impose on emancipation. As the inequities of industrialization became too glaring to ignore, those sensitive to the plight of the helpless rural populations flocking into urban centers like London and Berlin began to realize that larger forces were at play than most liberals imagined. The drive to liberty, whatever liberals hoped, would not stop once the middle-class elites were ensconced in power. What they had claimed for themselves others would seek as well—and under the same banner of liberty the middle classes had waved first. The spectre of a war of the classes came into being and was articulated in both imaginative and discursive literature through the remainder of the century. The liberal interest in protosocialist movements that one can observe in Varnhagen is partly due, as I shall argue in this chapter, to a bourgeois desire to domesticate the masses, initiating them into a more genteel, middle-class culture. The first impulse of those sympathetic to working class revolts and the idea of eliminating private property was to project the virtues they admired onto the common people.

Reportages like Varnhagen's on the insurrections of 1848 are replete with references to working class nobility manifest in attributes like courage, honesty, loyalty, and unselfishness. The abandonment of the cause of the underclasses in the Atlantic community today may, if one can draw parallels, be due to the intervening alienation effected when our latter-day poor are reported to exhibit behavior associated in the middle-class mind with vice: drug addiction, thievery, murder, prostitution, etc. The image of the underclass person has undergone a profound transformation, at any rate, from sympathetic and even admirable hero(ine) striving for approved goals like liberty to criminalized and dehumanized monster devouring the civil body. In both the United States and Europe, the alienation of the underclasses from the governing classes is heightened by the fact that they are generally outsiders by virtue of race, culture, nationality, and, in the case of the devout Moslem minorities, religion.

LIBERAL DISENCHANTMENT AND THE CONTINUING QUEST

The escalation of economic and social inequity violated everything most liberals had hoped from their regime. It was simply not supposed to happen. Yet with the production of an increasing quantity of goods and services, the extension of the franchise, the development of national consciousness, and the elimination of the aristocracy came an increase not of the general welfare or well-being of the population, which might have confirmed the essential goodness of humans and the bounty of the world, but of discontent. Even with aristocratic arrogance put behind them, Europeans did not experience a rise in general good. Neither did conflict vanish. Instead, human rights abuses became more frequent and spread far beyond Europe. The abuse of children and women in the emerging industrial labor markets was enough, for instance, to disturb even the dullest Christian sensibility typical of a previous age.

Mixed with the brave assertions of progress and the often bland optimism about the future, there was also a growing consciousness that any human order that makes happiness and satisfaction possible had since vanished. Both accessibility to goods and services and a consciousness of participation in the political processes were greatly expanded, so optimism was keen but mixed with hopelessness. The technology responsible for such material blessings also provided the means of turning every conflict into a lethal nightmare beyond human comprehension. Even the affluence enjoyed by the expanding governing classes still appeared to be created out of the misery of the alienated classes.

During the decades of the 1830s and 1840s, and especially after the insurrections of 1848, the former liberal classes throughout Europe found themselves comfortably in the ranks of a new bourgeois conservative establishment flush with industrial wealth. Meanwhile, the unparalleled brutalization of the former peasant classes and their reduction to penury made it easier than ever to despise their need. Many of the very minds and hearts that had hated the excesses and arrogance of the aristocracy lost all touch with their former humanitarian tolerance; they had, even more devastatingly, no recollection of the aristocratic concern to delimit and control conflict as well as to exercise noblesse oblige. Instead of the continuation of a balance of power and the peace established by the grand seigneurs of the *ancien régime*, the new elites moved inexorably toward hegemonial wars and imperial adventure. By substituting history for God and shifting emphasis from divine ordinance to the dictates of human passion, liberalism helped to create the conditions of the twentieth century. Its troubled conscience led it to seek new justifications for authority in which contrary principles were established; and these include a commitment to the sanctity of established borders and a belief in self-determination.

The two irreconcilable political principles are the political analogues of the philosophical principles of individual self-direction (i.e., autonomy) and the sanctity of individual human life built on the eighteenth-century anthropology of desire. Expressed in these principles are dualities that resonate down through the past two hundred years. On the one hand, the human heart asserts an autonomy of desire; on the other, reason struggles to bring it to its "right mind," to have it recognize the inviolable integrity of human life as the innermost sanctum and source of all things. National communities strive analogously to establish themselves institutionally but must also find their place within larger state constellations, where there is seldom possibility of anything like true autonomy without hegemonial domination of neighboring states.

The oppositions are hardly different from those in which the ancient world had come to an ethical deadlock before the advent of Christianity brought an exciting new hope. In the modern analogue, realism (i.e., reason) provides the brake to hubris; romanticism (i.e, the exaltation of desire) encourages it. The ancient circle in which human existence was locked began with the arrogance of unchecked desire, proceeded to violation, and ended in vengeance. It is the lethal cycle of violence that Christianity broke and that was treated in magnificent pre-Christian works like Aeschylus' *Oresteia*. The history of the modern nation-state parallels the drama of personal destiny as the modern world rejects universalist justifications of authority and resorts increasingly to various particularist anthropologies, all of them, moreover, children of the larger humanitarian anthropology of modernity that we explored through the lives and works of Herder and Goethe.

Domestic and foreign dissension, conflict, and war have not yet had a decisively deterrent effect on either our expectations or our behavior. We still believe incessantly in the absolute importance of individual autonomy. Our renewed attempts to reconstruct a viable order out of the destruction wrought in our wars, for instance, are never successful because they are governed by our fundamental humanitarian faith. There is, nevertheless, some indication that, at the end of the second millenium, a return to more universalist justifications is possible. The devastation of World War II had sufficient impact to drive Westerners into new systems in spite of themselves.

In addition to the traditional alliance system that was set up in the North Atlantic Treaty Organization (NATO) and that depended on the leadership of the hegemonial power, the United States, an indigenous trading partnership was initiated that now threatens to become a larger Pan-European community. The problem is that the sanction for the community is still anchored in arguments that appeal almost exclusively to an ethic of (economic) expedience. Human beings resist and find ultimately unsatisfactory relations based solely on expedience. Neither can the traditional modern justification of humanitarianism be invoked because it has been thoroughly discredited by the unspeakable atrocities committed by Western humans. It is far too early, at any rate, to suggest that the European Union begins in any way to resemble the spiritual symbiosis of Christian Europe. Indeed, Europe continues to behave as a civilization robbed of spiritual resource; the only commitment it can summon is to questions of food, shelter, and amusement. The nation-state still remains the only truly effective vehicle for authority and force in Europe, as elsewhere.[8]

The global history of modern times is the record of the spread of the Atlantic infatuation with the ethic of an individual, self-directive autonomy beyond its borders. In the West itself, the history of the ethic records the see-saw between the two contradictory principles of modernity (the demands of individualism) and the needs of community. The Western mind has divided itself into partisan camps. The liberal has opted for individualism and its demand of self-direction. Nationalists have attempted to transform liberty into a communal enterprise.

The nationalist succeeded early in infusing the national idea with religious fervor, and a nationalist advocate like Jahn provided a reasonably comprehensive ethnogeny for Germany. Liberals have continued to appeal to the Herderian anthropology to justify authority. Finally. a third group began to emerge by the third decade of the nineteenth century that sought a new solution to the problem of an ordering authority. Its advocates agreed with many liberals that private property was a form of oppression and conflict and needed to be eliminated and replaced by other forms of distribution. Private property, they felt, was at the bottom of the inequities that plagued European society because it privileged avarice.

We have seen how, in his tribute to Goethe in 1833, Varnhagen wrote that the social order in Europe was largely "a perversion" because the European realm had been seized and dominated by a small elite. He went on to urge that the inequities and other existing social and political evils were due to the unequal ownership of space and resources, excluding most people from any real access to Europe's bounty. It was not the first or the last time he would promote a viewpoint that is consistent with the liberal belief in equal opportunity and its corollary concern with material wealth. From the liberal perspective, the individual must be given access to resources before he or she can achieve a minimal degree of self-direction. Bread first, freedom later, liberals declared as they came upon the intersection between liberalism and a newly emerging justification that would come to be called *socialism*.

One might say that early socialists were liberals concerned with finding some way around an intransigent status quo. Communitarian radicals like the Scottish industrialist Robert Owen founded communities outside the reach of European political authority in the new world. These protosocialist communities attempted to decenter authority in order to distribute it equally among its members, providing each with the desired level field of oppportunity through cooperation. Today we know a lot more about Marxist and Leninist Communism and their cynical and bloody use of the state to coerce the dismantling of free markets than we do about early communitarian idealism. The early spirit of the Saint-Simonists, Fourierists, and other liberal socialist movements was antistatist and communitarian in emphasis. These groups sought to liberate the individual from the suppressive tyranny of the state by forming voluntary egalitarian networks of shared authority.

THE ORIGINS OF SOCIALISM

Socialism came into being as an attempt to base human authority in voluntary association rather than coerced system. The Saint-Simonists were, for instance, very conscious that any viable and lasting human community must be built around spiritual principles. They called themselves a religion. The anticlerical revulsions of the late eighteenth century had such a profound effect on sentiment, however, that later socialist movements abandoned the idea of religion and eventually picked up the term *ideology* to apply to the explanations they generated and the doctrines they adopted.

Ideology attempts to accomplish many of the same things that religion does (to explain, for example, in a convincing manner why we exist, to what ends we act and live—in short, to provide an intelligible explanation that enables us to set up affirmable relations with others). The Herderian anthropology had begun the process of providing a new explanation, but it had not really confronted the problem presented by the obstacles to humanitarianism that were embedded in the established economic and political order. Ethnogenesis merely tried to co-opt these obstacles, transforming them into a national property. The princes became, for instance, *German* princes. Industrialists became *German* industrialists, just as their products became *German* goods and a subject of shared pride. Nationalism circumvented the problems of inequity and sanctified the old order to a considerable extent.

The key difference between religion and ideology has to do with mystery. Whereas religion relishes mystery, ideology hates it and strives to banish it with clarity. Ideological movements are always continuations of the Enlightenment project of rationality: an attempt to make life intelligible through the discovery of the laws, principles, or rules that govern the cosmos. The orthodoxy of modernity is contained in the view that discovery and not revelation is the epistemological instrument through which knowledge comes into being. Religion is rejected in modernity's orthodoxy because it assumes that knowledge is revealed. The three traditions—liberalism, nationalism, and socialism—I have chosen to put here in critical perspective share modernity's orthodoxy, which in turn is built on certain assumptions about the meaning of life best articulated for our purposes in the work and life of Herder and Goethe. Neither Herder, nor Goethe, nor later Varnhagen, Jahn, or any other person associated with them believed seriously that their explanations and understanding had been revealed to them by any divine agency. They had come to their views as reasonable human beings engaged in discovering meaning in human experience that, however, pertained to the world generally.

There is a sense in which the religious experience of revelation does creep into the experience of reasonable apprehension. Charles Fourier was convinced that his protosocialist system had been revealed to him as being congruent with the nature of the cosmos. It is safe to conclude, on the whole, however, that a belief in revelation is unorthodox and inappropriate and disguises what is actually a kind of exceptional perceptiveness on the part of distinguished and gifted individuals. Explaining such revelations as inspiration, unconscious reasoning, and insight gave rise to the notion of the genius as a person not blessed but specially empowered.

Of the three "idols" considered, liberalism is the most closely tied to the original anthropology. Varnhagen was much closer to Herder and Goethe in his devotion to human liberty than was Jahn. Early socialist thought is really another liberal strategy to overcome the obstacles intrinsic to the status quo, as well as to circumvent the exclusivist propensities of nationalism. It is a continuation of modernity's concern for providing ample scope for the development of individual autonomy and self-direction. The affinity between socialism, liberalism, and Herderian anthropology can best be illustrated in the career of a person who became pledged to a socialist agenda. Here I have chosen the American and New Yorker Albert Brisbane, because he acted as intermediary between the Parisian Saint-Simonists (and later the Fourierists) and Varnhagen's circle in Berlin; but also because he brought Fourierist socialism back home with him to New York. His promotion of Fourierism in the United States permits us to understand better the motives and idealism that drove the modern imagination to accept, promote, and develop a socialist agenda.

AMERICA AND EUROPE: ETHICS IN THE ATLANTIC COMMUNITY

The first part of this study showed how the anthropology of modernity developed into an orthodoxy that has governed most behavior since the early nineteenth century. Europe was the focus, with only a side glance at American developments. These developments were, nevertheless, evident throughout the Atlantic region, wherever European civilization had taken hold; and in each locality there were and continue to be representatives whose work parallels or resembles that of Herder, Goethe, Varnhagen, and Jahn. As a product of European civilization and, at the same time, an intermediary between new and old worlds, Brisbane is an instructive case for understanding how liberalism's beliefs and attitudes pledged a person to a socialist agenda, at least during the third and fourth decades of the nineteenth century.

The American side of the story begins before Brisbane's birth. In the eighteenth century, the thin settlements along the eastern coasts of North America provided a secure site at some remove from the European homeland for the urgent metaphysical oppositions of that day to be played out at a very practical level, in the drama of commerce and politics. The romance of liberty was juxtaposed at an early date to the realism of community. Puritan and pietist New England began an experiment in that its settlers sought to build a city on a hill, an American Zion, a promised land.

The theistic source of the millenarian expectations that infused those early settlers was lost, however, during the course of the eighteenth century, just as it had been in Europe. If a belief in Zion did not evaporate but continued to live in the minds of the descendents, the focus was shifted to the establishment of a material paradise in which every individual human being could share in the general happiness. The problems of inequity were, perhaps, not as acute as they were in Europe, but they were compounded by periodical economic depressions and an industrial revolution that left many in often desperate straits.

Citizenship in Zion was at first reserved for true believers. After secularization, citizenship was extended and became a kind of general entitlement. All had a warrant to participate in a prosperous America in which individual self-direction was maximized, fostered, and protected. One's humanity was the only criterion for membership in the community well-being and, in fact, there were no established legal criteria to control access for non-native populations. Those who could afford a boat ticket could enter into the new American dream. Moreover, beginning in the 1850s, millions did become immigrant participants. Brisbane was himself the son of a Scots father and an English mother.

Coexisting with the idea of universal entitlement was another moral field that valued hard work as prerequisite to achieving meaningful fulfillment. These two moral notions are not necessarily compatible. General entitlement actually conflicts with the idea that advantages must be earned. These oppositional principles of authority are, nevertheless, embedded in the founding documents of the United States. In the *Declaration of Independence*, for instance, rebellion against constituted authority is justified by an appeal to a God-given entitlement to inalienable rights:

When, in the course of human events, it becomes necessary for one people to dissolve the political bands which have connected them with another, and to assume, among the powers of the earth, the separate and equal station to which the laws of nature and of nature's God entitle them, a decent respect to the opinions of mankind requires that they should declare the causes which impel them to the separation.

The pantheistic fundament is clear in the appeal to the non-Christian idea of "nature and nature's God." Ethnogenetic thought plays its role in the entitlement assigned a "people" to a "separate and equal station" in the world. Modernity's anthropology is an essential component when human nature is "endowed by their Creator with certain inalienable rights; that among these are life, liberty, and the pursuit of happiness." Indeed, "to secure these rights, governments are instituted among men." Political authority is justified as the instrument by which the new anthropology is to be realized, and ultimately in obedience to the "laws of nature."

Neither the sanction (the laws of nature) nor the behavior being sanctioned (life, liberty, and the pursuit of happiness) are strictly Christian. The *Declaration of Independence* is as contrary to Christianity as is Herder's clear articulation of modernity's anthropology of entitlement and autonomy. There is no admonition in Christian Scripture to suggest that governments should be instituted with the sole purpose of assuring life, liberty, or the pursuit of happiness. There is in the entire expanse of biblical literature little to suggest that either happiness, good health, or liberty are inalienable characteristics of the human condition. In virtually every great theism, life is not an inviolable right because death is recognized as an inevitable and even determining part of humanity. If anything, Christian Scripture speaks to the issue of liberty with assurances that the condition of mundane freedom or slavery is irrelevant to the value of human existence. A premium is placed in the great theistic systems upon obedience to divine ordinance.

The arguments in the *Declaration of Independence* move from the character of human nature to the meaning of political authority. Here we discover a crucial, destiny-laden leap of faith that sets up an inexorable revolutionary dynamic:

Whenever any form of government becomes destructive of these ends [i.e., the achievement of life, liberty, and the pursuit of happiness], it is the right of the people to alter or abolish it, and to institute new government, laying its foundations on such principles, and organizing its powers in such form, as to them shall seem most likely to effect their safety and happiness.

It is clear in what follows that the argument must have seemed excessively dangerous even to its authors. The foregoing call is followed by a passage designed to moderate the previous assertion of revolutionary right. An appeal is made to "Prudence," which dictates that "governments, long established, should not be changed for light and transient causes," after which twenty-seven complaints are lodged against the government of Great Britain.

The other founding document, the *Constitution of the United States*, was drafted after the successful conclusion of the rebellion of the Colonies, as well as a trial period in which they formed a loose confederation and expressed a need for a centralized authority. The concept of a "people" is employed in the American document a quarter of a century before it figured in Jahn's impassioned ethnogeny as the *Volk*. The establishment of a new political authority is, moreover, justified because the "people" *desire* a more "perfect union." The union, or a centralized authority, is organized to "establish justice, insure domestic tranquillity, provide for the common defense, promote the general welfare, and secure the blessing of liberty for ourselves and our posterity."

There is no appeal in the *Constitution* to the laws of nature or to nature's God or a Creator. There is, on the other hand, the assumption that centralized government is an unmitigated blessing and the sole agency through which justice and equity can be enforced. The meaning of liberty, justice, and the other general qualities the Constitution seeks to assure are set out in a number of articles and amendments designed to leave no doubt about what the founders meant and intended; in this sense they were true liberals and advocates of clarity. They were definitely not nationalist mystifiers, though they served the cause of the state as effectively as any nationalist, seeking to establish it as the sole effective authority over the public weal and, moreover, reserving only those "powers" it did not claim for itself for any other existing interests or institutions. A strong central government or state was moreover sanctified and hallowed by the enormous sacrifices brought on its behalf during the American Civil War (1861–1865).

The American state was established on liberal principles of self-direction, while the European state was jusified in ethnolinguistic terms. The effect was, nevertheless, the same. In either case, the establishment of states signaled the ascendency of a single authority over the affairs of human beings. Although established on different principles, there is no difference between the behavior and functions of the American state and the major European nation-states. Domestically they both operate to extinguish rival authority centers, while externally they seek to achieve hegemonial influence over their neighbors.

Psychopolitically speaking, the modern state, whether liberal-American or ethnolinguistic nation in principle, interprets the world in largely bipolar terms. Externally there are clients and allies grouped as friends and the remainder relegated to the enemy camp. Internally the state regards the inhabitants of its realm as being either patriots or aliens. Both the liberal state and the nation-state employ force to protect established domestic elites from threats from emergent rival power centers. There is in either scenario little to restrain the state from the exercise of maximum force whenever the resources are available to project it.

The patriot in either liberal state or nation-state is pledged to support the state agenda. In the liberal state loyalty is the only criterion, while the nation-state still requires nativity and/or native speakers of the national language. When the American Robert E. Lee shifted his allegiance in crisis to his home state and the community to which he was most closely tied, in spite of a lifetime of federal service, he became an alien. On the other hand, in the nation-state even generations of loyal service rendered by non-nationals do not necessarily qualify them for insider acceptance, as German Jews discovered to their dismay and pain.

The modern state is insatiable in its regime and can tolerate no rival. Americans who supported the Confederate cause only comprehended the merciless pursuit of total authority to which the state is committed at the end of a long and bloody war. Others who have opposed federal force, including Indians, coal miners, and domestic dissenters, have also discovered the inhumanity with which the state's coercive mechanism can deliver punishment to every rival and against all defiance to its regime. The external behavior of the modern state can be gauged by the vicious wars fought since the advent of the new atheistic anthropology. The new order makes authority capable of lethal action far in excess of any force needed to effect a rational purpose or to secure a reasonable interest.

Socialism was from the beginning an oppositional or antistatist ideology that recognized in both the liberal-constitutional and the nation-states serious threats to the West's humanitarian anthropology. Those like Brisbane, who began to seek remedy in socialist strategies, had first to be thoroughly disillusioned by the chauvinism and petty particularism of ethnogenesis, as well as revolted by the ineptness of liberalism in effecting meaningful reform.

NOTES

1. "Im Sinne der Wanderer," *Ueber Kunst und Alterthum* (1832), drittes Heft des sechsten und letzten Bandes, 541.

2. Recent interest in Renan in Europe is reflected in such articles as Walter Euchner's "Vom Recht der Nation," *Die Zeit*, No. 16, 22 April 1994, p. 20.

3. Karl Marx, Friedrich Engels *Werke* (Berlin, 1974), Vol 30, No. 116, 27 November 1861: "Der Kerl is aber doch ein ganz schäbig feiger Lauskerl gewesen" (p. 202).

4. Haym, "Varnhagen von Ense. Tagebucher von K. A. Varnhagen von Ense. Sechs Bande," *Preussische Jahrbücher* XI (1863), 445–515. On the last page, Haym wrote, "In unserem politischen Leben steht er als das Symptom einer Krankheit: in unserer Literatur als eine immerhin höchst beachtenswerthe, ja, unumgängliche Erscheinung da."

5. Pickett, *Varnhagen*, p. 94.

6. *The Letters of Varnhagen von Ense to Richard Monckton Milnes. Anglistische Forschungen*, Heft 92 (Heidelberg, 1965), 8.

7. Feilchenfeldt, *Varnhagen als Historiker*. Amsterdam: Erasmus Verlag, 1976.

8. "The nation-state is dead. Long live the nation-state," *The Economist*, December 23, 1995–January 5, 1996, pp. 15–18.

10

THE AMERICAN AS SOCIALIST: ALBERT BRISBANE (1809–1895)

Brisbane's career shows why so many men and women of universalist sympathies chose socialism at a time when liberalism, with its laissez-faire capitalism and new industrial elites, had failed to achieve the goals its advocates had set for emancipation and enfranchisement. The strength of his example also lies in the fact that he was American and, therefore, as a socialist an anomaly of sorts. In both his success and failure, Brisbane clarifies the ideological currents on the Western shores of the Atlantic community: the strong belief in the future and self-directive individualism mixed with a concern for social cohesion that found both conservative and radical expression.

If Brisbane's roots placed him very close to Europe, he was also an American through and through. His canny Scots father made a fortune as a merchant, agent for the Holland Land Purchase, and founder of Batavia and Buffalo, New York. His English mother gave him a good dose of secular idealism. She could, Brisbane remembered in later life, expound on human destiny in cosmological terms.[1] On the other hand, Brisbane had grown up, as he himself later testified, almost wild, with little formal education, freely ranging through the forests and country around Batavia. He was a superb rider and, perhaps, penultimately American because he exhibited a behavior of intense contrasts. He assaulted the highest social citadels of Europe and America with a fearless and boundless confidence that recognized no limitations of class, wealth, office, or power. But he also wallowed at times in self-doubt that prohibited his acting at all.

From a home environment characterized by skepticism and reformist idealism, Brisbane had gone at the age of fifteen to New York City where he learned French from Jean Manesca, an aging Frenchman who had escaped intact from the slave insurrections in his native Santo Domingo. It was under the tutelage of Manesca that Brisbane developed his obsession with idealist thought. By the time he had finished with his pupil and was ready to dispatch him to Europe, Manesca had successfully inculcated Brisbane with the belief that mundane, everyday reality was of little consequence. The young man set out believing that a life of higher, abstract thinking was the only life worth living. Brisbane sailed in May of 1828 at the age of eighteen for France with the intention of sitting at the feet of the great thinkers of that continent. It was an odyssey that would last some six years.

At the Sorbonne in Paris, the young American was one of the very few of his compatriots to hear the lectures of Victor Cousin. Like certain French intellectuals since, Cousin was an intermediary between the American intelligentsia and German thought. It was not too long, however, before Brisbane discerned that he was listening to a kind of translation from the German. He then determined to proceed to Berlin to hear the ideas at their source. Although Brisbane later presented himself in his autobiographical writings as a single-minded intellectual pilgrim, in reality he always had time to stop along the way to make acquaintance with men such as Goethe. His travels were meanderings of a young man intent on finding his vocation and having the help of Great Minds in the bargain.

Although Brisbane's diaries reveal more than one might expect of uncertainty and lack of confidence, there were areas such as his fluency in French in which he was very secure—perhaps naively so. Later, in commenting on his achievements, Brisbane was somewhat given to exaggeration. The extant letters he wrote to Varnhagen von Ense show that he was in command of a fluent but erratic French characterized by very eccentric turnsofphrase and occasional anglicisms that are incomprehensible.[2] There is no record of what he achieved in German, though he did reach Berlin and attended Hegel's lectures for awhile. In his social relations in Berlin, he most likely used French because any of the Berlin hosts and hostesses whose salons he frequented could speak it well.

Whatever his limitations, the youth moved easily among the intellectual elites of the European capitals he visited. Part of the attraction he held for the intelligentsia was, of course, his nationality. An American was still a relative novelty abroad, and few indeed had ever reached some of the places Brisbane would visit during the course of his extended sojourn. One can follow his travels handily by reading his diaries (they are deposited in the George Arendt Research Library at Syracuse University and have not yet been published). He records much about the people he met, his feelings about them, and the occasional intellectual epiphanies he enjoyed.

The diaries tell us that the schematic version of his life reported in the quasi-autobiography put together by his last wife, Redelia, misrepresents the certainty with which he moved to his life's calling. On the other hand, since young Brisbane was anxiously searching for some guidelines for his life, his occasional insights into the meaning of social relations really did seem to him, as Redelia reports the old man having said, of greatest moment in his life. These insights or epiphanies opened up to him a new level of social understanding and served as milestones in his development that remained important to him all his life and to which he could refer when seeking stability in his otherwise rather peripatetic life.

As a boy, Brisbane recalled how he had suddenly had a vision, while throwing a stone into a brook, of collective humankind spreading out like ripples in the water and including himself as a kind of tiny, atomic constituent of its dynamic movement. The image is indeed symbolic of two of the strongest currents of the nineteenth century, for in it one can recognize the perennial naturalism that haunted the Western mind with desolate visions of humankind's cosmic insignificance. There is also, on the other hand, a glimpse of the pantheistic faith in a grand future as the world emanates outward into ever greater articulation and self-expression, coming into its own, as it were. Another such moment, experienced in Paris while eating ice cream during the intermission at the opera, occurred when Brisbane suddenly understood how his enjoyment of leisure's aesthetic luxuries depended on the complex social and economic system that enabled him to operate by drawing on the product of labor invested by other people. The two visions combined made him psychologically ripe for socialist doctrine.

After a year in Paris, Brisbane was impatient, restless, and convinced that he had learned all he could from French savants. Establishing a pattern that accompanied him all his life, he itched to leave France and go to Berlin. There he intended to hear the great Hegel. Since his wealth made it possible for him to obey his impulse, he left. In Frankfurt am Main there was a fateful meeting with Jules LeChevalier, a Saint-Simonist who would later introduce him to the social thinker, Charles Fourier. When he reached Berlin, Brisbane found easy access to the salons and soon met Rahel Varnhagen and her husband. It was his ideological conquest of Rahel that he considered the triumph of his sojourn there. Although she was old and sick at the time, she and the young man joined forces to promote the new protosocialist teachings he had brought from Paris.

Although Varnhagen was much less inclined to enthuse, he did produce a series of articles in 1832 promoting Saint-Simonism. The young American must have impressed him, for he carried on a correspondence with Brisbane for years after he had left Berlin.[3] Brisbane was at first as enthusiastic about Germany and Germans as he had been about France and the French. He made a determined attempt to romance Henriette Solmar, a hostess of one of Berlin's salons, and failed. Once again his restlessness triumphed, and, in October 1830 he left Berlin for Vienna on the first leg of what became a remarkable journey and an adventure which few Americans of the time undertook.

Brisbane's wealth enabled him to move on before he had submitted to the profound discipline necessary to master the most difficult material. In one sense, it was his wealth that provided him opportunities for permissiveness and self-indulgence that characterized his personal life while, at the same time, assuring a constant amateurism in the social, political, and intellectual projects he undertook. He never followed through to the logical consequences of any enterprise, intellectual or practical. After abandoning Cousin and the wisdom available at the Sorbonne, then Hegel and the whole liberal establishment in Berlin, Brisbane went on to leave Saint-Simonism for Fourierism. Back in America at last, he continued throughout life to leave behind him a swath of deserted or abandoned systems, schools, projects, mistresses, wives, and children.

During the next three months, his travels took him as far as Turkey and through war-torn Greece. His diaries are a record of his struggle to find adequate expression for the events and social conditions he observed during this journey. His exploits and observations during his journey are alone worthy of note and exceedingly rare in the American experience. What he witnessed in moslem Turkey initiated his life-long commitment to the question of improving women's rights. The status of women in Moslem society outraged him. In Greece he narrowly escaped being murdered as he climbed up to visit ancient ruins. Later he was conveyed by Russian and British warships until he found himself in quarantine in Malta.

Brisbane's habits of sexual promiscuity were also established during these youthful travels. His appetite for random encounters with young women stayed with him all his life. His preference for frequent changes in sexual partners would involve him in protracted legal negotiations that would finally darken his last years. Part of the attraction of the new socialist thought of Fourier had to do with its justification of promiscuity, though he shrewdly hid that when promoting Fourierism in the United States. It was during his confinement on the island of Malta that he records how easily a young man with money could gain sexual access to the destitute young women of the region. Brisbane's moralizing observations are, after that time, mixed with blatant sexual episodes. When he asked a maid in a hostel in Italy if she would sleep with him, the simplicity of her direct reply he thought worth recording. She answered, "good."

Brisbane had little interest in the psychological aspects and feelings of others. He spent his energy analyzing social and historical forces he observed at work in the societies he visited. His negative view of English society may have been given him by his English mother who had left England and was filled, if we can believe her son, with reformist ardor. It was confirmed when he witnessed a shipside whipping of a sailor while sailing on a British frigate. As Brisbane wrote in his diary entry dated December 1, while en route to Syracuse to Calabria,

I think there must before a great while be a Revolution in England: the general organisation of Society. . . must produce some changes. I am surprised only it has lasted so long. . . I should, for one, like to see it come: the general advancement of the spirit of nations interests me too much to wish to see it stoped [sic] for individual wellfare [sic]—England must be baptized with the spirit of the New Century behind which it is lagging [Entry of Wednesday, lst Decem, from Syracuse to Calabria].

After that time, Brisbane's perspective remained remarkably constant throughout his life. The youth's reflections during his travels provide the essential configuration that would determine the thought and character of the man. In one respect, Brisbane is the epitome of the American Whig. Society is, in his view, dynamic and composed of competing forces engaged in a dialectical movement guided by a national spirit which sets certain limits and lends society a characteristic flavor. Revolution is viewed romantically as an opportunity for resolving conflict and restoring harmony; it is, therefore, an acceptable social mechanism and was also very much on young Brisbane's mind during his sojourn in Europe. He also provides a pattern for future American presence in Europe, for generations since have taken a radical stance while in Europe, only to modify their views on returning home.

Brisbane did, in some respects, moderate himself after returning to New York. He abandoned the idea that revolution is a desirable instrument of social change. Fourierism gave him the American answer. It was a creed that, while promising the idea of peaceful associationism, in no way challenged the capitalist status quo—at least in the abridged Fourierst doctrine that Brisbane formulated for his compatriots.

In the meantime, Brisbane came back to Paris from his travels in Asia Minor and points south. There he quickly penetrated the circle of the Saint-Simonists. Writing in his diary on October 9, 1831, he recounts attending a meeting in which he met the chief leaders of Saint-Simonism, Enfantin and Bazard. The first meeting he attended, he wrote, had "all the appearance of a fashionable soirèe. Some looked rather more genteel than others, but there are many remarkably handsome faces among the women." After speaking with Enfantin, Brisbane declared that "their ideas contain more, are deeper, fuller of life, and a vast deal more important than the ideas of *Schelling,* or *Hegel.* Pure systematizing without having humanity constantly before you and your systems is good for nothing".

The period of initial enthusiasm for the Saint-Simonists and their cause, however, was soon followed by agonizing over whether he could commit himself adequately to their cause. Brisbane bewails what he perceived as a lack of feeling in himself, very much as Varnhagen had done as a young man: "Feeling is what I want, is what I have need of. I would wish to feel deeply, profoundly, and let it sooner be melancoly [*sic*] sad, anything, than not at all" (p. 51). In a sentimental age it was not uncommon that young people should discover they could not generate enough feeling to satisfy the conventions. Brisbane also did what he often did when he began to wrestle with the necessity of committing himself to something concrete: He left Paris and returned to Berlin once again.

In Berlin, Henriette Solmar's lukewarm reception displeased him. He took her in his arms "and pressed her several times; (but she did not kiss me, that is she did not return it as I gave it)" (p. 110). After the young women of Malta and Italy, her measured affection was inadequate for the twenty-two year old. Soon Brisbane decided that he did not really even like her. He also rejected another acquaintance, the chief pupil of Hegel, distinguished scholar, and one of Varnhagen's best friends, Eduard Gans, as just another "liberal." Michelet he also found "flat, and stale, and altho' the ideas may be well worked out, they remain without life, and interest." There was, in short, little that pleased him the second time around in Germany.

The time in Berlin was not wasted, however, and if we are to believe the reminiscence of Brisbane as an old man, he worked together again with the Varnhagens to promote the cause, left them writings of Fourier, and distributed more copies of the *Globe,* the Saint-Simonist newspaper, in Berlin coffee houses. Not given to a small estimation of himself, Brisbane went so far in his autobiography as to claim that during 1831–1832 he was responsible for bringing socialism to Germany. His progressive disillusionment with academic philosophy he recorded in his diary: "Philosophy now appears to me a thing dead, without life, in which the thoughts and faculties of mind become the mere playthings of themselves" (p. 119). Although he "loved Germany very much" he decided that the German people will not give "humanity its futurity" (p. 120).

Brisbane's disillusionment encompassed Europe and included the people with whom he associated. His view of "futurity" did not include the European bourgeoisie and its mode of socializing. Liberalism he spurned because it advocated a revolution "in favour of the middle classes...although that revolution has already been accomplished by the people" (pp. 124–125). Back in the United States, on the other hand, he would show himself perfectly willing to work with the propertied classes—of which he himself was a distinguished member—to affect only very limited social change.

It may to some extent have been homesickness that prompted Brisbane to record his deepening disillusionment and dissatisfaction with the state of affairs he believed he observed in Europe:

At present there is no God, no Providence in the world. And the larger portion of society is plunged in ignorance and poverty, are unseen, unheard of...and that harmony which God seems to have placed in the universe is not in the least reflected in the social world of man,—everywhere there is war, envy: hatred—that antagonism replaces harmony: and instead of a foresight of love, we find a blind hasard.(p. 133)

Brisbane later recalled the frustration he felt in his attempts to promote socialist ideas in Berlin at the time:

What, then, was my surprise to find that these men, whose whole intellectual lives had been devoted to the old philosophical theories, remained indifferent to everything in the shape of new ideas. They did not perceive the originality in what we presented; they did not appreciate the importance of what I might call the philosophy of labor—the philosophy of the material interest of men and a complete change in the system governing them. This mental obtuseness, as it seemed to us, made Madame Varnhagen and myself militant disciples of Fourier in all the circles in which we moved. (p. 173)

Although it is evident in the letters Brisbane wrote to Rahel Varnhagen in late 1831 and early 1832 that it was not Fourier but the Saint-Simonists they promoted, it is safe to assume that the frustration they experienced was quite real.[4] Brisbane apparently left Berlin on June 7, 1832 and returned to Paris.

BECOMING A DISCIPLE OF FOURIER

It was during the autumn of 1832 that Jules LeChevalier introduced Brisbane to Charles Fourier.[5] According to Brisbane, he hired Fourier, at the rate of five francs per hour, to teach him his system. The two men met twice a month, which must have cost the American a total of $12.00.[6] Brisbane lingered in Paris and did not return to the United States until some time in early 1834. By May 22, 1834 he was writing to Varnhagen from Batavia, requesting a copy of the sensational *Rahel* book Varnhagen published at his own expense and sent out to friends after his wife's death. Brisbane also spoke in his letter of his sense of destiny as an American:

It gave me infinite pleasure to return to my country and to walk down the streets I know so well. I have a sense of being very free....In Europe I was no more than a simple student; I was not a citizen: I did not have the right to speak and act—but here, I am a citizen and can speak and act, and raise my voice in the affairs of my country: which gives me a sense of value and liberty.[7]

He also spoke of consolidating his financial affairs and outlined plans he had for building rental units in the new city of Buffalo.

Brisbane did indeed devote much of his energy to his investments during the period from 1834 until 1839, though he also complained of a general malaise he experienced which he attributed to Europe's lack of sufficient oxygen. It is entirely possible that some of his investment schemes were designed to generate money needed to effect Fourierism.[8] His friend and teacher, Jean Manesca, had died in late 1838, vacating the office of secretary of the Fourier Society in New York. Manesca's death may have been one of the factors that led to Brisbane becoming more active in the movement. On April 7, 1839 he gave a speech in New York commemorating Fourier's birthday and thereafter entered upon the most active public period of his life.

In the aftermath of the Panic of 1837, the American communitarian movement had grown out of a post-Ownenite renewal of interest in alternatives to industrialization in an increasingly urban setting. Serious economic depression had led American industrialists to abandon the paternalist programs that had shown so much promise for a humanitarian treatment of labor. Conditions for industrial workers worsened sharply, and downward wage pressures soon made the plight of American labor desperate. Brisbane's diaries during the period 1830–1831 indicate that he had anticipated the disenchantment of many of his compatriots when he decided that industrial society was corrupt and badly in need of radical reorganization.

Brisbane was soon joined by a growing number of Americans in his concern for finding humanitarian alternatives to the status quo. He was far from alone in believing that the root of the problem lay in a society that encouraged conflict rather than harmony in human beings. If he was out of sorts with liberalism and its American equivalents, Brisbane was nevertheless always ready to join ruthlessly with any person or group, whether or not he was in fundamental agreement with them, if they promised to assist the cause. His patriotism also led him at first to compare the United States favorably to the inequitable societies of Europe, though he soon included his own country among the social problems of the world.

"We condemn merely the present social organization, which, as we will endeavor to prove, is monstrously defective," he wrote in the first treatise he published.[9] The treatise was a 480-page exposition of the theories of Fourier which appeared in 1840 as *The Social Destiny of Man: or Association and Reorganization of Industry*. What especially appealed to Brisbane about Fourier's system was the idea that cooperation could be substituted for coercion and competition—even at the cost of subverting what then passed for human nature. His vision was the original modern fantasy of a harmonized society in which conflict had been banished from human relations; it was a world in which the individual could devote himself or herself in uninhibited pursuit of desire while not being threatened by the demands of contrary interests.

To propagate Fourier's ideas among Americans, Brisbane was not reluctant to suppress his mentor's more controversial notions, particularly those that promoted the dismantlement of marriage and traditional childrearing. Brisbane also did not elaborate on Fourier's extravagant cosmological speculations, though they were certainly conceived as the undergirding for his entire system. Brisbane's abridgement focuses more on the practical side of organizing a philanstery (in this case, a community of six thousand), with the intent of creating a nearly self-sufficient industrial cooperative that would, concurrently, provide a benign social environment for productive individuals.

Horace Greeley was destined to be Brisbane's most important ally and supporter. When the Whig journalist and newspaper publisher was persuaded, his impact on the spread of utopian communitarianism was immense. The first step was taken when Greeley and Brisbane founded the short-lived periodical *The Future* to propagate Fourierist ideas. When the publication failed, Greeley made room for a column in the New York *Tribune* for Brisbane, providing him with a very important propaganda vehicle for the price of about $500. Brisbane's column proved to be one of the most effective propaganda vehicles of modern American history. In it he developed a popular version of Fourierism to which thousands of readers could relate. For Whigs like Greeley, Fourierism offered not an alternative but a supplement to industrial capitalism. American socialism emerged not as a program for complete and radical social change but rather as an additive that would help ameliorate the growing tensions between the classes.

Brisbane more than rose to the challenge. He proved a very effective propagandist, a convincing writer, and a persuasive public speaker. The tall, gaunt Yankee with the abstracted and absent-minded demeanor became a vivid and powerful public figure with great influence over large numbers of people looking for a leader and options. Disparate elements throughout western New York and the Mississippi valley began to crystallize into a movement. For his part, however, Brisbane was not keen on the experimental communities that arose. He was afraid that they were premature and undercapitalized. Among the many experiments, only the well-known New England community at Brook Farm was the recipient of his intensive engagement and interest.[10]

Brisbane's appearance on the scene at Brook Farm precipitated a crisis that threatened the Farm's survival. His manner and rhetoric proved persuasive to the New England intellectuals who inhabited the place, and Brook Farm was converted to a Fourierist phalanstery. It was only after the inevitable failure of the experiment that Brisbane was perceived as a destructive meddler.[11] In recalling Brisbane, some of the former Brook Farmers hit on a criticism of his character that was repeated in other testimony and was related to his wealth. Brisbane apparently generated expectations of financial assistance in his auditors which he neither intended nor was prepared to meet. When nothing was forthcoming, the faithful often felt betrayed and recalled him with bitterness.

More intriguing is the question of how such early socialist ideas could have had appeal for a broad spectrum of Whigs, Democrats, and Transcendentialists, the latter who viewed any challenge to individualistic self-reliance as anathema. Brisbane's persuasive gifts doubtless contributed to the acceptance of Fourierism among those from whom one would otherwise expect a certain fundamental hostility. His willingness to disguise, suppress, and simply falsify Fourier's doctrines for the sake of gaining tactical allies certainly is behind Fourierism's adoption by people of such diverse political views. On the other hand, what appears on the surface to be a broad spectrum of social and political views proves—as I have maintained throughout this book—on closer examination to be woven from the same American (and even Western) cloth we have already described, with the common thread being the shared hope for secular redemption, the belief that a city on a hill can and should be achieved as a civil society, and the positing of all value in some fantasized future. There was an expectation that one need only find the correct formula and then apply it for the new, redeemed age to become a reality. The formula is what one later came to call an ideology.

It may be that Brisbane went farther afield than most of his contemporaries in quest of the formula. What he discovered in the work of the eccentric Charles Fourier Brisbane considered not formula, not ideology, but *science*. When he brought it back to America, it was not as an idea or notion that he peddled it. Fourier had unlocked the secrets of nature, and Brisbane was, therefore, not merely a spokesman for another interpretation of reality. He was an apostle and co-prophet. What he propagated was not merely a new promise but word from the fundamental structures of the cosmos. Brisbane's version of Fourierism, after all, was little different from the Brook Farmers' hope of establishing a regime of "freedom, self-culture, the integration of thought and labor, and humane relationships."[12]

It was because Brisbane perceived himself as the apostle of ultimate truth that he had little qualm in manipulating others and feeding them only that version of the truth that they, in his judgment, were capable of digesting. His lack of scruple is a preview of the ruthlessness exhibited later by ardent socialists. The believer resorts happily to deception if it leads to conversion. When Brisbane alienated people who felt betrayed, he was able to ignore it. The true prophet must be courageous in the use of any expedient moves that brought humankind farther along the road to the "futurity" that the prophet conceived himself or herself as serving so faithfully.

It was said that Brisbane was afflicted by a particularly intellectual form of insanity evidenced in his utter indifference to mundane affairs and human relationships. There is an echo of Marx living in isolation in London and working daily in the British Museum; a kind of splendid indifference. While Marx could be tyrannically indifferent, abusive, and almost violently contentious, however, Brisbane was abstracted and even gentle. Anecdotes recalling his extreme absent-mindedness are legion. His last wife, a young woman enamored of reformist causes, discovered him admid the shambles of what was left of his house after a major fire, his children unwashed, the condition of the household filthy—and yet Brisbane seems to have been utterly unmindful of these conditions. At another point, he was said to have sat across from his own child and nurse on the streetcar without recognizing them until they both got off at the same stop.[13]

Brisbane's eventual willingness to use coercion to force people to cooperate is evident in a "Plan of the Transitional Organization of Industry," which he sent in halograph to T. C. Durant in 1868 and which provides a taste of the future. Durant had instructions to make useful additions and then to forward the document to E. P. Grant, who in turn was supposed to pass it on to Victor Considerant. Considerant, a fellow Fourierist from Paris, was in San Antonio attempting to set up a Fourierist-style colony. Like so many before him, he awaited Brisbane's sending him more than just moral support and advice.

Brisbane's plan was authoritarian. His ideas about cooperation had undergone a change. By the 1860s, he thought he had located part of the reason for the earlier failures of the communtarian experiments in their tolerance of unproductive members. Thus did he come to the belief, as he expressed it in the Plan, that "there must be introduced *a just and wise authority*, which may be *absolute* when necessary". He continues by remarking that "We must go on the assumption that men will not be *harmonizable* at once; but that they will be animated by many of the false instincts with which civilization has imbued them."

Brisbane proposed a quasi-military structure of authority in order to enforce the discipline necessary to transform participants to a harmonizable state. There is no evidence, on the other hand, that Grant accepted his argument; indeed, the document may never have reached Considerant in San Antonio, whose experimental community, in any case, never got off the ground. Even these French Fourierists apparently harbored feelings that Brisbane had failed to live up to certain agreements he had made about supporting them.

BRISBANE'S ELITIST ROMANTICISM

For all the differences that have been explored in numerous studies in our own century, the different perspectives of the last century agree in their most fundamental assumptions about the nature of the world and the condition of the human race. One of the charms of studying Brisbane's writings lies in the forthright and naive faith he showed in the noble purpose of elite culture that belies his idealism. He imagined, for instance, that the tight-knit community created by a phalanstery would enable the leaders to eliminate the "coarseness and rudeness of the lower classes." Although a strong program of education within the phalanstery was not supposed to eliminate the social classes, it was designed to create an environment of politeness.

Through all his work this consistent theme spins its didactic thread: The masses are to be pacified and converted to a genteel mode of behavior because

communtarianism can obviate the causes of social conflict. The fortunate ones
(such as Brisbane) would thus be left in an even more enviable position because
they would be free to continue the enjoyment of their advantages without anxiety.
In short, we are returned in surprising fashion to the humanitarian universe of
Goethe and Herder in which individual human beings are all depicted as striving
toward noninjurious relations simply because they know in their hearts that such
behavior is best.

The high ideal is presumed to be a projection of human nature: Humanity is
that to which human nature inclines us. Brisbane leaps on Fourier's own formu-
lation of the passional drives which echo Herder's "higher impulses" (*Triebe*).
Anybody deviating from the idealist pattern of striving toward humanitarianism
falls short of humanity. Through certain humanitarian instruments, even the great
unwashed masses can be domesticated and persuaded into cohesive community
through the idealist apology—and without demanding equal empowerment.
Modern education provides the intense indoctrination; social welfare produces
the pacifying oil; the philanstery creates the context of good feelings that mollify
real grievances. Thus does the great bourgeois justification for authority emerge
in its fantasy of a world in which privilege (i.e., the satiation of desire) can be
enjoyed unchallenged.[14]

The supremacy of the better classes would be assured in Brisbane's scheme
through an organization that depended upon injections of private capital, beginning with a $100,000 up front that Brisbane thought necessary for the basic estab-
lishment of a phalanstery of 6000 members. Nor would all property be held in
common, any more than the nuclear family remain intact, for the phalanstery
would operate more like a joint stock company in which larger stockholders would
also command more rights—and, perhaps, a broader sexual access among members. When all of this is considered, it is not suprising that, in a tract published in
1856 with the title *Theory of the Function of the Human Passions*, Brisbane turns
out to have been an ingenuous Romanticist thinker who placed primary emphasis
on what he calls the "Passional Forces."

To understand humankind's social destiny, which is, according to Brisbane
in a chapter entitled "General View of Man," the "end for which it was created
and placed on the Planet it inhabits," one must "comprehend the nature of that
passional and intellectual Motor in him, called the SOUL". Since these passions
are natural forces, it is not they which require modification or adjustment; instead
they require a "Social Organization" to suit them. Brisbane was certain that these
"Passional Forces" were simply not being accomodated by any given "Social
Organization."[15]

As if Brisbane's classification of the human passions in the text were not
enough, he included a fold-out sheet bearing the title "Synoptical Table of the
Functions of the Human Passions." Both his explication of Fourier's theories on
the human passions and his *Introduction to Social Science* (1857, 1876) are his
responses to the widespread sentiment that communitarianism had been tried on
American soil and failed. Brisbane argued again that the circumstances had been
inauspicious and that the experiments had been severely hampered by

undercapitalization. In his survey of socialist thought, he considered St. Simon, Auguste Comte, Krause (whose work he became acquainted with while stopping in Munich), Robert Owen, and Herbert Spencer, and he asserted that Fourier's main contribution lies in his having deduced a plan of social organization only after having "discovered" what he calls "Laws of Universal Order."

Since Fourier's "Laws" are the crucial aspect of his philosophy, Brisbane admitted that he had not hesitated to abridge his other teachings, for the "editor was solicitous that doctrines in antagonism with the fundamental principles of our civilization should not be broached." At this point, we can relate his view that the social order must be modified to accomodate the natural passions to Herder's work. Once again the eighteenth-century anthropology that replaced Christianity in the critical forum dictates a progressivist scheme through which humankind can pass into a happier future. Futurity, as Brisbane put it many times, was the utopian goal toward which all moral behavior inclined. In Brisbane and most socialist thought, the focus is not on the troublesome and, in any case, complex individual but on the collective destiny of mankind; or, as Brisbane put it in *Social Science*: "The Human Race is a collective, continuous, progressive WHOLE."[16]

Brisbane's mind was never a hospitable haven for ideas of state ownership. He knew about Karl Marx and wrote from Kansas City on January 3, 1883 that

Collectivism in France is the same as Communism in Germany—as the Communism founded by *Karl Marx*. Collectivism asserts that natural wealth of the world belongs to Humanity *collectively*—Socialism asserts second that a certain Class in Society, and very limited in numbers, has monopolized the Wealth of the world belonging to Humanity, it must be dispossessed, and the wealth—called also, property, capital—returned to the true, natural owners, the people as a whole. Violent revolution will be necessary to effect this; at least, unless a *scientific solution* of the problem is discerned.[17]

It was obvious that he preferred his own brand of syndicalism to a Marxist state and cooperative communities in which the upper-middle class was still comfortable to the rule of a proletariat. The world was simply, so he concluded at last, not ripe for revolution. Humankind still existed on a rather primitive level of development, which he liked to call the "Social Childhood of the Race."

A CAREER MANQUÉ?

In old age, Brisbane became convinced that his true vocation had been not as a social reformer but as a teacher. In writing to Redelia on October 28, 1875, he made one of his rare bitter charges against Horace Greeley, whom he held responsible for having diverted him from the "great task" of teaching a new religion and turned his energies to the "low, practical idea" of promoting industrial reform. He complained that he had "flittered away" his life and felt himself to be a failure at age sixty-six.[18]

Brisbane's sense of failure and frustration represents a relapse to his youthful insecurity and was magnified in 1879, when a sordid controversy erupted over the issue of a sexual relationship he had once had with a former housekeeper.

After the death of his first wife, Brisbane had begun in his usual fashion a casual liaison with his housekeeper, who, though she left him, renewed their relations shortly before he departed for Europe to observe the insurrections in 1848. Brisbane apparently heard nothing more from her until her daughter styled herself "the only daughter of Albert and Lodoiska Brisbane" in her wedding announcement.

Brisbane unleashed Pandora's box when he publicly denied having ever been married to Lodoiska. As his brother George was quick to point out, his denial was tantamount to "branding her [Lodoiska's daughter] a bastard in the New York Herald."[19] Charges of bigamy and a divorce trial followed. George managed to expose publicly how Brisbane had muddled his private relations with four different women who were consecutively and sometimes simultaneously married to him. The resulting scandal also indicated that he had been involved in the free love movement.

In the extended feud that ensued, Brisbane's brother remained his archenemy, exploiting every opportunity to do him damage. Brisbane meantime removed himself from the conflict by simply staying in Paris. The media treatment of the trial made it apparent, however, that associationism was no longer taken seriously in America. In an editorial entitled "A Fourierite Apostle," the *New York Times* on May 31, 1883 attacked Brisbane vehemently and referred to his advocacy of "that form of socialistic insanity known as Fourierism." His domestic squabble was, according to the newspaper, evidence enough of the "disgusting immorality of the dirty Frenchman's dreams." Similar editorials appeared throughout the United States.

Brisbane lived another seven years, employing his financial resources to appeal the divorce decision and prevent Lodoiska from receiving any court settlement; in effect, he left the problem to be resolved by his heirs. Until the very end, he was true to a lifelong pattern of escaping the more mundane responsibilities. Although he was attended during the last years by his adoring younger wife, Redelia, all her efforts were not successful in bringing him to any kind of systematic reminiscence. After his death, she had to gather the facts and details into some coherent narrative.

Like the Saint-Simonists with whom Brisbane first flirted, the Fourierist advocates thought that society would need to be transformed through structural changes that would institute a new order more hospitable to humanitarian values. The inequity and injustice that existed in the established institutional reality of the European order must, according to advocates of these views, be overcome. The resulting cooperative society would cancel the need for conflict and resolve inequity, facilitating general affluence. The analysis of what was perceived to be wrong with society was shared by liberals and nationalists; the prognosis of socialist thinkers was merely at variance with these other perspectives. Many European socialists not only agreed with nationalists about the importance of the state or governmental mechanisms, but they entertained similar notions about the use of coercive force by the state to assure conformity.

CONCLUSION

The idea of the phalanstery that Brisbane took over from Fourier was conceived as a kind of large resort hotel in which everybody could live together in an eternal vacation. It is not surprising that a person of education and means like Brisbane should find the convenience, comfort, and comraderie of a hotel or boarding house congenial as a plan for an ideal society. Such living conditions were customary during much of the nineteenth century. Americans of every socioeconomic category found it convenient to pool resources in such establishments, and there was the added advantage that boarding house life reduced the drudgery of daily chores for residents. Since there was no ideal of domestic privacy manifest in the ownership of single-family dwellings such as we have today, sharing rooms and a bed with acquaintances or strangers was an accepted daily habit.

Turning the United States into a network of phalansteries promised to assure for the entire population the standard of living Brisbane enjoyed. Like so many social reformers who came to seek alternatives to the exigencies of self-interest, Brisbane imagined that improving the living conditions would also have a morally uplifting effect on the general population. Drawn into the life of the phalanstery, the masses could be socialized to genteel and civil behavior. Cooperation was to be the motor that drove history upward toward utopia. Just as nonnationals became the moral reprobates of a nationalist order or conservatives and reactionaries became the villains of liberal history, so uncooperative behavior was to be ruthlessly suppressed in socialism. If an individual was unable voluntarily to recognize the benefits of humanitarianism, he or she was to be coerced into moral conformity.

NOTES

1. Redelia Brisbane, *Albert Brisbane: A Mental Biography*, p. 51.

2. Terry H. Pickett and Francoise de Rocher, eds., *Letters of the American Socialist Albert Brisbane to K. A. Varnhagen von Ense*. Heidelberg: Carl Winter Universitätsverlag, 1986.

3. Werner Vortriede argues in "Der Berliner Saint-Simonismus," *Heine-Jahrbuch* 75, 14 Jhrg. 93–110, that Varnhagen's conversion was largely due to Brisbane, but the notion seems to have originated with Brisbane himself. Varnhagen's articles on Saint-Simonism are available in Klaus F. Gille, ed., *Karl August Varnhagen von Ense: Literaturkritiken*. Tübingen: Max Niemeyer Verlag, 1977, pp. 111–123.

4. Brisbane's Diaries, pp. 24–15.

5. Brisbane congratulates Rahel in a note on December 20, 1831 for her sympathy for the Saint-Simonist doctrine, and he speaks again in a letter in late January 1832 of Enfantin's book, which he entitles "Economie Politique." In January 1832, he entered in his diary under the heading "Politics" that "the first thing of the St. Simonisme I knew was one of their works, which I bought in Holland." Since he proceeded to note that he had seen Madame Varnhagen the previous Saturday and observed that she "appears to comprehend St. Simonisme, and thinks it must realise itself in the world," it is safe to assume that Brisbane's autobiographical reminiscing was not in accordance with the facts and that his knowledge of Fourier and his theories came after his sojourn in Berlin.

6. Johnathan Beecher quotes Brisbane's report of his meeting with and description of Fourier in his definitive biography, *Charles Fourier. The Visionary and His World.* Berkeley: University of California Press, 1986, p. 441.

7. The original letter is in French and can be found in the work listed in note 2, pp. 44–47.

8. Carl J. Guarneri, *The Utopian Alternative. Fourierism in Nineteenth-Century America.* Ithaca: Cornell University Press, 1991, p. 31.

9. *Social Destiny of Man.* Philadelphia: C. F. Stollmeyer, 1840, p. 98f.

10. Brisbane also showed some interest in the phalanx at Red Bank, New Jersey. "John Humphrey Noyes, the founder of the Oneida Perfectionists, uses the data left by A. J. Macdonald, a contemporary student of Association, to show that there were approximately thirty-five phalanxes scattered about the country, with a total membership of over 3,000 people during the 1840s," quoted from Noyes, *History of American Socialism*, pp. 15–18, by Richard Francis, "The Ideology of Brook Farm," *Studies in the American Renaissance* (Boston, 1977) p. 17. Other journals designed to propagate Fourierst ideas include *The Phalanx* (1843–1845), *The Present* (1843–1844), *The Harbinger* (1845–1849), and *The Liberator* (1840–1845).

11. Zoltan Haraszti reflects the attitude of other historians of Brook Farm when he concludes the monograph, *The Idyll of Brook Farm* (Boston, 1937), with the following comment (p. 46): "Albert Brisbane—the pivotal figure—went on merrily from one adventure to another....And so he continued, sauntering with the same profound conviction to ever-new mysteries." On the other hand, John Thomas Codman, hardly an admirer of Brisbane, wrote in his *Brook Farm: Historic and Personal Memoirs* (Boston, 1894), p. 249: "We are first indebted to Albert Brisbane, and it is a great debt which the future will certainly appreciate and pay." A further very useful survey of contemporary remarks on Brisbane's character can be found in Richard N. Pettitt, Jr., *Albert Brisbane: Apostle of Fourierism in the United States, 1834–1890* (Dissertation: Miami University, 1982, IV, pp. 110–139), and it includes Emerson's comment on Fourier and Brisbane: "Their conversation is always insulting; for they have no other end than to make a tool of their companions."

12. Guarneri (footnote 8), 48.

13. Oliver Carlson's biography of Brisbane's son, Arthur, who became a famous journalist and editor under W. R. Hearst, contains a scathing chapter on Brisbane's neglect of his children after his wife's death. Such statements as the following abound: "Though he tried to remember when to feed them, when to change their clothes, and when to wash their faces, such matter of fact things were very frequently forgotten." *Brisbane. A Candid Biography* (New York: Stackpole Sons, 1937), p. 72.

14. *General Introduction to Social Science*. New York: C. P. Somerby, 1876. Brisbane explains just how human beings are to be elevated: "Elegance, convenience, refinement, and splendor will be connected with everything relating to Industry and its prosecution; the gardens, orchards, parks, woodlands, fields, etc. will be laid out with the greatest taste and beauty, and Art and Science will be associated in every way with agriculture." (p. 100).

15. *Theory of the Functions of the Human Passions*. New York: Miller, Orton & Mulligan, 1856, p 2ff.

16. *Intro. to Social Science* p. 23.

17. Microfilms from the George Arent Research Library at Syracuse University, Box 1, Folder 10. 12.

18. *Ibid.*

19. Pettit, "Appendix A, Exhibit F," p. 334, April 17th, George to Albert: "Your letters to your daughter in which you ask her for all concerned her mother *herself* and mine (yours) not to bring her suit is worthy of such a miscreant as you after having branded her as a bastard in the New York Herald."

11

CONCLUSION: WANDERING IN THE SYNTAX OF PROGRESSION

We began with Herder's thoughts about the meaning of human destiny as a progression from one state of efficacy to another. In retrospect, it is important to remember that Herder was not a single, lonely philosophical giant spinning out new departures. Like Charles Darwin somewhat later, Herder found his way to creating a comprehensive syntax for a vision he shared with other thinkers, a vision seminal to the modern order prevailing in the Atlantic community and exported elsewhere. The notion that human nature is impelled by good urges toward ever higher stages of improvement was in general circulation at the time. Karl Fink has written that

Herder's use of proportional syntax is basic to his use of analogy as a means for showing the process of events from one state of existence to another. Thus Herder's language informs his theory that stages of life are forms of geometric progression; and at the same time it conforms to his pattern of thought emphasizing the extent to which he, too, is a creature of language.[1]

It was Herder's genius not merely to take up a new worldview that he found compelling but to invent for it a syntax that successfully transformed it into the common sense of a new age. The architecture of our thought is constructed of a syntax of progression in which we wander both in thought and spirit, taking its forms, opportunities, and limits for granted, permitting it to inform our assumptions and thus our behavior. Most significantly, we also appeal to it to justify our behavior; it thus endows presumptions to order with *authority*.

All the paradoxes and weaknesses of the three chief modern ideologies can be traced not merely to the original comprehensive view of human existence that has been illustrated through Herder's thought and Goethe's life, but they can be found wholly manifest in the conceptual structures of justification through which we have since lived. It is indeed the aggregate forms of human life first established through the great and shaping events that took place between 1750 and 1850 that continue to determine the course of our civilization; it is in this sense that we have fallen victim to a syntatically determined course that, while holding us in thrall, paradoxically promises us autonomy.

We wander through landscapes of syntatical disjuncture: assertions of autonomy are punctuated by demands for a disciplined response to human needs of cohesive rather than mere conflictive relations. This book has been concerned first with the syntatical paradoxes and then with the moral unaffirmability of their promise. One cannot have it both ways. An entity cannot be proudly sovereign one moment and humbly submissive the next. Human freedom has discriminate limits.

In our survey of the three chief justifications for authority in modern Atlantic civilization, we have seen that the claims to autonomy cannot be affirmed without escalating conflictive relations. Neither can cohesive relations be established under a regime pledged solely to the promotion of autonomy. Goethe explored the paradoxes and their destructive consequences in his work *The Sorrows of Young Werther*, which we reviewed early in this book. Werther's subjectivist drive to realize (his) desire led him not only to commit willful injury to himself and his friends but to relish it. The equation has been repeated on a historical scale ever since by real human beings and not fictional characters. Lenin, Hitler, and numbers of others have played out the scenario to the hilt. Obsessive pursuit of the objects of one's desire leads, as events have shown, to the impoverishment of mind and spirit. Many subsequent attempts to live out the claims of the new anthropology of autonomy have signally failed to achieve Herder's ideal of humanitarian relations toward which he believed autonomy drives us. Good intentions and high-mindedness appear not to change the paradoxes at all.

Our modern age not only has an accumulation of historical experience in which the worst about human nature is repeatedly proven, it has also produced a large and compelling body of imaginative literature and art that makes the same point. In spite of a strong belief to the contrary, human beings have, during the past two centuries, created systems of exclusionary particularism that match or exceed anything the traditional, premodern past can offer in antihumanitarian and injurious behavior. In spite of the incessant talk of happiness and fulfillment, modern authority, whether clothed in liberal, nationalist, and socialist justifications, has wrought havoc, abused the gentle inclinations of love and charity, and made a mockery of our sense of communal ties, *Heimat*, and *patria*.

Invoking the authority of the nation-state, rulers have marshalled vast armies of miserable humanity to participate (often unwillingly or even unwittingly) in titanic acts of injury that recognize no division between military and civilian. The field of lethality has been expanded in the name of sundry ideal futures into every nook and cranny of human life. Experience during the present century has shown how each of the claims made on behalf of the three major justifications cannot be affirmed because they not only have failed to work but, in fact, have produced behavior quite the obverse of what is claimed.

Herder's ideal of humanitarian universalism appears in retrospect to have been based on a specious assumption that nature in general and human nature in particular are fundamentally benevolent forces. Although many observers have recognized that such a claim is not borne out in behavior, it has not yet had a visible effect on the justifications for authority. Even when we urge ourselves to a reconsideration of the assumptions on which prevailing authority is founded, we do it in conformance with the principles of a Herderian anthropology of (as Brisbane termed it) "futurity." While calling for change, we are still besotted with an unchanging reverence for what we perceive to be the ineffability of desire. The full realization of the self continues to be the measureless standard by which we are confounded.

There is a caution with which I conclude. A philosophy of humankind which exalts humans themselves, setting up the ego as the authority for behavior, was not something Herder or his immediate generation invented. Myths of subjective authority have inhabited the imagination since the beginning of thought. There is an ancient tradition in which humans are a law unto themselves, but it has been a minority position, consigned to the civilized periphery. The Western traditions of the Atlantic community—traditions shaped first by Greece and then by Christianity—are defined by the fact that, at least until the advent of modernity, the god Anthropos has been forced to live subject to the authority of external powers.

Until the advent of modernity, Western history was a story that encompassed more than the repetitive follies of human nature. The imagination of the Atlantic community was animated by a divine spectacle in which people's behavior and relations were a mere constituent in a larger drama of eschatological significance, not moving in pallid spasms from one failed ideal to another, from slaughter to slaughter, or from ideology to ideology, but to a divine conclusion that applied both to each individual and to humankind as a body made sacred through its participation. The seat of authority was, in any case, outside the ego/self, and it appealed to justifications beyond the myopic confines of solipsism. We have seen how the situation changed after the success of Herderian anthropology, when every ideal was defined in terms of the subjective ego. Anthropos (or the new plebeian) was unleashed to a novel freedom and a decisive authority over the affairs of the world.[2]

INTO THE LOOKING GLASS: NARCISSUS AS KING

The scepter of authority passed to a people, a nation, an individual, to us, and to me, and every new justification for acting in the world resorted to a single source of authority centered in ourselves. Humankind has since been divided into those who are legitimate authorities (i.e., the mature, the authentic, the enfranchised, the successful, the people of achievement, our sort of folks, *me*), and those who are not (i.e., the poor, the asocial, the derelict, the lazy, the unsuccessful, the mediocre, the non-citizen, the unenfranchised, the foreign, *them*). Such a duality generates a need for control mechanisms to regulate and define it, thus justifying the aggrandizements of the state against other authority and setting a new calculus of power in motion.

There is a certain ambivalence in my statements in the previous narrative that needs now to be resolved. I argue, on the one hand, that the state was born as a fateful entity through the fatherhood of the absolutist princes. Machiavelli's *The Prince* signals the theoretical underpinnings of that new system of statecraft. What must now be apparent is the career by which the state was launched on a course independent of service to any authority but itself. On the other hand, I describe the defeat of the nobility and the church as a process by which *nation* co-opts the state for its own purposes—and that was, at least, the intention of the new generation of liberal patriots. The thrust of the modern or Herderian anthropology was to free Europeans from their bondage and to use the mechanisms of coercion of the state when necessary to achieve the desired effect. Unfortunately, the result has not been a new age of happiness.

In establishing the principle of individual right(s), the founders and patriots of the modern age successfully neutralized any counterclaim that had formerly obstructed the exercise of state supremacy. During the nineteenth century, often well-meaning and earnest men and women proceeded to dismantle the great structures of diverse authorities by which European civilization had lived. Americans stumbled over the tangle of questions intrinsic to the interplay between regional and central authority, choosing finally the costly demolition of provincial culture. It is hardly surprising that, during the course of these events, Atlantic civilization moved toward the complete destructuring of the authority of the Christian church. Most recently, this process has proceeded into its advanced forms under the rubric of religious diversity. While every trace of Christianity is eliminated from the public forum, the most exotic "religious" notions are encouraged because they pose no perceptible threat to state supremacy. In the meantime, the pogroms of National Socialism eliminated European Jewry, while American secularization has proceeded to turn the synagogue and Hebrew faith in America into vacant halls at best memorializing a dead religion. The a-theism of the founders of modernity has become a reality among their spiritually dwarfed successors.

Now what is left but the state? The modern view of human destiny permits state authority to make perpetual war against all rivals in the name of the people and its individual rights. Not even a prayer can be said in school by children whose spontaneous habits exude reverence for a world so wonderfully diverse and inexplicable. The state prefers to marshall these yet unfinished beings into its regulatory channels and pump them full of its dreary versions of naturalistic determinism. These prescriptions need only be called "science" to achieve legitimacy. Instead of prayer, we are by all means inundated with the perplexities of expert jargon. During recreation we are served up the trivializing (not to say dehumanizing) quiddities of popularist relativism (i.e., the widely held view that values in different cultures should be assigned equal moral weight). In short, the state has used its force to bulldoze every elevation into a lowland of sunken and exhausted mind, which it can easily survey and control.

Since the advent of the new calculus of state supremacy, vast numbers of people have been injured in wars, conflicts, and atrocities. Injuries continue to occur regardless of whether one has membership in one category or the other; indeed, most of us are members of both. If we are citizens in one state, for instance, we are foreigners in another—at any rate, always strange to ourselves and unsure who we really are. When we are sent off to war for a noble cause, we are startled to find that we die or are maimed as readily as the enemy. Violence is not at all like the cinema presents, happening only to the other person.

The disjuncture of our age lies in the gulf between our professed dedication to humanitarianism and our inability to experience its universalist sympathies, our belief in our deity and our very real mortality. If we could become admirable people, we would make very poor gods. The enormous breach between what we profess to be true and what we do is as great as that between who we are and who we pretend to be. We have only to dress ourselves in uniforms and venture out in order to do willful and calculated injury. In those moments our despicable propensities are undeniable, though they are always present. Out of a civilization pledged to charity, we have created a society regulated by military science and dedicated to war.

Modern government is a travesty of the pursuits of traditional governing elites. Combat has turned viciously upon the innocent rather than being the limited reserve of the privileged. Modern war requires the maintenance of vast enterprises euphemistically termed "defense establishments." These institutions are part of the state police mechanism and intrude politically, economically, and socially into every sphere, even those formerly and traditionally civilian. Actual behavior during the modern age has exposed as patently false the claim that these military enterprises are separate from the *civilian* areas of life. Since Sherman's incursions into the South, military behavior has targeted civilian community. The purpose of the squandering of all that vast resource of energy is to reduce as many human beings as possible to abject misery.

The disjuncture of modernity is evident in the distance between the public appeal to noble ends and the reality of injury that is the consequence of our behavior. Defense establishments exist, according to the public line, to assure liberty and happiness. Wars are fought to good and noble purpose. Carniverous business ravages communities on behalf of anti-monopolistic free enterprise. Great networks of highways are built to "assist" people, to hurry them to work, and to facilitate the distribution of goods and services, while in fact they deconstruct neighborhoods and towns, isolating them one from another and, moreover, contaminating a blessed silence with the ubiquitous noises of traffic.

Once the distance between what is professed and what actually exists would be called *lying*. Today the interpretive elites insist that, since there is no truth, there can be no lie. Everything is a little true or, perhaps, true in its own way (i.e., not true at all). We can look for points of sympathy with a person who destroys a Vietnamese village, murders an innocent person for a pittance, or abandons his or her children to pursue self-development and self-expression, chasing after desire. In the modern equation there are no longer the admirable and the despicable, there are only victims, with whom we are obligated to find some common and sympathetic ground.

Those in authority who have been responsible for orchestrating mass injury have almost without exception continued to applaud their dedication to the Good or, at least, the necessary. Robert McNamara's recent repentance of his role in Vietnam stands virtually alone among the acts of human beings who have exercised an authority that led to the injury of millions of their fellow human beings. Everyone else has protested vigorously and to the very end (when they have spoken of their roles at all outside the usual public pronouncements) that they have faithfully served the ideals to which they were publicly pledged. Such public ideals are promoted across a broad front and include notions such as democracy, liberty, autonomy, future happiness, social welfare, social security, general health insurance, free markets, racial and national purity, peace, equity, and any number of variations on the themes of humanitarianism and autonomy.

A literary tradition has arisen as well in which acknowledged people of achievement from every area of endeavor produce memoirs and autobiographies that treat their roles in events. Like that other modern literary genre, the novel, these works seek to resolve the disjunctures between desire and possibility and provide a justifying account for behavior that has unavoidably fallen short of expressed humanitarian ideals. Despite the fact that these accounts are usually full of transparent hypocrisy, the moral incongruity of modern life they record for us persists and mocks every new appeal to goodwill. Even the leading protagonists in the oppositional modern tradition, those who recognize the hypocrisy and despise it, cannot discover for us any alternative but a despairing nihilism. Nietzsche, Schopenhauer, the existentialists, the deconstructionists, and numerous other schools of negativism participate in modernity's devotion to change. They are like workers in the fields of desolation, deeply committed to the work of dismantling the last remnants of human shelter. Humankind is to have no respite from the aggrandizements of state force. Instead of a brotherhood of happiness, modernity has steadily expanded the fields of misery.

The aspiration to autonomy also demands that desire be self-interpreting. The passional drives that govern us are not to be violated by the intrusions of an independent reason. Our histories are depicted as journeys by which desire is driven by its passional force to its own unique and inexplicable conclusion. The work of enlightenment Kant promoted in his essay titled "What is Enlightenment" could never actually begin because it required the instrument of a passional drive to move human nature out of its "natural lethargy." More than two centuries later, we discover that it was not we who were set free but passion. Mature judgment never had a chance to develop since the orthodox measuring stick for progress (the only meaningful movement in the modern paradigm) was the complexion of desire: If it were intense, all else did not matter. The modern age has thus been like the nurse who is so obsessed with tending to the fever that she forgets the patient.

Reason's sole legitimate function has been to provide the tools for desire to magnify itself. Those tools fall under the rubric of technology. Werther's total abdication before his desire for Lotte now seems quaint, his tearful sentimentality embarrassing if not ludicrous. But Werther remains the exemplary modern plebeian who abdicates his humanity in order to serve (his) desire with abandon. It did not matter if Lotte desired him. Anything extraneous to the desiring ego is irrelevant. Questions of humanity—such as consideration, appropriateness, morality, ethics, legality, or prudence—are out of the question and can only be entertained by members of the conventional race of men who Lotte's fiance cum husband, Albert, represents. Only a person like Albert could ask desire to account for itself or could seek to interpret, much less condemn, passion.

Werther throws the exemplary modern tantrum, unleashing his ire upon Albert and his kind. Such creatures of judgment and restraint are the scourge of passional autonomy. It is no wonder that they have become the villains of our age, stubborn and practical sorts who challenge the majesty of desire and who insist that there are things in life more important than its fulfillment. It is Albert's heresy that challenges the fundament of the modern worldview. If desire is not sacred there is little reason to invest the ego with authority. The mind derives its principles from other sources.

Goethe established an abiding polarity in his early work. Werther rages as a law unto himself; Albert can neither comprehend nor tolerate his destructive behavior and recognizes that Lotte is his intended victim. When Werther borrows the pistol from Albert with which he blows out his brains, it is clear how prudence provides the instrument with which excess destroys itself. The orthodox modern subjectivist has sought to make history his last rage so that humanity itself is consumed by the intensity of his passion. It is really his only method of self-confirmation, like Hitler being consumed in the conflagration he ignited or Satan being dashed into hell after defying heaven's King. The last frantic gesture of the egoist comes no doubt to these tormented spirits when they are confronted not with the grandeur of their drama but with its numbing tedium. Nothing is less interesting to the vibrant mind than the ego's fantasies of self-exaltation.

THE NATION-STATE IN THE WORLD

The supremacy of the modern order of the nation-state transcends its geopolitical area of origin. Countries with emerging economies, places in which the native culture is in no way related to European developments, are now attempting to implement its claims. In Asia and Africa they seek to build new orders on the fundament of Herderian anthropology, integrating into it all the errors of Jahn's nationalism and/or Brisbane's socialism (or some other version thereof). In those non-European places nationalist rhetoric and agenda dominate the public forum. Often the claims made are an attempt to justify regimes run by Western-trained plutocracies.[3]

Western parliamentary governments have managed to institutionalize a system in which partisans of all three chief views participate in justifying prevailing authority. Liberals, nationalists, and socialists each take their turn at the helm.

Usually the political parties represent an amalgam of the three justifications and divide for functional reasons into two opposing camps. Each justification is employed to mobilize sufficient force for sustaining state authority. Although the structural transformation of Western authority predates the philosophical *revolution* from theology to anthropology, the establishment of its supremacy depended on the development of new principles of order. Now that these principles are in general and even global use, these matters are no longer of simply European or Atlantic concern. It is, therefore, crucial that we examine the evidence of escalating violence that has marked Western history since Herder and understand how it is connected to its view of human destiny and the claims it makes on that basis.[4]

VOICES OF THE SURVIVORS OF THE HOLOCAUST

There is one last category of complaint to add. In addition to the oppositional critics of nihilism, there are also the survivors of its nightmares who have confronted modern orthodoxy with its failure. After both World War I and World War II veterans returned from a life in hell with the message that none of the justifications invoked to support the barbarism they had participated in and survived were valid. Their message was simply that there is no ideal that can suffice to justify the injuries they had experienced. Clear depictions of the savage meaninglessness of modern war reached mass audiences in works like Erich Maria Remarque's *All Quiet on the Western Front.*

There were also other writers such as Ernest Hemingway and Ernst Juenger who celebrated and romanticized the violence. Almost as if in anticipation of Hitler, the German Juenger not only produced several potent and convincing fictions based on his experience at the front; he wrote in 1922 that "war is that which has made humankind and its times what they are."[5] Apologists of violence are joined by a vast state propaganda machinery and a commercial media that promote injurious behavior both as a patriotic duty and for its thrills.

Operating with the encouragement of the War Ministry in Germany, for instance, the Ullstein Verlag turned out best-sellers like the reportage by Captain Paul Oskar Hoecker published in 1914, *At the Head of My Company* (*an der Spitze meiner Kompagnie*). The most successful book about the war in Germany, Hoecker's work depicts the German incursion through Belgium and into France. At the start, the author is confronted with a challenge to his sense of humanity. Under orders to execute local inhabitants caught hiding firearms, he begins during the first week by having a young Belgian farmer shot.

While expressing his extreme reluctance to deal injury, Hoecker shows how individuals under state discipline ultimately feel they have no choice. They accept the notion that they are instruments of the state and that their moral commitment requires them to act lethally. In memoirs written a quarter of a century later, Hoecker exhibits no regret or change of heart; rather he evaluates a new political crisis in 1939 from the perspective of an unrepentant nationalist.[6]

Literature written by participants in and victims of modern combat and atrocity is large and rich. Civil War diaries continue to be published monthly in the United States. Vietnam literature has become an acknowledged genre and recognized scholarly specialty. The genocide of European Jewry is an established institution with its own literature, public rites, and museums. If numbers of scholarly and popular journals are devoted to the most lethal events of the past two centuries and reach a specialist readership, compelling pacifist fictions continue to reach mass audiences. The chamber of modern horrors has been memorialized as well everywhere in stone. It is, thus, rather odd that none of the literature of the survivors has made any discernible difference in the character of the justifications still invoked to sanction the exercise of authority in our world.

Often, too, those urging us to remember the terrible events are the very voices that appeal most earnestly to the formulas of orthodox modernity, imploring us to act on goodwill and in the interest of conventional humanitarian progress. In the urgency of their appeals, one can hear the anguish of their moral perplexity. Their resources are limited because they remain in bondage to the progressivist syntax with which the architecture of their conceptual landscapes is constructed. The history of injury we have committed in the twentieth century simply has not sufficed to jar us loose from our attachment to the modern progressivist fantasy.

Civilization is not rightly understood, even in the view of the survivors, as a state of disciplined order wrested over ages of misery and struggle out of the anarchy of barbarism; it is perceived instead as a drama of liberation. Rather than look beyond the syntatical landscapes they have inherited, survivors begin a wild goose chase after new ideals generated out of that syntax. The peculiar problem of the survivor is exemplified in the autobiography of the Jewish-German Ernst Toller, who published an account of his eventful life just six years before his suicide in New York in 1939, the day his works were burned by the Nazis. Toller began life as the son of a German nationalist who was determined to escape any rudimentary pariah status by identifying with German culture and German language and siding with the German community against the Poles in the eastern province where he grew up. During World War I Toller fought on the front for Germany and survived the war to become a leading Expressionist dramatist. He also abandoned nationalism for socialism.

Toller participated in the Communist revolution in Bavaria in 1918, played a key role in its ephemeral government, barely escaped execution, and was imprisoned for five nearly hopeless years. When by happenchance he survived so many tribulations, he emigrated first to England and then to the United States, where he continued to pursue socialist and humanitarian projects. During these ups and downs, he continued to forge an active and public identity as an honest and courageous modern warrior who fights for a humanitarian future. His autobiographical narrative is haunted, at the same time, by that other identity he had neither chosen nor professed, an identity that had been given but that conveyed on him more than he ever desired or was willing to profess. Toller's given identity as a Jew contradicts modernity's insistence on the ultimate importance of autonomy and self-determination. Rather than experience it as a rich blessing, he spent his life avoiding or ignoring it.[7] It is one of the paradoxes of modernity that it was, nevertheless, thrust upon him again and again.

Toller hardly stands alone. Most moderns are urged to pursue concocted identities and to abandon or destroy the relations in which they are naturally bound through birth. And, yet, when that is done, the way is fraught with anxiety and danger. Nationalism appears to be the only ideology that approves of the natural matrix of relations we call community. The problem with ethnogenesis is, as we have seen, that it pushes an agenda hostile rather than hospitable to Herder's humanitarianism because it does not provide for those not included in the national body. Indeed, the only moment left in which modern human beings are permitted the mutually supportive transcendence promised by Herder is to be found in the highest cultural achievements.

Every Western nation-state maintains an establishment that subsidizes and encourages the production of cultural artifacts that meet Goethe's standard of universal appeal while advertising the nation that produced them. The universality does not mask, in the view of its apologists, an exclusivist elitism because both the creators and those who enjoy the works are enfranchised citizens of this high country of human attainment. Writers, poets, composers, scientists, artists, dramatists, actors, musicians, and politicians all are confirmed in their role as a personified universal ideal and, at the same time, national heroes who exemplify the best the nation can give. Their entitlement is grounded in their unique achievements; these, however, are owed to a combination of personal genius and national inspiration. The public promotion and celebration of high cultural achievements is thus an important mode by which modern authority celebrates the success of its claims. Those who do not number among the company of the high achievers are assigned the more humble but still important role of benefactors who appreciate, support, and approve.

When the notion of a universality of achievement is turned into political coin, it becomes a doctrine of world status and provides a channel for the rivalry that exists between nation-states. It is significant that these rivalrous relations are characterized by a syntax of combat and battle. Just as works of individual genius articulate the inaccessible specificity of the inner soul of an individual, so does their political analogue express the uniqueness of a people and its national culture. Finally, hidden within that inmost essence is something that cannot and will not be shared but that demands acknowledgment. Such a claim constitutes a noxious assertion of entitlement: that we must acknowledge the significance of something to which we are barred access and can, therefore, never comprehend, which is like doing blind homage before an empty idol.

NOTES

1. Karl J. Fink, "Herder's Life-Stages as Forms of Geometric Progression," *Eighteenth Century Studies* VI (1981), 46.

2. A more contemporary example of the perennial revival of Gnostic ideas can be found in Elaine Pagels's *The Gnostic Gospels* (1979). Pagels's career and ideas find glowing endorsement in a review of her latest work by *New Yorker* critic David Remnick entitled "The Devil Problem," April 1, 1995, 54–65.

3. Hugh Tinker, "The Nation-State in Asia," in *The Nation-State: the Formation of Modern Politics.* New York: St. Martin's, 1980, 119: "The nation-state served a genuine purpose in Europe in the shift from the traditional society to modernity. In Asia, it proved to be an invaluable instrument in getting rid of Western colonialism....It does little or nothing to help Asians solve their most immediate problem: that of institutionalizing the relations of communities and groups, whom geography has made neighbors but who possess no real feeling of a common identity." Irving Leonard Markovitz also concludes in *Power and Class in Africa: An Introduction to Change and Conflict in African Politics* (Englwood Cliffs, N.J.: Prentice-Hall, 1977) that indepedent African nation-states can have a happy future (pp. 347ff).

4. Benedict Anderson links Herder's anthropology of Volk to a private-property language, which he credits with generating nationalism. He also believes that the great shift to an anthropocentric worldview was due largely to the "profound shrinkage of the European world in time and space that began already in the fourteenth century, and was caused initially by the Humanists' excavations and later, paradoxically enough, by Europe's planetary expansion": *Imagined Communities. Reflections on the Origin and Spread of Nationalism* (1983), pp. 66–67.

5. Ernst Juenger, "Der Kampf als inneres Erlebnis," in *sämtliche Werke*, 19: "Der Krieg ist es, der die Menschen und ihre Zeiten zu dem macht, was sie sind."

6. Paul Oskar Hoecker, *Gottgesandte Wechselwinde. Lebenserrinerungen eines Fünfundsiebzigjährigen.* Bielefelt and Leipzig, 1940. Wolfgang Natter's unpublished manuscript, "Literature for the Warrior: Literature at War, 1914–1918," has proven very useful and is in the author's possession.

7. Ernst Toller, *I Was a German.* New York: William Morrow, 1934.

SELECTED BIBLIOGRAPHY

Allen, Diogenes, *Christian Belief in a Postmodern World.* Louisville: Westminster/John Knox Press, 1989.

Anderson, Benedict, *Imagined Communities. Reflections on the Origin and Spread of Nationalism.* London: Verso, 1983.

Anderson, Quent, *Making Americans: An Essay on Individualism.* New York: Harcourt Brace, 1992.

Arendt, Hannah, *On Violence.* New York: Harcourt Brace, 1969.

Armstrong, John A., *Nations before Nationalism.* Chapel Hill: University of North Carolina Press, 1982.

Ball, Hugo, *Critique of the German Intelligentsia.* New York: Columbia University Press, 1993

Barnard, F. M., *Self-Direction and Political Legitimacy: Rousseau and Herder.* New York: Oxford UP, 1988.

Blackstone, William T., *Francis Hutcheson and Continental Ethical Theory.* Athens: University of Georgia Press, 1965.

Borsody, Stephen, *The Tragedy of Central Europe: Nazi and Soviet Conquest and Aftermath.* New Haven: Yale University Press, 1980.

Bowman, Shearer David, *Masters and Lords. Mid-19th Century U. S. Planters and Prussian Junkers.* New York: Oxford UP, 1993.

Brandmeyer, Rudolf, *Biedermeierroman und Krise der ständischen Ordnung.* Tübingen: Niemeyer, 1982.

Breuer, Stefan, *Max Webers Herrschaftssoziologie.* Frankfurt: Campus Verlag, 1991.

Brumbaugh, Robert S., *Western Philosophic Systems and Their Cyclical Transformations.* Carbondale: Southern Illinois University Press, 1992.

Chaudhuri, K. N., *Asia before Europe: Economy and Civilization of the Indian Ocean from the Rise of Island to 1750.* Cambridge: Cambridge University Press, 1990.

Cheyfitz, Eric, *The Poetics of Imperialism.* New York: Oxford UP, 1991.

Crick, Francis, *What Mad Pursuit: A Personal View of Scientific Discovery.* New York: Basic Books, 1988.

Dahrendorf, Ralf, *Reflections on the Revolution in Europe.* London: Chatto & Windus, 1990.

Dawkins, Richard, *The Blind Watchmaker*. White Plains, N.Y.: Longman, 1986.

Desmond, William, *Beyond Hegel and Dialectic. Speculation, Cult, Comedy*. Albany: State University of New York Press, 1992.

Donoghue, Denis, *Connoisseurs of Chaos: Ideas of Order in Modern American Poetry*. New York: Oxford UP, 1984.

Elazar, Daniel, *Building Toward Civil War*. Lanham, MA: Madison Books, 1992.

Evans, Richard J., *Rethinking German History*. London: Allen & Unwin, 1987.

Fichte, J. G., *Addresses to the German Nation*. New York: Harper & Row, 1968.

Fichte, J. G., *The Vocation of Man*. Indianapolis: Hatchett, 1987.

Frank, Ernst, *Friedrich Ludwig Jahn. Ein moderner Rebell*. Heusenstamm bei Offenbach: Orion, 1972.

Gellner, Ernest, *Nations and Nationalism*. Ithaca: Cornell University Press, 1983.

Glenny, Misha, *The Fall of Yugoslavia. The Third Balkan War*. London: Penguin, 1992.

Glenny, Misha, *The Rebirth of History. Eastern Europe in the Age of Democracy*. London: Penguin, 1990.

Goody, Jack, *The Taming of the Savage Mind*. Cambridge: Cambridge University Press, 1977.

Greenfeld, Leah, *Nationalism. Five Roads to Modernity*. Cambridge: Harvard University Press, 1992.

Gruner, Rolf, *Philosophy of History*. Aldershots: Gower, 1985.

Guarneri, Carl J., *The Utopian Alternative. Fourierism in Nineteenth Century America*. Ithaca: Cornell University Press, 1991.

Hatfield, Henry, *Aesthetic Paganism in German Literature*. Cambridge: Harvard University Press, 1964.

Hawking, Stephen W., *A Brief History of Time*. New York: Bantam Press, 1988.

Henderson, Charles Jr., *God and Science: The Death and Rebirth of Theism*. Atlanta: John Knox Press, 1986.

Herder, Johann Gottfried, *Against Pure Reason: Writings on Religion, Language*. Minneapolis: Fortress Press, 1992.

Hobsbawm, E. J., *Nations and nationalism since 1780. Programme, myth, reality*. Cambridge: Cambridge University Press, 1992.

Horten, Michael Scott, *Made in America: The Shaping of Modern American Evangelism*. Grand Rapids: Baker Books, 1991.

Immanuel Kant, *Zum ewigen Frieden. Ein philosophischer Entwurf aus dem Jahre 1795*. Berlin: Verlag der Nation, Reprint, 1987.

Jackman, Robert, *Power without Force: The Political Capacity of Nation-States*. Ann Arbor: University of Michigan Press, 1993.

Johnson, Phillip E., *Darwin on Trial*. Washington, D.C.: Regnery, 1991.

Johnston, Otto W., *The Myth of a Nation: Literature and Politics under Napoleon*. Columbia, S.C.: Camden House, 1989.

Kedourie, Elie, *Nationalism*. 4th edition. Oxford: Blackwell, 1993.

Keegan, John, *The Masks of Command*. London: Johnathan Cape, 1987.

Kessler, Stanford, *Tocqueville's Civil Religion. American Christianity and the Prospects for Freedom*. Albany: State University of New York Press, 1994.

Keulman, Kenneth, *The Balance of Consciousness. Eric Voegelin's Political Theory*. University Park: The Pennsylvania State University Press, 1990.

Lambropoulos, Vassilis, *The Rise of Eurocentricism*. Princeton: Princeton University Press, 1993.

Loewenhaupt, Wilfried, *Politischer Utilitarismus und buergerliches Rechtsdenken*. Berlin: Duncker & Humblot, 1972.

Loewith, Karl, *From Hegel to Nietzsche: The Revolution in Nineteenth Century Thought.* Trans. by David E. Green. New York: Holt, Rinehart & Winston, 1964.

Luebbe, Hermann, *Säkularisierung: Geschichte eines ideenpolitischen Begriffs.* Freiburg: K. Alber, 1965.

Luepke, Johannes von, *Wege der Weisheit. Studien zu Lessings Theologiekritik.* Göttinger Theologische Arbeiten, Bd 41. Göttingen, 1989.

Markovitz, Irving L., *Power and Class in Africa. An Introduction to Change and Conflict in African Politics.* Englewood Cliffs, N.J.: Prentice-Hall, 1977.

Markus, R. A., *The End of Ancient Christianity.* Cambridge: Cambridge University Press, 1990.

Marsden, George M., *Fundamentalism and American Culture: The Shaping of Twentieth Century Evangelicalism, 1870–1925.* Oxford UP, 1980.

McDonald, Forrest, *Novus Ordo Seclorum. The Intellectual Origins of the Constitution.* Lawrence, Kans.: University of Kansas Press, 1985.

McGowan, John, *Postmodernism and Its Critics.* Ithaca: Cornell University Press, 1991.

McKee, Christopher, *A Gentlemanly and Honorable Profession.* Annapolis: Naval Institute Press, 1991.

McKnight, Stephen, *Sacralizing the Secular. The Renaissance Origins of Modernity.* Baton Rouge: Louisiana State University Press, 1989.

Mead, Walter Russell, *Mortal Splendor: The American Empire in Transition.* Boston: Houghton Mifflin, 1987.

Medina, Vicent, *Social Contract Theories: Political Obligation or Anomaly.* Savage, Md.: Rowland & Littlefield, 1990.

Montgomery, Marion, *Liberal Arts and Community.* Baton Rouge: Louisiana State University Press, 1990.

Montgomery, Marion, *Virtue and Modern Shadows of Turning.* Lanham: University Press of America, 1990.

Morton, Michael, *The Critical Turn: Studies in Kant, Herder, Wittgenstein, and Contemporary Theory.* Detroit: Wayne State University Press, 1993.

Morton, Michael, *Herder and the Poetics of Thought.* University Park: Pennsylvania State University Press, 1989.

Moynihan, Daniel Patrick, *Pandaemonium. Ethnicity in International Politics.* New York: Oxford UP, 1993.

Nell-Beuning, Oswald von, *Gesellschafts-Ordnung: Wesensbild und Ordnungsbild der menschlichen Gesellschaft.* Nuremberg: Glock und Lutz, 1947.

Norris, Christopher, *What's Wrong with Postmodernism: Critical Theory and the Ends of Philosophy.* New York: Guilford, 1991.

Nye, Joseph S., Jr., *Bound to Lead: The Changing Nature of American Power.* New York: Basic Books, 1990.

O'Toole, Patricia, *The Five of Hearts. An Intimate Portrait of Henry Adams and His Friends, 1880–1918.* New York: Clarkson Potter, 1990.

Pfaff, William, *The Wrath of Nations. Civilization and the Furies of Nationalism.* New York: Simon & Schuster, 1993.

Plantinga, Alvin, *The Twin Pillars of Christian Scholarship.* Stob Lectures of Calvin College, 1989.

Pohlman, H. L., *Justice Oliver Wendell Holmes and Utilitarian Jurisprudence.* Cambridge: Harvard UP, 1984.

Repgen, Konrad, *Von der Reformation zur Gegenwart.* Paderborn: Schoeningh, 1988.

Riley, Patrick, *The General Will Before Rousseau. The Transformation of the Divine into the Civic.* Princeton: Princeton University Press, 1986.

Roochnik, David, *The Tragedy of Reason: Towards a Platonic Conception of Logos*. London: Routledge, 1990.

Russell, Greg, *Hans J. Morgenthau and the Ethics of American Statecraft*. Baton Rouge: Louisiana State University Press, 1990.

Rutler, George William, *Christ and Reason. An Introduction to Ideas from Kant to Tyrell*. Front Royal, Va: Christendom Press, 1990.

Schaeffer, John, *Sensus Communis. Vico, Rhetoric and the Limits of Relativism*. Durham, N.C.: Duke University Press, 1990.

Schroeder, Gerald L., *Genesis and the Big Bang. The Discovery of Harmony between Modern Science and the Bible*. New York: Bantam, 1990.

Schulze, Hagen, *The Course of German Nationalism: from Frederick to Bismarck, 1763–1867*. Cambridge: Cambridge University Press, 1991.

Sontheimer, Kurt, *Von Deutschlands Republik. Politische Essays*. Stuttgart: Deutsche Verlags-Anstalt, 1991.

Stampp, Kenneth, *America in 1857: A Nation on the Brink*. New York: Oxford UP, 1990.

Starr, Chester G., *The Aristocratic Temper of Greek Civilization*. New York: Oxford UP, 1992.

Stern, Karl, *The Flight from Woman*. New York: Paragon House, 1986.

Stout, Jeffrey, *The Flight from Authority: Religion, Morality, and the Quest for Autonomy*. New York: Harper & Row, 1981.

Timm, Eitel F., *Ketzer und Dichter: Lessing, Goethe, Thomas Mann und die Postmoderne in der Tradition des Haeresiegedankens*. Beiträge zur neueren Literaturgeschichte, 88. 3. Folge. Heidelberg, 1989.

Timm, Eitel F., *Subversive Sublimities: Undercurrents of the German Enlightenment*. Columbia, S.C.: Camden House, 1992.

Vallee, G., J. B. Lawson, and C. G. Chapple, eds., *The Spinoza Conversations between Lessing and Jacobi*. New York: University Press of America, 1988.

Verheyen, Dirk, *The German Question: A Cultural, Historical, and Geopolitical Explanation*. Boulder, Colo.: Westview Press, 1991.

Voegelin, Eric, *From Enlightenment to Revolution*. Ed. John H. Hallowell. Durham, N.C.: Duke University Press, 1975.

Wagner, Nancy Birch, *Goethe as Cultural Icon. Intertextual Encounters with Stifter and Fontane*. New York: Peter Lang, 1994.

Wallace, Robert, *The Legitimacy of the Modern Age*. Cambridge: MIT Press, 1983.

Walsh, David, *After Ideology. Recovering the Spiritual Foundations of Freedom*. San Francisco: HarperCollins, 1990.

Walther, Eric, H., *The Fire-Eaters*. Baton Rouge: Louisiana State University Press, 1992.

Watson, Michael, *Contemporary Minority Nationalism*. London: Routledge, 1990.

Wiedenmann, Ursula, *Karl August Varnhagen von Ense. Ein Unbequemer in der Biedermeierzeit*. Stuttgart: J. B. Metzler, 1994.

Wood, Allen W., *Kant's Rational Theology*. Ithaca: Cornell University Press, 1978.

Yack, Bernard, *The Longing for Total Revolution. Philosophic Sources of Social Discontent from Rousseau to Marx and Nietzsche*. Princeton: Princeton University Press, 1986.

INDEX

About the Author

TERRY H. PICKETT is Professor of German at the University of Alabama, where he has taught since 1969. He is the author of a monograph on the American Fourierist Albert Brisbane and a biographical study of the German man of letters K. A. Varnhagen von Ense. In addition, he has published numerous articles.

ISBN 0-313-29891-2

90000>

EAN

9 780313 298912

HARDCOVER BAR CODE